Tire Tread and Tire Track Evidence

Recovery and Forensic Examination

CRC SERIES IN
PRACTICAL ASPECTS OF CRIMINAL AND FORENSIC INVESTIGATIONS

VERNON J. GEBERTH, BBA, MPS, FBINA *Series Editor*

Practical Homicide Investigation: Tactics, Procedures, and Forensic Techniques, Fourth Edition
Vernon J. Geberth

The Counterterrorism Handbook: Tactics, Procedures, and Techniques, Third Edition
Frank Bolz, Jr., Kenneth J. Dudonis, and David P. Schulz

Forensic Pathology, Second Edition
Dominick J. Di Maio and Vincent J. M. Di Maio

Interpretation of Bloodstain Evidence at Crime Scenes, Second Edition
William G. Eckert and Stuart H. James

Tire Imprint Evidence
Peter McDonald

Practical Drug Enforcement, Second Edition
Michael D. Lyman

Practical Aspects of Rape Investigation: A Multidisciplinary Approach, Third Edition
Robert R. Hazelwood and Ann Wolbert Burgess

The Sexual Exploitation of Children: A Practical Guide to Assessment, Investigation, and Intervention, Second Edition
Seth L. Goldstein

Gunshot Wounds: Practical Aspects of Firearms, Ballistics, and Forensic Techniques, Second Edition
Vincent J. M. Di Maio

Friction Ridge Skin: Comparison and Identification of Fingerprints
James F. Cowger

Footwear Impression Evidence, Second Edition
William J. Bodziak

Principles of Kinesic Interview and Interrogation, Second Edition
Stan Walters

Practical Fire and Arson Investigation, Second Edition
David R. Redsicker and John J. O'Connor

The Practical Methodology of Forensic Photography, Second Edition
David R. Redsicker

Practical Aspects of Interview and Interrogation, Second Edition
David E. Zulawski and Douglas E. Wicklander

Investigating Computer Crime
Franklin Clark and Ken Diliberto

Practical Homicide Investigation Checklist and Field Guide
Vernon J. Geberth

Bloodstain Pattern Analysis: With an Introduction to Crime Scene Reconstruction, Second Edition
Tom Bevel and Ross M. Gardner

Practical Aspects of Munchausen by Proxy and Munchausen Syndrome Investigation
Kathryn Artingstall

Quantitative-Qualitative Friction Ridge Analysis: An Introduction to Basic and Advanced Ridgeology
David R. Ashbaugh

Practical Criminal Investigations in Correctional Facilities
William R. Bell

Officer-Involved Shootings and Use of Force: Practical Investigative Techniques
David E. Hatch

Sex-Related Homicide and Death Investigation: Practical and Clinical Perspectives
Vernon J. Geberth

Global Drug Enforcement: Practical Investigative Techniques
Gregory D. Lee

Practical Investigation of Sex Crimes: A Strategic and Operational Approach
Thomas P. Carney

Principles of Bloodstain Pattern Analysis: Theory and Practice
Stuart James, Paul Kish, and T. Paulette Sutton

Cold Case Homicides: Practical Investigative Techniques
Richard H. Walton

Practical Crime Scene Processing and Investigation
Ross M. Gardner

Practical Bomb Scene Investigation
James T. Thurman

Practical Analysis and Reconstruction of Shooting Incidents
Edward E. Hueske

Tire Tread and Tire Track Evidence

Recovery and Forensic Examination

William J. Bodziak

CRC Press
Taylor & Francis Group
Boca Raton London New York

CRC Press is an imprint of the
Taylor & Francis Group, an **informa** business

CRC Press
Taylor & Francis Group
6000 Broken Sound Parkway NW, Suite 300
Boca Raton, FL 33487-2742

Printed in the United States of America on acid-free paper
10 9 8 7 6 5 4 3 2 1

International Standard Book Number-13: 978-0-8493-7247-6 (Hardcover)

Library of Congress Cataloging-in-Publication Data

Bodziak, William J.
Tire and tire track evidence : recovery and forensic examination / author William J. Bodziak.
p. cm. -- (Practical aspects of criminal and forensic investigations)
Includes bibliographical references and index.
ISBN 978-0-8493-7247-6 (alk. paper)
1. Motor vehicles--Tires--Identification. 2. Criminal investigation--United States. I. Title.

HV8077.5.T57B63 2008
363.25'62--dc22 2007042612

Visit the Taylor & Francis Web site at
http://www.taylorandfrancis.com

and the CRC Press Web site at
http://www.crcpress.com

To my grandchildren—
Haley, Peyton, Ryan, Jordan, Griffin, and Will

Editor's Note

This textbook is part of a series titled *Practical Aspects of Criminal and Forensic Investigation*. This series was created by Vernon J. Geberth, New York City Police Department lieutenant commander (retired), who is an author, educator, and consultant on homicide and forensic investigations.

This series has been designed to provide contemporary, comprehensive, and pragmatic information to the practitioner involved in criminal and forensic investigations by authors who are nationally recognized experts in their respective fields.

Contents

Preface

Millions of cars and trucks are currently in use in the United States. Since the early twentieth century, the automobile has been a part of our freedom of movement, of choice and convenience. Today, young boys and girls frequently learn to drive at the age of 16, while our senior citizens often drive into their 80s and 90s. Unfortunately, our highly mobile society also provides criminals the means to travel discreetly to and from the scenes of the crimes. In fact, with the exception of domestic crimes, neighborhood burglaries and crimes committed by juveniles of pre-driving age, it is difficult to find many other examples of major crimes that do not involve the use of a vehicle. Criminals drive to commit burglaries, to stalk or abduct their victims, to rob banks and stores, and to distant locations where they might dispose of victims. Their vehicles not only provide a quick entrance into and exit from the crime area but provide a certain degree of secrecy and security.

In the Oklahoma City bombing incident, surveillance cameras recorded Timothy McVeigh as he drove the Ryder rental truck on the way to the Alfred P. Murrah Federal Building. That morning he innocently appeared like any other driver, arousing no suspicion as he parked the Ryder truck in front of that building and activated the truck bomb that minutes later killed 168 men, women, and children and injured countless others. Just prior to the explosion, McVeigh safely exited the area in his old Mercury Marquis that had been previously parked nearby.

In the famed sniper homicides in the Washington, DC area in 2002, John Muhammed and Lee Malvo used their car to convey them to and from the various areas where they committed these crimes. In some instances they actually used the converted trunk of their car from which to shoot their victims. In child abduction cases, Amber Alerts have become a commonly used and sometimes successful method of utilizing the mobile public to look out for any perpetrators escaping the area in their vehicles. Some of these cases have resulted in the return of the victim, but in other cases the vehicle provided the perpetrator the means to abduct and harm the victim.

Long before modern forensics and the use of tire impression evidence in court, the wheels of horse drawn wagons left their tracks over unpaved roadways that retained their distinctive features and visual proof of their passage. Interpretation of those tracks was made by those who out of necessity and experience acquired the observation skills, knowledge, and experience to do so. The invention of the horseless buggy that led to today's modern automobile and the invention and evolution of the pneumatic tire have only provided increased numbers of vehicles and a different set of features to examine.

Today's modern tires are highly engineered and complex items built from rubber, fabric, and steel components and then molded to take on their final tread design, sidewall design, and final shape. A tire's complexity and variations along its full circumference require a general understanding of its construction and features in order to assure that tire evidence is properly recovered, documented, and evaluated.

Police laboratories around the world have long provided forensic examination of tire evidence. Their long-standing success in linking vehicles to crime scenes through the impressions and tracks vehicles have left behind have served as successful and reliable forensic tools in countless cases. Today, crime scene technicians routinely search for, document, and recover tire tracks and impressions when collecting evidence from a crime scene. Once that evidence is collected, forensic examiners with specialized knowledge, training, and expertise in this discipline compare this evidence with the tires and track dimensions of suspect vehicles.

I first examined tire evidence as a trainee in the FBI laboratory in 1973 and have since conducted thousands of tire evidence examinations. I've been fortunate to have accumulated a great deal of information and experience that has resulted from working with several very knowledgeable FBI Laboratory examiners, visiting numerous tire manufacturing facilities, interacting with examiners from other laboratories, from educational seminars, and years of casework experience. I am hopeful that sharing the information I have provided in this book will not only encourage the increased use of tire evidence, but will be informative, useful, and provide assistance to those tasked with its collection, recovery, and examination.

Acknowledgments

Many provided considerable support during the preparation of this book. I would like to extend special thanks to Sandra J. Wiersema for the considerable amount of assistance she provided. I would also like to extend my sincere appreciation to David Bicigo, Anthony Brinkman, Harvey Brodsky, Karen Elliott, Nancy Garfield Chychrun, Paul Gage, James Garfield, Rocky S. Stone, Teresa A. Stubbs, and Mark Thomas for their generous contributions of time and support.

Love and appreciation go to my wife Shirley for her patience and understanding during its preparation.

About the Author

William J. Bodziak is a forensic consultant and operates Bodziak Forensics in Palm Coast, Florida. He received a Bachelor of Arts degree in Biology from East Carolina University in Greenville, North Carolina, and a Masters of Science in Forensic Science degree from the George Washington University in Washington, DC. In January 1970, Mr. Bodziak was appointed a Special Agent of the Federal Bureau of Investigation, serving in an investigative capacity in FBI offices in Connecticut, Maryland, and Florida. In 1973 he was assigned to the FBI Laboratory in Washington, DC, where he served for nearly 25 years in the Laboratory as an examiner of questioned documents and footwear and tire impression evidence until his retirement in 1998.

He has testified as an expert witness in federal, state, and local courts throughout the United States and also in courts in Guam, Puerto Rico, the U.S. Virgin Islands, South Africa, and Canada. He has lectured and provided instruction on footwear and tire tread impression evidence at the FBI Academy in Quantico, Virginia; at the FBI International Law Enforcement Academy in Budapest, Hungary; and at numerous seminars, classes, and conferences throughout the United States, Europe, Australia, and New Zealand.

Mr. Bodziak authored the text, *Footwear Impression Evidence* (Elsevier, 1990 and CRC Press, 2000) and has also authored chapters in other books as well as articles in professional journals in the areas of questioned documents and impression evidence. He is a member of the International Association for Identification where he is a certified footwear examiner, has served as the chairman of the Footwear and Tire Track Section, and in 2006, was the recipient of the John A. Dondero Memorial Award. In addition, he is a Fellow of the Questioned Document Section of the American Academy of Forensic Sciences and has served as both secretary and chairman of that section. He is a member of the American Society of Questioned Document Examiners and is a certified Diplomate of the American Board of Forensic Document Examiners.

General Tire Information

1

Tires…round, black and expensive! That is the impression of most consumers who often consider them a low-tech commodity and make purchasing decisions based solely on price. Those with an opportunity to tour a tire production facility are surprised to learn that there are 20 or more components, with 15 or more rubber compounds, assembled in a typical radial passenger car tire and marvel at the massive amount of machinery and processing involved to achieve the finished product. Tires are highly engineered structural composites whose performance can be designed to meet the vehicle manufacturers' ride, handling, and traction criteria, plus the quality and performance expectations of the customer. The tires of a mid-sized car roll about 800 revolutions for every mile. Hence in 50,000 miles, every tire component experiences more than 40 million loading-unloading cycles, an impressive endurance requirement.[1]

From the Wheel to the Tire

The wheel has long been used to facilitate the movement of carts, wagons, bicycles, and other items, and eventually, covered with a tire, the movement of automobiles. But tires mounted on wheels, as we know them today, did not always exist. Early wheels consisted of wood covered with leather or steel, as depicted in Figure 1.1. Not until after 1844 and Charles Goodyear's discovery of a process of curing rubber known as vulcanization could rubber be used to cover wheels. These wheels were covered with a thin layer of solid rubber, as depicted in Figure 1.2. Later, the size and shape of solid rubber tires changed. They were absent of any design, but were still stronger, resisted cutting and abrasion, and provided more shock absorption than wood alone or wood covered with steel. In 1845, Robert William Thomson of England patented the first

[1] National Highway Traffic Safety Administration, U.S. Department of Transportation. The Pneumatic Tire. Washington, DC: NHTSA; August 2005: Chapter 1 (B. E. Lindenmuth), page 2.

pneumatic tire.[2] The word "pneumatic" means "filled with air under pressure." Thomson's pneumatic tire used materials other than rubber and was not very successful. Not until years later in 1888 did John Boyd Dunlop of Belfast, Ireland create a commercially practical version of the pneumatic tire for a bicycle.[3] Although Dunlop's pneumatic bicycle tire was not used on automobiles, he is still generally credited as the inventor of the pneumatic tire that we know today. Dunlop's pneumatic tire was inflatable and used rubber to encapsulate the air. But it was still many years later before the first successful pneumatic tire for cars, using an air-filled inner tube, saw more common usage.

Figure 1.1. Wooden wheels covered with steel, as on this old wagon, were also used on very early motorized carriages and automobiles.

Figure 1.2. A wooden wheel covered with solid rubber on an early motorized carriage.

[2] The Goodyear Story, by Maurice O-Reilly, p. 13.
[3] World History of the Automobile, by Erik Eckermann, 1989, p. 37.

The Pneumatic Tire

In the pneumatic tire, the air compresses and acts as a shock absorber when the tire goes over a bump, providing a smoother ride than solid rubber tires. The pneumatic tire can be described as a donut-shaped piece of material placed around the circumference of a wheel for the purpose of both cushioning the vehicle and protecting the wheel from wear and tear. Tires are a highly engineered item and more complicated than most of us know. Like shoes, its tread often leaves its features at the scene of a crime. Although the tire is far more complex than a shoe, its complexity, if understood, can provide the forensic examiner the ability to apply that information to conduct a more accurate and successful forensic examination.

Most people think tires are just a large piece of molded rubber, but actually they consist of numerous components including the tread rubber, sidewalls, liner, plies, beads, and belts. These components are composed of three materials: (1) various rubber compounds; (2) textile fabrics, such as nylon, polyester, and rayon; and (3) steel. Using a tire building machine, these components are assembled to form what is known as a green tire. The green tire is then placed in a mold where the tread and sidewall designs are impressed into the rubber as it is cured to acquire its final shape and design. During this process, known by the industry as "mold cure," the various rubber components used to build the tire are bonded together through the process of vulcanization.

The role of the pneumatic tire is of immense importance on the automobile. Tires are the only components of the vehicle that make contact with the road. Tires both carry the load of the vehicle and transmit the forces that drive, brake, and guide it. While doing this, the tire deforms to fit an area of contact on the road that is less than the surface area of a sheet of paper. It must endure hundreds of thousands of revolutions or flex cycles, yet have adequate structural rigidity to carry the vehicle and endure the drive, brake, and side forces. A tire's tread compound must provide wear resistance and be tough and resilient to minimize cuts, tears, and cracks, as well as protect the tire body from bruising impacts. The tire tread carries a design to ensure adequate removal of water and other contaminants from the road surface and to create frictional adhesion between the tire and the road to keep the vehicle from slipping and sliding. To this day, the only type of material which has been successfully used as the tread is rubber or a synthetic rubber-like material.

Tire Footprint or Contact Patch

A tire that is not under load is round. When that tire is placed on a vehicle under load, the portion of the tire having contact with the road surface

Figure 1.3. A footprint of a radial tire. The footprint is the contact area the tire makes against a hard flat surface under load.

flattens. This flattening is known as deflection and is a significant variable governing the area of contact between the tire and the roadway. The flattened area that makes contact with the road is known as the tire's footprint or contact patch. A footprint of a radial tire is depicted in Figure 1.3. Technically defined, the tire footprint is the contact area of a tire against a flat hard surface under load. The length of the footprint increases as tire inflation decreases or the load increases.

How a Tire Carries the Load

The term *deflection* is defined by the tire industry as the free radius minus the loaded radius of an inflated tire. Free radius is the distance from the wheel axis of rotation to the unsupported tire surface. Loaded radius is the distance from the wheel axis of rotation to a supporting surface at a given load and stated inflation. This is illustrated in Figure 1.4.

The tire plies are composed of fabric cords covered with rubber. In an inflated but un-loaded tire (thus not deflected) the cords are tensioned by pressure within the tire. The tire casing takes up its equilibrium shape as determined primarily by the cord paths. As the tire is placed under load and is pressed against a surface such as a flat roadway, the tread rubber is compressed and the tire casing loses its axial symmetry and takes on a flattened contact patch at the point of deflection. The resultant upward force on the upper half of the ring becomes greater than the resultant downward forces on the lower half. This causes the sidewall tensions in the upper half to be greater than the lower half, and this force pulls the bead coil against the base of the wheel rim and transmits a resulting upward force to the wheel. This upward force against the wheel, illustrated in Figure 1.5, is what largely supports or carries the vehicle.

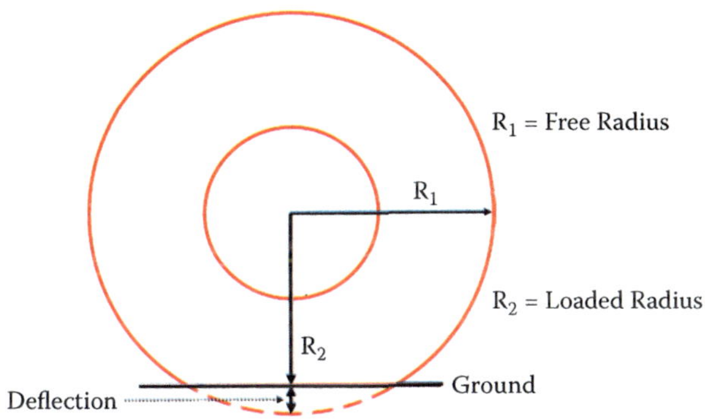

Figure 1.4. The loaded radius is the distance from the hub to a supporting surface of the tire. The free radius is the distance from the hub to a nondeflected (unsupported) area of the tire surface.

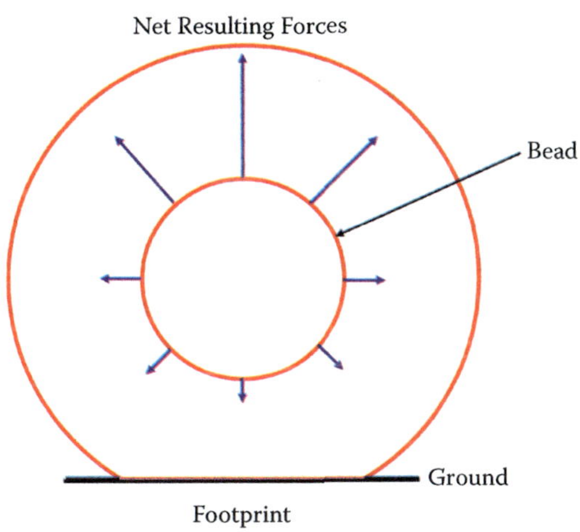

Figure 1.5. The resultant upward forces causes the sidewall tensions in the upper half to be greater than the lower half, transmitting an upward force on the wheel.

Tire Evolution

Tires have evolved considerably over the years, keeping pace with the evolution of the automobile. The first rubber pneumatic tires were of bias ply construction. Bias ply tires were named as such because the fabric cords that were imbedded in the rubber plies ran at a bias, i.e., diagonally from bead to bead. Bias tires were later improved and reinforced with belts that were placed beneath the tread surface. The belts helped stabilize the bias tire and offered added protection against punctures and road hazards. In 1948 Michelin patented and introduced the radial tire in Europe. Radial tires are so named because their plies run radially at a 90-degree angle from bead to bead. Radial tires allow for longer tread life, better handling, less rolling resistance, and increased gas mileage. American automobile manufacturers and tire companies resisted the change from bias tire construction to the more expensive radial construction until, in the early 1970s, when gasoline prices went from 30 cents to 1 dollar per gallon, the demand for more efficient radial tires grew.[4] Today, virtually all tires used, particularly on automobiles and small trucks, are radial tires. Figure 1.6 depicts differences in the ply construction of a bias belted tire and a radial tire.

Tread designs have also evolved. Early pneumatic tires were without any tread design. Eventually, early bicycle and automobile tires used buttons of rubber or leather that were attached to the surface of the tire to provide some extra traction. In 1897, C. J. Bailey invented and patented the "Bailey's Won't Slip" tire for bicycles, which consisted of added buttons of rubber that were raised slightly above the tire's surface.[5] Some early automobile tires also made similar adaptations to tires. Eventually automobile tire widths increased. This added width actually increased skidding on wet surfaces, as the weight of the vehicle was now spread over the wider tire's larger surface area. In 1908 Harvey Firestone introduced his "Non-Skid" tire. This tire actually had the words "Non-Skid" repeated at an angle across the tread of the tire. Figure 1.7A shows an ad for the Firestone non-skid design and Figure 1.7B depicts an ad for another early tire design, the Goodyear diamond tread tire. Thus the development of molded tread designs began.

Both tire and wheel sizes have also changed dramatically over recent years to accommodate the faster, higher performance vehicles. For example, in the year 1985, of 64 rim sizes on the market, one was 12-inch, fourteen were 13-inch, nineteen were 14-inch, twenty-six were 15-inch, and four were 16-inch. In 2006, there were 269 rim sizes, ranging from 12-inch to 23-inch,

[4] The Goodyear Story, p. 158.
[5] Cycling Trade Review, March 1897.

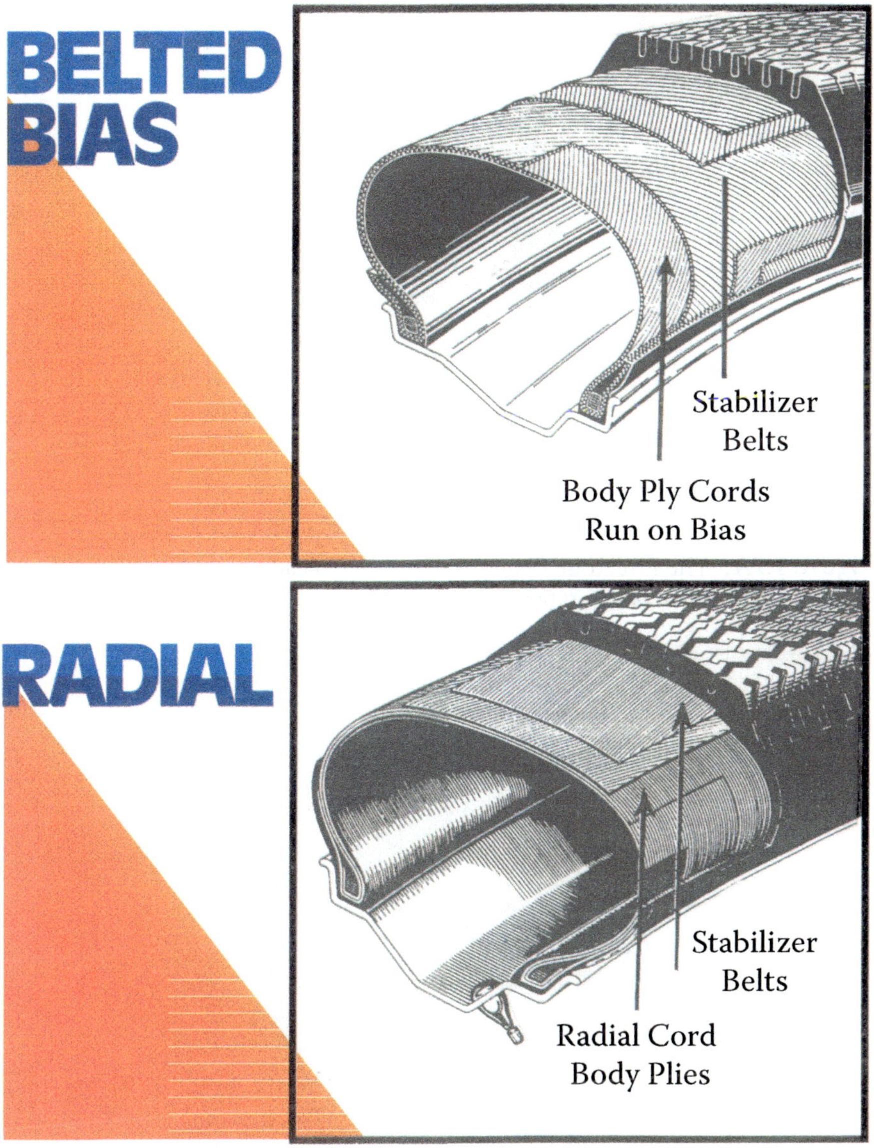

Figure 1.6. The ply construction of a bias and bias belted tire runs on an angle (on the bias). The ply construction of a radial tire runs radially from bead to bead.

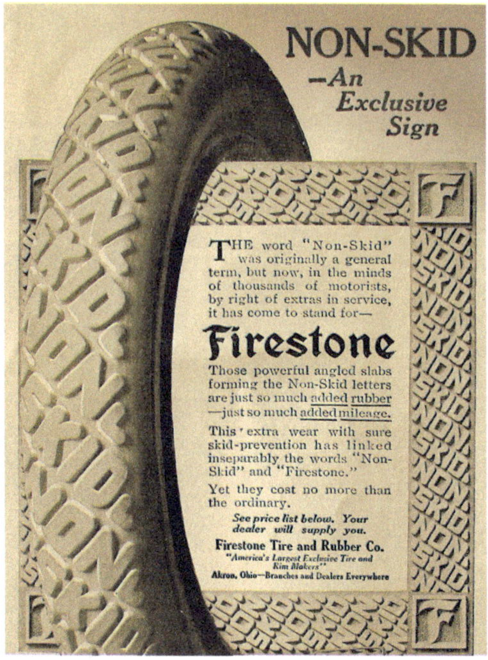

Figure 1.7A. The Firestone "Non-Skid" design as advertised in 1915. The tread design is composed of the repeating words "Non-Skid."

Figure 1.7B. An advertisement for an early Goodyear diamond tread design.

including forty-seven that were 15-inch, fifty that were 16-inch, fifty-two that were 17-inch, and fifty that were 18-inch.[6]

Tire aspect ratios have changed as well. At one time, most tires had an aspect ratio of either 70 or 75. In 1985, of 64 aspect ratios produced, seven were 80, thirteen were 75, nineteen were 70, thirteen were 60, and twelve were 50. But by the year 2006, there were 269 aspect ratios which ranged from 30 to 80 of which the median number was between 50 and 60.[7] These lower profile tires, i.e., those with lower aspect ratios, provide better response and handling when driving. Today, an ordinary passenger car is often equipped with tires having aspect ratios of 40 to 55.

Along with the many changes, the average passenger tire life has increased from about 5,000 miles in 1923, to 24,000 miles in 1973, to about 45,000 miles in 2004.[8]

Original Equipment Manufacturer Tires (OEM)

In 2003, it was reported there were in excess of 200 million cars, trucks, or sport utility vehicles operating in the United States.[9] Some of these still contain the tires that were on the vehicle when it was new, while others have had to replace those tires. Tires that come on a new vehicle are known in the industry as Original Equipment Manufacturer (OEM) tires. Most in the industry simply refer to OEM tires as OE tires. In 2006, U.S. tire shipments for OE tires for combined passenger cars and light trucks were reported to be 53.2 million.[10] Years ago, OE tires were not made for a particular model car or truck. Buying a new car usually involved considering tire options. Those options included brand options as well as the option of whitewalls and also possibly upgrading the quality or size of the wheels and tires. As the automobile continued to evolve, vehicle and tire manufacturers learned that performance of a vehicle was related to the tires on that vehicle and began designing certain tires for certain vehicles. When designing a tire for use as original equipment on a particular vehicle, the tire manufacturer must choose the tire attributes that are desired for that particular vehicle; however, compromises must be made. For instance, a stiffer sidewall on a sports car tire may provide better responsive handling desired for that car but will also reduce the comfort of the ride. Likewise, a tire with tread compound that enables a softer ride on a sedan would reduce the miles that tire would travel

[6] Tire and Rim Association, published in Tire Business, February 26, 2007
[7] Tire and Rim Association, published in Tire Business, February 26, 2007
[8] Goodyear Tire published in Tire Business, January 31, 2005
[9] DOT Federal Highway Administration figures reported 221 million total vehicles in the year 2000.
[10] Tire Business, February 26, 2007, p. 10.

before wearing out. The vehicle manufacturer and tire manufacturer often work together to develop tires that produce the most satisfactory and desirable traits. In fact, tires now play such an important role in the personality of some vehicles that manufacturers are beginning to require their tire suppliers to identify some of their OE tires with symbols or codes branded on the sidewalls, thus confirming the tire's original use.

Replacement Tires

As the OE tires wear or become damaged, they eventually need replacing. The tires used to replace OE tires are simply referred to in the industry as "replacement tires." In 2006, U.S. tire shipments for replacement tires for passenger and light trucks were reported to be 229.3 million.[11] The owner of the vehicle will have a choice with regard to the replacement tire or tires they purchase. It is normally a choice that is influenced by price, convenience, availability, and other factors.

Tread Design

Tread design is discussed more specifically in Chapter 7, but some basic information is provided here. The tread design of a tire is an arrangement of tread blocks of various shapes separated by grooves and slots. In many tire designs, tread blocks will contain sipes, which are very small grooves placed there for added traction and flexibility. In almost all passenger and light truck tires, tread blocks vary in size (pitch lengths) and are arranged in a mixed arrangement around the circumference of the tire, known as a pitch sequence. The various sizes and the mixed arrangement of the tread blocks is to reduce noise generated by the tire, thus it is referred to as "noise treatment" by the industry. Included within the grooves of the tread are tread wear indicators, also known as wear bars. Tread wear indicators are bars of rubber that rise 2/32 inch across the bottoms of the grooves of the tread design, so that when the overall tread design eventually wears down to 2/32 inch, they will become noticeably visible and signal the owner that the tire should be replaced.

Information on Sidewalls

The two sidewalls of the tire provide coverings for the inner components of that tire and are the portion of the tire that connects the beads to the tread. Of

[11] Tire Business, February 26, 2007, p. 10.

the two sidewalls, the serial side of the tire is the side that is intended to face inward. The non-serial side is cosmetically designed and intended to face outward and will contain the whitewall or raised white lettering of the tire. (Some of the newer directional tire designs are actually made so that either sidewall will be cosmetically acceptable to face outward. This enables rotation of the directional tire by mounting it differently on the opposite side of the vehicle.) On both sidewalls of the tire are names, letters, and numbers that have been transferred to those surfaces during the mold cure of the tire. Some of this information is of forensic and/or investigative value and significance while other information, although of interest, has little or no forensic value.

Since 1968, the U.S. National Highway Traffic Safety Administration Department of Transportation (DOT) has had labeling requirements that cover the information that must be placed on the tire sidewalls.[12] This includes the DOT number, size designation, tread wear and traction grading, temperature grading, and speed and load information. Figure 1.8 is a drawing

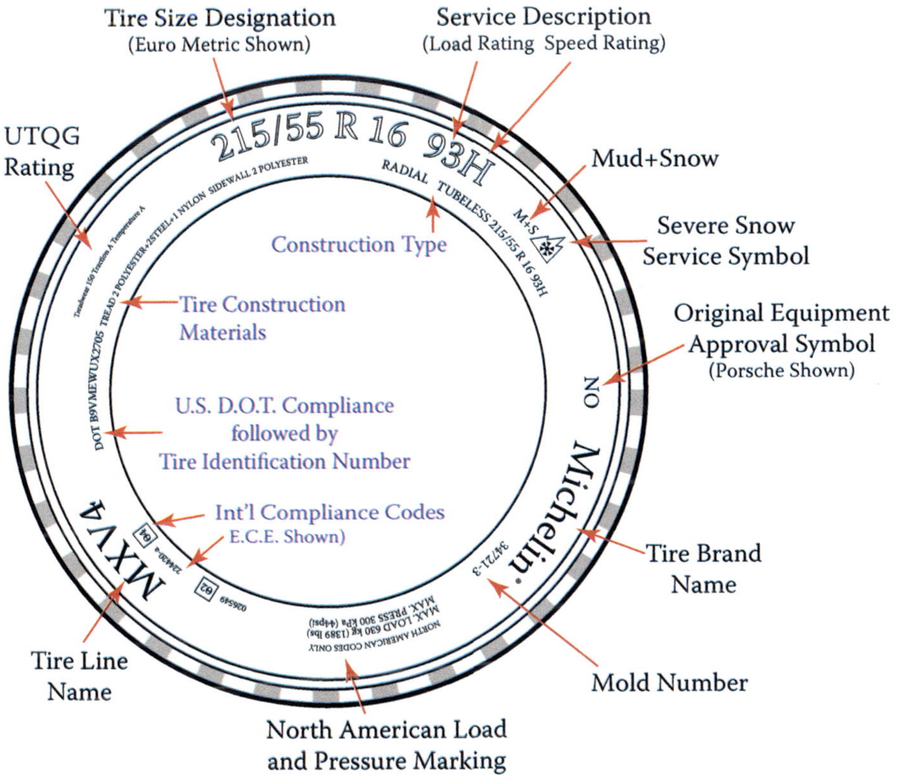

Figure 1.8. This drawing depicts some of the information that is molded on the sidewalls of a tire.

[12]National Highway Traffic Safety Administration, U.S. Department of Transportation regulations, § 571.139.

that represents the sidewall of the tire and some of the information contained thereon. On the sidewall are the following:

Tire Brand

The brand name or manufacturer name, such as Michelin, Bridgestone, Goodyear, Cooper, and so forth, normally receives the largest lettering on the tire.

Manufacturer's Line of Tire

Each particular tire design will have its tire line name. For instance, a particular line of Goodyear tires will bear the Wrangler name. Likewise, a particular line of Continental tires will bear the Conti-Trac name. Some consist of words, others consist of numbers and/or letters, and some consist of both. Examples would be Goodyear Wrangler AP, Bridgestone Turanza LS-T, Cooper Lifeliner Touring SLE, or Michelin Pilot MXM4.

Tire Size Designation

All tires sold in the United States must meet the size standards for bead shape, width, diameter, and other parameters established by recognized standardizing organizations such as the European Tire and Rim Technical Organization and the Tire and Rim Association.[13] Virtually all passenger tires on the market today use the systems established by these bodies. The tire size designation, an example of which is depicted in Figure 1.9, is a multicomponent item that provides the section width, aspect ratio, construction type (the letter *R* for radial construction, the letter *B* for belted bias construction, or the letter *D* for bias or diagonal construction), and rim size. Various tire size designations are set forth in the inset in this chapter, including those used in the past as well as those used today.

Figure 1.9. The P-metric tire size designation of a passenger tire.

[13]The Tire and Rim Association, Incorporated, is the technical standardizing body of the tire, rim, valve, and allied part manufacturers for the United States. It was first organized in 1903 and is located in Copley, Ohio. See http://www.us-tra.org/tra-About.htm.

Rim Diameter

The rim diameter is expressed in inches with numbers such as 16, 17, and 18. There have been millimetric rim sizes, but they are not very common.

Section Width

Section width is the linear distance measured between the outer sidewalls of an inflated tire without load. It is included as part of the tire's size designation. As an example, for a tire with a size of P195/70R14, the "195" is the section width of 195 millimeters.

Aspect Ratio

The aspect ratio is a number that provides the relationship of the height of the tire section to its width. On the tire, it is included as part of the tire size designation, as illustrated in Figure 1.9. As shown in Figure 1.10, a tire whose section height is 55% of the section width has an aspect ratio of 55. That would be expressed as part of the size as P195/**55**R14. Section height is calculated by taking the diameter of the tire, minus the diameter of the wheel, divided by 2. Thus a tire diameter of 26 inches minus a rim diameter of 16 inches divided by 2 equals a section height of 5 inches. Appearance wise, tires with lower aspect ratios have shorter sidewalls than those with higher aspect ratios. Those tires with lower aspect ratios have the general appearance of being flatter and are referred to as "low profile" tires. Tires with lower aspect ratios, like the tire depicted in Figure 1.11A, have added handling and cornering ability in contrast to those with higher aspect ratios, like the one depicted in Figure 1.11B.

Load Index

Two-digit numbers such as "90" (P195/70R14 **90**S) are now often located at the end of the tire size designation. The numbers denote the tire size's assigned numerical value for relative load carrying capabilities. In the case of this example, the 90 identifies the tire's ability to carry approximately 1,323 pounds. A load index scale is provided in Table 1.1.

Speed Ratings

In countries where selected highways such as the Autobahn do not have speed limits and high-speed driving is permitted, speed ratings were established to match the speed capability of tires with the top speed capability of the vehicles to which they are applied. Speed ratings are based on laboratory tests where the

Numeric Sizing System

This is the oldest standardized tire sizing system for passenger car tires. When this system was adopted, tire aspect ratios were either 92 or 82. For example, 7.00-14 tires had a section width of 7 inches, a rim diameter of 14 inches and an aspect ratio of 92. The lower profile equivalent size tire with an aspect ratio of 82 would be 7.35-14.

7.35-14

Approximate Section Width — Rim Diameter

Alpha-Numeric Sizing System

This system was established in 1968 and is based on the tire's load carrying capacity, rather then its measurements. The tire's capacity and size are indicated by letter designations from "A" (smallest tire, lowest capacity) to "N" (largest tire, highest capacity). An example of an Alpha-numeric tire size is BR78-13. "B" shows size/load. "R" indicates radial construction, "78" is the aspect ratio, and "13" is the wheel size in inches

BR 78 -13

Radial Construction — Load Rating — Aspect Ratio — Rim Diameter

P-Metric Sizing System

This system was established in 1976 and is commonly used today. P-metric stands for Passenger-Metric. This was designed to be used on domestic vehicles primarily used as passenger vehicles, such as cars, minivans, smaller SUV and light duty pickup trucks.

P215/70R14

Section Width (millimeters) — Radial Construction — Passenger Car — Aspect Ratio — Rim Diameter

Metric Sizing System

This is a European tire sizing system sometimes referred to as a Eurometric system. It evolved from the numeric system, except that the section width is now expressed in millimeters and the aspect ratio has been added. This example also includes the Load Index and Speed Symbol after the size.

215/70R14 82H

Section Width (millimeters) — Radial Construction — Load Index — Aspect Ratio — Rim Diameter — Speed Symbol

Light Truck Numeric System

This is similar to the Numeric system for cars. It lists the section width in inches, the construction type, the rim diameter in inches plus a light truck designation.

7.50R-15LT

Radial Construction — Light Truck Designation — Section Width — Rim Diameter

Light Truck Metric Sizing System

Similar to the P-Metric system, except the LT now signifies the tire is a size designed to be used on vehicles capable of carrying heavy cargo or towing trailers. This includes medium and heavy duty trucks, pickups, SUV and full size vans.

LT215/75R15

Section Width (millimeters) — Radial Construction — Light Truck Designation — Aspect Ratio — Rim Diameter

Light Truck High Flotation Sizing System

This is the same as the Light Truck Numeric system but the tire diameter is added at the beginning. Flotation sized tires have wider overall widths than their LT-Metric and LT Numeric designated counterparts.

31x10.50R-15LT

Tire Diameter — Radial Construction — Light Truck Designation — Section Width — Rim Diameter

ST or T designations

If the size begins with "ST" it signifies the tire is a Special Trailer Service" size, only to be used on boat, car or utility trailers. If the size begins with "T", this signifies the tire is a "Temporary Spare" only to be used until a flat tire can be repaired or replaced.

T135/90D17

Section Width (millimeters) — Bias Construction — Temporary tire — Aspect Ratio — Rim Diameter

Inset 1.1. Old and New Tire Size Designations

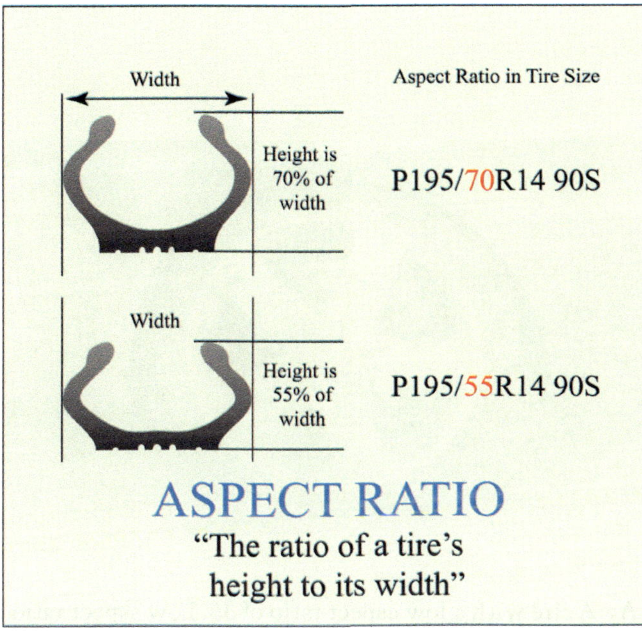

Figure 1.10. The aspect ratio on some tires is lower, while on other tires it is higher.

tire is pressed against a large diameter metal drum to reflect its appropriate load and run at ever-increasing speeds until the tire's required speed has been met. Early tires had their speed rating symbol shown within the tire size, such as 195/70**S**R14. Tires using this type of branding were not to have been produced after 1991. Beginning in 1991, the speed symbol denoting a fixed maximum speed capability of new tires must be shown only in the speed rating portion of the tire's service description, such as 195/70R14 90**S**. This is commonly provided after the load index which comes after the tire size designation (Figure 1.9). Table 1.2 provides a list of speed ratings. Speed ratings are established in kilometers per hour and subsequently converted to miles per hour. This is why the speed ratings for miles per hour appear at odd-number increments.

Tire Pressure

Tire inflation pressure is the level of air in the tire that provides it with the ability to carry a load. The tire inflation pressure is measured in pounds per square inch (psi). The proper tire pressure for a tire is not what is listed on the tire itself but what the vehicle manufacturer has listed on the vehicle placard. The tire pressure recommended is the cold inflation pressure.

Figure 1.11A. A tire with a low aspect ratio of 35. Low aspect ratio tires appear almost flat.

Figure 1.11B. A tire with a higher aspect ratio of 70.

Table 1.1. Load Index Scales

LOAD INDEX	LOAD	LOAD INDEX	LOAD	LOAD INDEX	LOAD
30	234	61	567	92	1389
31	240	62	584	93	1433
32	247	63	600	94	1477
33	254	64	617	95	1521
34	260	65	639	96	1565
35	267	66	659	97	1609
36	276	67	677	98	1653
37	282	68	694	99	1709
38	291	69	716	100	1764
39	300	70	739	101	1819
40	309	71	761	102	1874
41	320	72	783	103	1929
42	331	73	805	104	1984
43	342	74	827	105	2039
44	353	75	852	106	2094
45	364	76	882	107	2149
46	375	77	908	108	2205
47	386	78	937	109	2271
48	397	79	963	110	2337
49	408	80	992	111	2403
50	419	81	1019	112	2469
51	430	82	1047	113	2535
52	441	83	1074	114	2601
53	454	84	1102	115	2679
54	467	85	1135	116	2756
55	481	86	1168	117	2833
56	494	87	1201	118	2910
57	507	88	1235	119	2998
58	520	89	1279	120	3086
59	536	90	1323	121	3197
60	551	91	1356	122	3307

Table 1.2 Speed Ratings

Symbol	Maximum Speed (mph)	Maximum Speed (km/h)
J	62	100
K	68	110
L	75	120
M	81	130
N	87	140
P	93	150
Q	99	160
R	106	170
S	112	180
T	118	190
U	124	200
H	130	210
V	149	240
W	168	270
Y	186	300
ZR	Over 186	Over 300

Department of Transportation (DOT) Number

The Department of Transportation number is known as the DOT number. It is an identification number required by the U.S. National Highway Traffic Safety Administration Department of Transportation to be permanently molded on the sidewall of each tire.[14] The DOT number was traditionally present only on the serial-side sidewall of tires. Effective June 1, 2007, the DOT number must now be molded on both sidewalls.[15] Figure 1.12 depicts a photograph of a DOT number on a tire, and Figure 1.13 provides an explanation of the information in that DOT number. The DOT number contains (1) two symbols representing the manufacturer's assigned plant code, (2) two symbols representing the tire size, (3) no more than four symbols to be used at the manufacturer's discretion, and (4) four numerical symbols identifying the week and year of manufacture (only three numbers were used for tires made in 1999 or earlier). Although these are United States regulations, tire manufacturers in other countries normally include the DOT number on their tires to certify they meet U.S. standards for import into the U.S. market.

[14] National Highway Traffic Safety Act, U.S. Department of Transportation, § 574.5, Tire Identification Requirements.

[15] U.S. Department of Transportation, Federal Motor Vehicle Safety Standards, § 571.109, Standard 109, S4.2.2.3.2C.

Figure 1.12. A DOT number on the sidewall of a tire.

DOT	APB3	8BXX	3704
Meets Department of Transportation Safety Standards	Manufacturer Plant Code "AP" = Uniroyal Goodrich Tire Manufacturer Ardmorc, OK "B3" = Size Code	Manufacturer's Optional Symbols	Date of Manufacture 37 = 37th Week 04 = 2004

Figure 1.13. An explanation of the DOT number in Figure 1.12.

Mold Number

Each tire also has a mold number. Because there are normally many molds in each design and size, mold numbers help distinguish which specific mold a tire was cured in. Mold numbers have traditionally been placed along the bead area of the sidewall and appear in small lettering and numbers. Some mold numbers may be as simple as "34721-01," which designates the mold design first (34721) and then the specific mold (01, 02, 03, etc.). Others may be more complicated and include a drawing number and/or a longer mold number, as pictured in Figure 1.14. The mold numbers are something that each manufacturer controls, and therefore there is no universal format. The examiner should always record these numbers on any tire they examine as

Figure 1.14. A mold number on a tire. The format of this number varies among manufacturers.

they might be needed in the event assistance from the tire manufacturing facility is requested.

Economic Commission for Europe (ECE) Symbols

In Europe, because so much travel extends beyond the borders of any one country, the ECE developed uniform motor vehicle standards. These include physical dimensions, sidewall branding, durability and high-speed endurance requirements, and, most recently, a sound rating for the noise a tire emits. The ECE symbol on a tire's sidewall means the manufacturer certifies that the tire meets all regulations. Tires produced outside of Europe do not require these; however, with the globalization of vehicle manufacturing, many tire manufacturers will include these numbers. Each country will have an assigned code that, for example, will read "E3 0259091-S." The letter *E* and the number following it will identify the country that originally granted approval. In this example, the number *3* represents Italy. Beginning in 2004, the addition of an *S* after the number indicates the tire also meets the "pass-by" noise limits.

Uniform Tire Quality Grading

The National Highway Traffic Safety Administration, U.S. Department of Transportation establishes standards for passenger car tires with regard to tread wear, traction, and temperature. These exclude tires having deep winter tread, spare tires, and tires with 12-inch rim diameters and less. A tire rated for treadwear at 150 would wear one and one-half times as well as a tire graded 100. For traction, the tires are rated from highest to lowest from "AA, A, B, and C." The traction rating represents the tires ability to stop on wet pavement. The temperature grades range from an "A" for the highest resistance to heat, down to "C."

Wheels and Rims

U.S. tire manufacturers participate in the Tire and Rim Association,[16] which establishes engineering standards for tires, rims, and related parts. Rim sizes are provided as a way to assure the rim or wheel size and the tire size are compatible. For almost all tires and wheels made today, the rim diameter is expressed evenly in inches and is part of the tire size designation. In the tire size P225/50R**16**, the number 16 denotes a rim of a 16-inch diameter.

[16] Joe Pacuit (executive vice president, Tire and Rim Association, Inc., Copley, Ohio), personal communication, January 4, 2007.

Rim sizes come in 8, 10, 12, 13, 14, 15, 17, 18, 19, 20, 22, 23, 24, 26, and 28 inches and are used on most cars, minivans, vans, sport utility vehicles, and light duty trucks. While less common, some medium and heavy duty trucks, may still use a rim diameter expressed in half inches (such as 17.5). Half sizes are becoming almost obsolete. Rim width is the linear distance between rim flanges in contact with the tire. Some rim terminology is provided in Figure 1.15.

Another aspect of a rim is the wheel offset. Wheel offset is the distance between the hub mounting surface and the centerline of the rim. Most vehicles' wheels have what is known as a positive offset, which occurs when the mounting surface of the rim is closest to the street side of the rim centerline. This arrangement holds the tires farther in toward the centerline of the vehicle. When the hub mounting surface is even with the centerline, it is referred to as a zero offset. Negative offset is when the hub mounting surface is on the brake side of the centerline of the rim. This arrangement moves the mounted tires outward. Figure 1.16 depicts positive, negative, and zero offset.

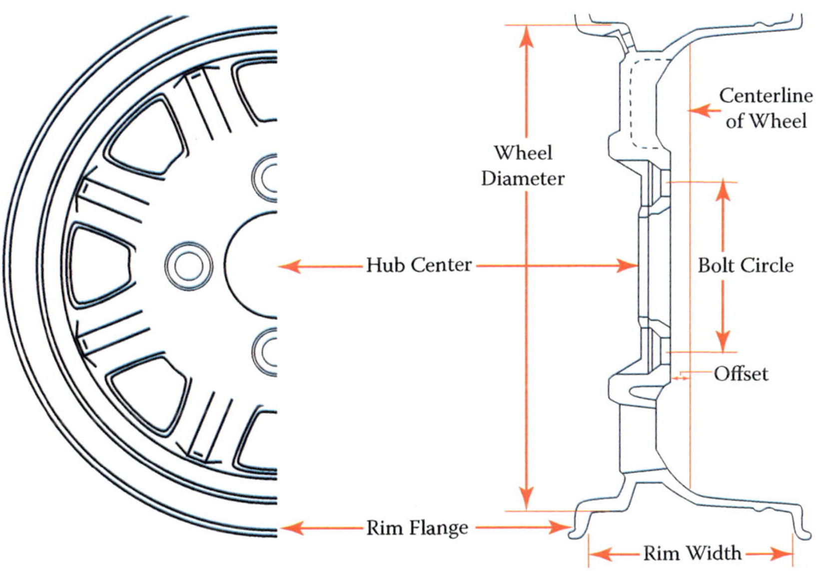

Figure 1.15. Rim terminology.

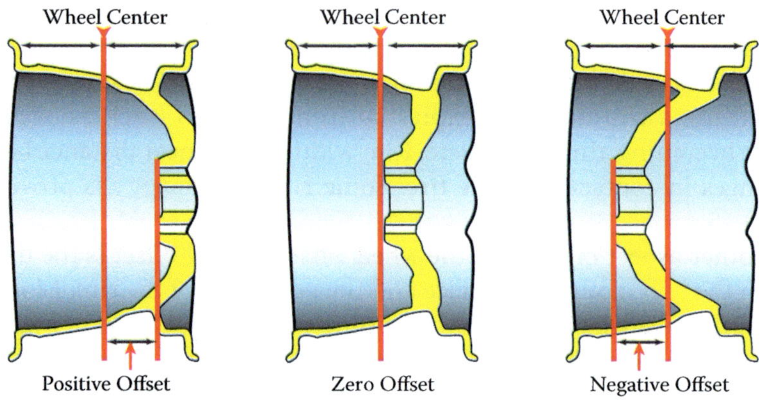

Figure 1.16. Wheel offsets can be positive, which is the most common, or neutral or negative. A positive offset will position the tire closer to the vehicle, whereas a negative offset will position the tire farther away from the vehicle.

Track Evidence

2

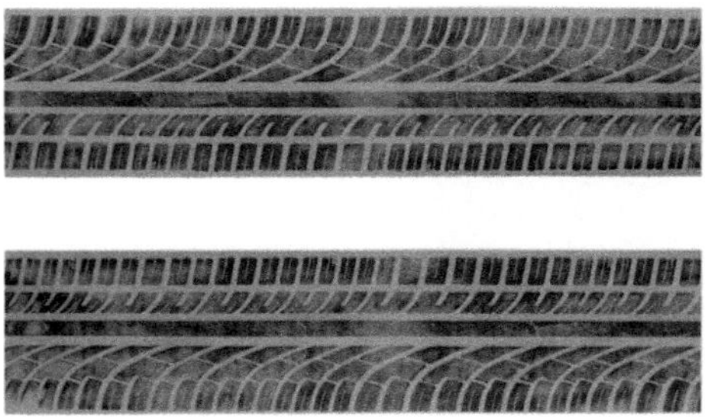

Track Evidence

Tracks are the results of the path each tire takes as a vehicle moves forward or backward. Track evidence involves the measurement and documentation of those tracks, which includes the track width, tread width, wheelbase, turning diameter, and rolling circumference. Collecting track measurements at the scene of a crime provides another way to include or exclude vehicles.

How Vehicles Track

When a vehicle is traveling straight forward, its four tires leave parallel tracks. The rear tires will take the same path as the front tires and will run across and obliterate most of the front tire impressions. With almost all vehicles, the exact track width of the front tires is slightly different from the rear tires. This difference creates a slight offset between the front and rear track paths. For example, the left rear tire may not track perfectly over the left front tire impression. This is illustrated in Figure 2.1. This can also be seen in the cast depicted in Figure 2.2, where the area between the arrows represents a small remaining portion of the front tire track after the rear tire tracked over the rest of it. It should be noted that a vehicle rarely travels perfectly straight, particularly when moving slow, and consequently any slight deviation from straight will also increase or decrease this slight offset between the front and rear tire tracks by shifting the rear tires left or right.

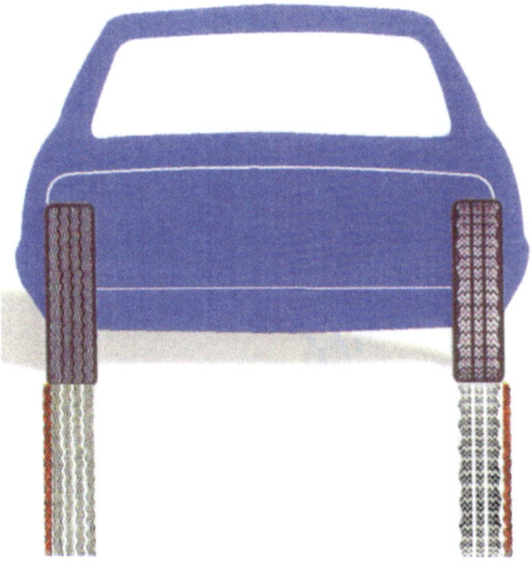

Figure 2.1. When a vehicle is moving straight forward, the rear tires will track over and obliterate the impressions of the front tires. In most vehicles, the track width of the front tires is slightly different from the track width of the rear tires, thus the track paths will be slightly offset and a small portion of the front tracks will survive. The small area in red represents an example of this where the track width of the front tires is slightly greater than that of the rear tires.

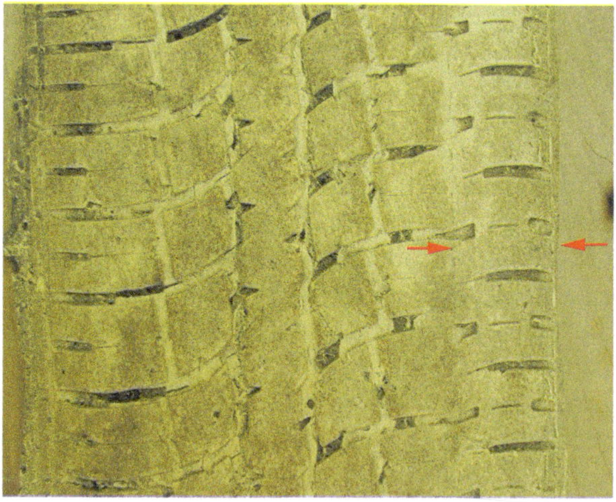

Figure 2.2. A cast taken from a scene where a small portion of the front tire impression has not been obliterated by the tracks of the rear tire. This portion is on the edge of the cast in the area between the red arrows. This is either due to the difference in track width between the front and rear tires and/or due to a slight turning of the vehicle.

When a vehicle's front tires turn left or right, their front tire tracks change direction as well. The rear tires follow this change of direction and track to the inside of the respective front tires on the same side. At the beginning of the turn, the separation between front and rear tracks is minimal; however, as the degree of the turn increases, the separation increases. The effects that turning has on the path of the tracks are illustrated in Figure 2.3. When turning left, the rear tires track to the inside of the front tires, on the left side of the turn. When turning right, the rear tires track to the inside of the front tires, on the right side of the turn. This relationship is the same regardless of whether the vehicle is traveling forward or backward. The example provided in Figure 2.4 is where a vehicle backed out of the driveway over a fresh dusting of snow. While backing out, the steering wheel was turned to the left sufficiently to provide good separation of all four tire tracks. The vehicle then came to a stop, indicated by the arrows, and then, after reversing direction and turning the steering wheel to the right, exited the area. The positions of the four tires are indicated in the illustration as LF (left front), LR (left rear), RF (right front), and RR (right rear). Figure 2.5 illustrates tracks from a vehicle that pulled into a parking space after a light snow. The vehicle then backed out while briefly turning the steering wheel to the right and then back to the left.

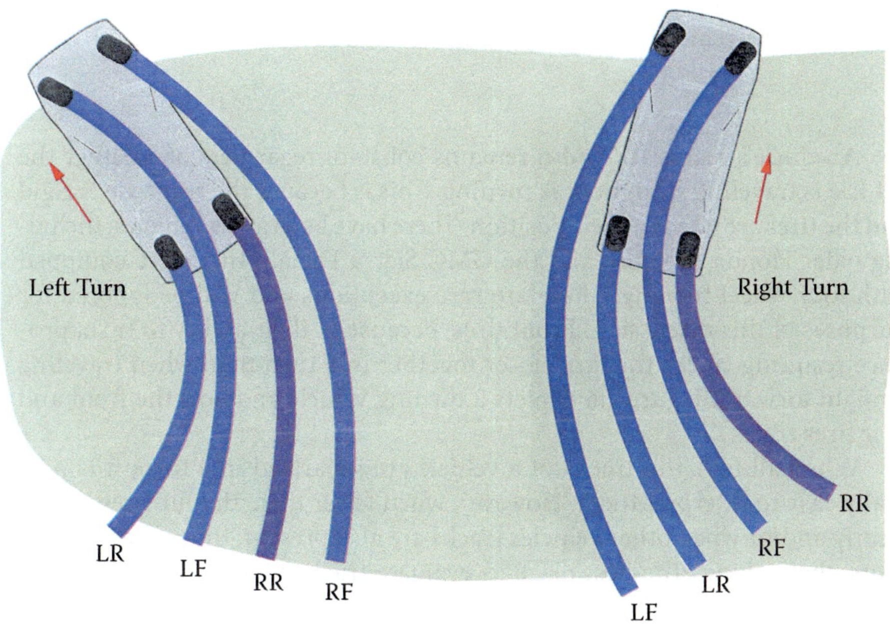

Figure 2.3. The paths and thus the tracks of all four tires separate during a turn. In a turn, the rear tracks will track to the inside of the tracks of the front tires.

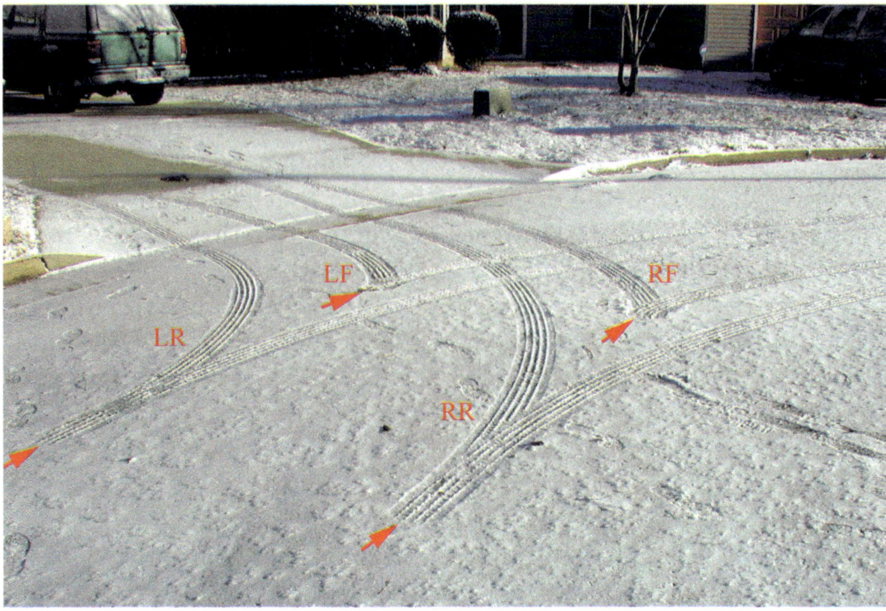

Figure 2.4. Crime scenes where a vehicle is turning and all four tire tracks have been recorded will allow for the determination and documentation of the respective four tire positions. In this photograph, a vehicle has backed out of the driveway over newly fallen snow and the four tire positions are clearly evidenced. Any differences in design or condition of wear can be attributed not only to a tire on the vehicle, but to the specific position that tire was mounted.

A vehicle's rear track width remains constant regardless of whether the vehicle is traveling straight or is turning. This is because the rear axle is rigid and the tires are fixed in their position. There have been a few vehicles, including older Honda Preludes and the GMC Sierra Denali, that were equipped with four-wheel turning. These are rare exceptions and will be ignored for purposes of this discussion. Front tires, because of their ability to turn, produce resulting tracks that are closer together in a turn than when traveling straight forward. Figure 2.6 depicts a turning vehicle and how the front and rear tires track.

When all four tire tracks of a vehicle are separated in a turn, it is normally easy to interpret them. However, when fewer than all four tires record clearly and/or when other vehicles tracks are also present, the process can be more challenging. The best place to evaluate track evidence is at the scene after which specific photographs can be taken. In many cases, attempting to evaluate track evidence later with only photographs can have serious limitations.

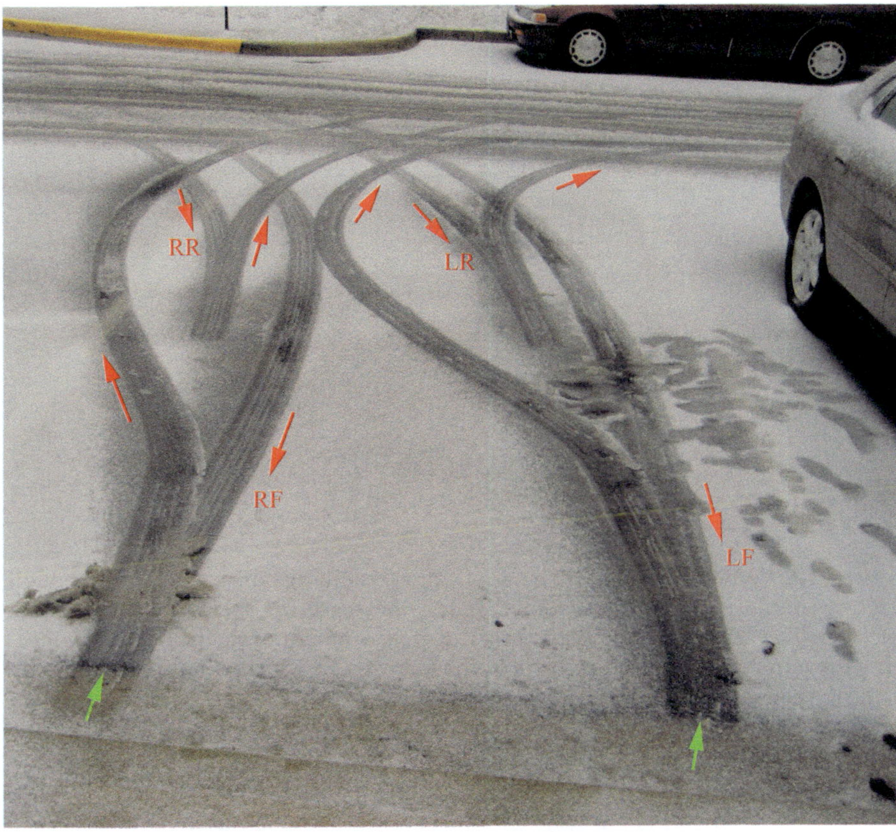

Figure 2.5. Another instance, this time in a previous snow, where a full set of tracks enables the documentation of the respective tire positions. This situation also provides a means to measure front and rear track width and wheelbase.

Tread Width

The tire industry defines the tread arc width as a measurement across a tire's full tread that coincides with the radially outmost surfaces of the various tread blocks, ribs, or lugs. However, when a tire leaves its impression at a scene, that impression rarely represents the entire tread arc width. Most passenger and light truck tires today have a round shoulder appearance with the tread design curving around the shoulder, as depicted in Figure 2.7. When that tire tread leaves its impression on a firm or hard surface, only a portion of the tire's arc width will be represented. On softer surfaces, more of the tread in the shoulder area will be recorded as the tire sinks into that surface. In a very soft and giving surface, the entire tread arc width could be recorded in an impression. This is best observed when taking known inked

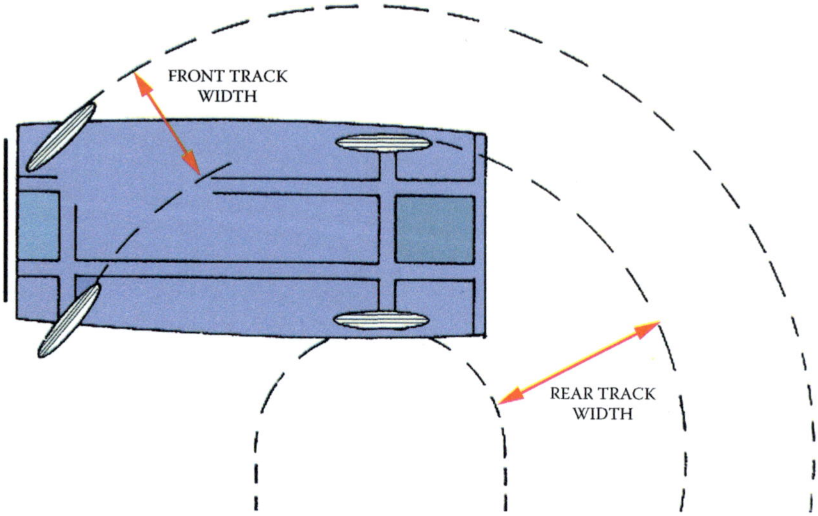

Figure 2.6. When a vehicle turns, its front tires change direction and although the tires remain the same distance apart, the resulting tracks become closer together. The greater the turn, the less the measurement of the front track width. This prevents useful measurement of the front track width when there are only turning tracks at a scene.

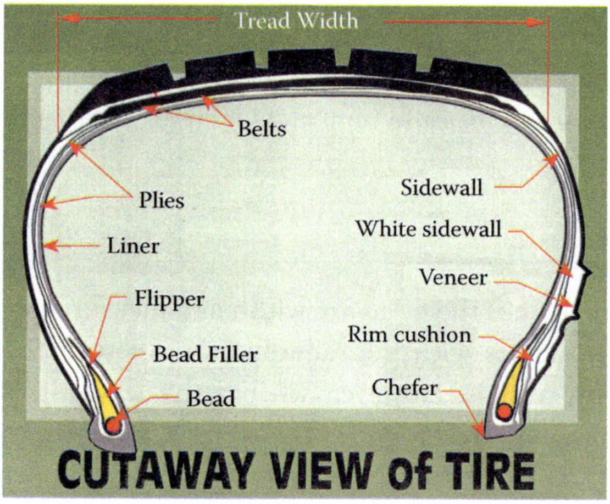

Figure 2.7. A cutaway of a tire shows the tread width. Most tires have a rounded shoulder. This rounded profile means that only a portion of the tread width will record on a hard surface.

standards of tires on a hard surface and later comparing them against casts or photographs of three-dimensional impressions in soil. As one example of this, measurements made of the recorded tread width of a tire on a full size vehicle showed 8.22 inches of its tread width recorded in soft soil, 7.32 inches of its tread width recorded in firm soil, and only 6.54 inches of its tread width recorded on a hard concrete surface. Some tire designs have a more square tread profile, and in those designs more of the tread arc width will likely be represented in any impression it leaves.

If a scene impression is two-dimensional, as would be found on an asphalt or concrete surface, the dimensions of the impression could be accurately documented either by measuring or through photography with a flat ruler. If a scene impression is three-dimensional, the tread width recorded could vary at different locations throughout the scene, depending on variations in the substrate conditions. If the tread width is being measured to be used in combination with track width calculations, the width of the tread should be measured for each tire at the points where the track width measurement is made. If recording the tread width is of importance for attempting to learn the size of the tire, a cast of the impression should be made from which more accurate measurements can be taken. For all of these measurements, be aware that for vehicles driving straight, the tracks at the scene are often combinations of both the front and rear tires.

Track Width

Track width has also been referred to as the "stance" of the vehicle. The industry track width dimension for both front and rear track widths is measured from the center of the tire tread (or impression) from one side of the vehicle to the center of the tire tread (or impression) on the opposing side of the vehicle. Inset 2.1 on track width provides instructions on measuring track widths and an illustration of the center-to-center measurement as well as optional ways to measure track width. Two of the optional ways involve measuring from the inside edge of the impression to the inside edge of the opposing impression, to which the width of the tire tread is added. Similarly, the outside-to-outside measurement subtracts the width of the tire tread. It will therefore be necessary to also measure the tread width at the point of these measurements. Relying later on the actual width across the tread of the actual tire or the width of an inked impression of that tire will not be accurate.

For those vehicles equipped with two tires, side-by-side on one assembly, known as a dual wheel assembly, the industry standard measurement for track width is made by measuring from the center between the tires (or track) from one side to the next. These points of measurement on a vehicle

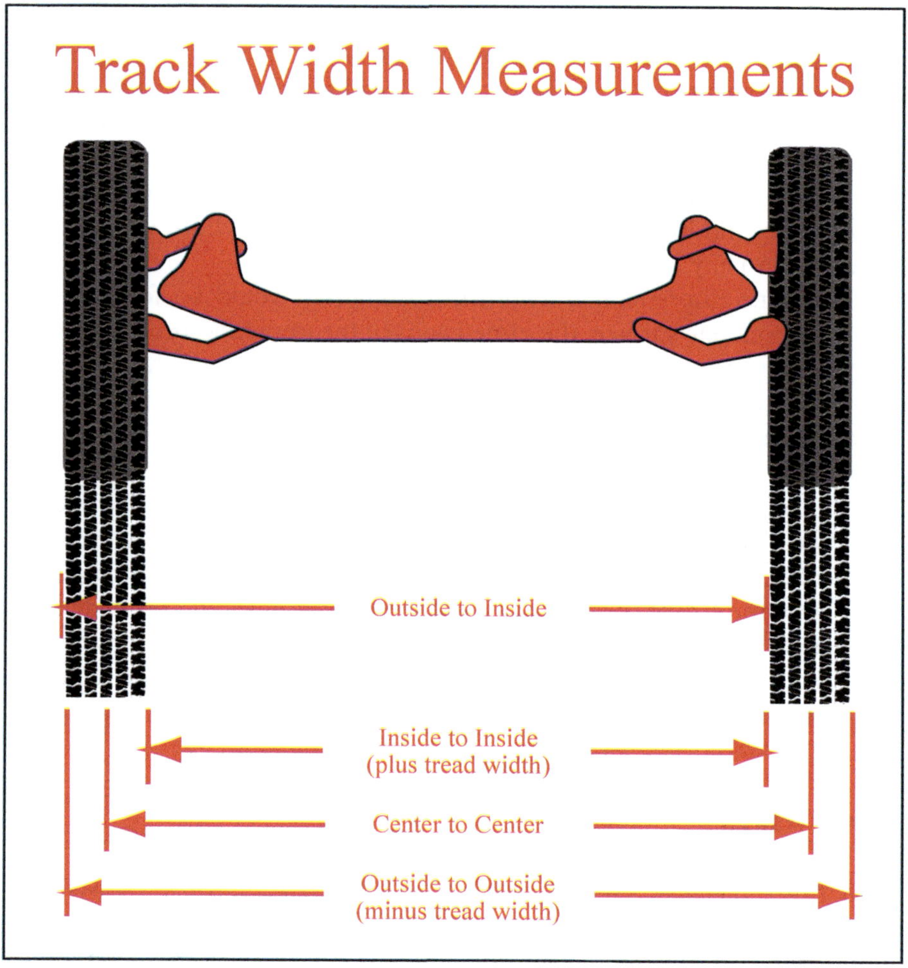

Measuring track width:

- Two persons are needed for this measurement.
- Locate areas of the impressions where good detail has been retained.
- Study the impressions on each side to evaluate the point from which the measurements will be made. In the case of center rib and directional tire designs, finding the center of the design will bee asier. In the case of asymmetrical, non-center rib and block designs, this may be more difficult.
- If the tracks are straight and parallel, beaware of impressions that are combinations of the front and rear tires.
- If the tracks are turning, only the rear track width measurement will be reliable.
- Extend a tape measure from the center of the tread design on one side to the center of the tread design on the other side and note the measurement in tenths of inches, e.g., 53.4 inches. Make sure the measurement is done perpendicular (90degrees) to the tracks.
- Make and record several measurements.
- In cases where a center-to-center measurement is not possible, make measurements from the inner and outer edges of one impression to the other and also measure the tread width at these locations.From these measurements, derive the equivalent of the center-to-center measurement.

Figure 2.8. The industry track width for dual tire assembly vehicles is from the center between the two tires on one side to the center between the two tires on the opposing side of the same axle.

are depicted in Figure 2.8. Taking this measurement from impressions on a three-dimensional surface is depicted in Figure 2.9. In Figure 2.9, a wide ridge has formed between the paired tires, and the center of this ridge is the point measured from.

The front track width of a vehicle is measured no differently from the rear; however, measuring impressions made by front tires in a turn will not accurately reflect the front track width, as illustrated in Figure 2.6. Scenes that only involve turning tracks may not provide an occasion to make a front track width measurement.

There are some opportunities to take measurements of the front track width if certain evidence is present. An example of a situation where front track width could be measured is illustrated in Figure 2.5, where the vehicle pulled straight in and the front tires stopped. A less common instance would be where a vehicle has been stopped in a position under the proper circumstances to have left four small indentations or impressions in soft soil or snow that represent the positions of each of the four tires.

Turning Diameter

Turning diameter is another measurement that, in combination with other track dimensions, can reduce the number of vehicles capable of leaving impressions at the scene of a crime. All vehicles have the ability to turn; however, some can make a tighter turn than others. Making a U-turn on a narrow road is the best reminder of this. In general, smaller vehicles will be able to turn in a tighter circle than larger vehicles. But this is not always

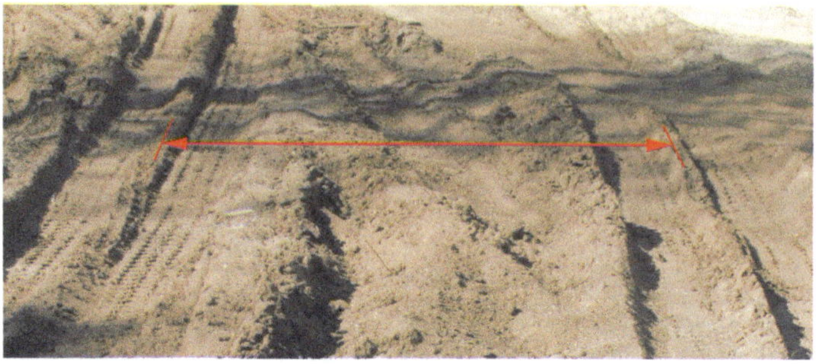

Figure 2.9. When the two tires on a dual tire assembly sink enough into a soft surface, a ridge forms representing the center area between the tires. The center of this ridge will be the reference point used to measure the track width.

true as there are different steering mechanisms on different cars. At a crime scene, if a tight turn is made in sand, soil, or snow, the calculation of the diameter of that turn can be useful in the elimination of certain vehicles that are not capable of making that sharp of a turn. The determination can also be made later as to whether the suspect vehicle could have made that turn for purposes of inclusion or exclusion.

The turning diameter is the minimum diameter in which a vehicle turns based on the outer edge of the arc of the front outside tire. Measuring the turning diameter of a vehicle's tracks is illustrated in Figure 2.10. In this example, any two positions on the turning circle are selected (x and x'). Both positions would be on the outside edge of the front tire impression that, depending on the direction of the turn, is on the outside of the turn. The distance from the selected x and x' positions is measured and half of that distance will be used as the value of B in the formula. At the point that represents the midway point between the x and x' positions, a second measurement is made perpendicular to the outside edge of the turning circle. This measurement will be the value of A in the formula. Using those two values, the turning diameter of the vehicle can be calculated. It is important to note that as a vehicle enters a turn, there is often some distance the vehicle moves while the operator is still turning the steering wheel, and at the end of the turn there is often some distance the vehicle moves as the turn decreases and the wheels straighten out. This means that some parts of the turning tracks will likely be tighter than others. If turning tracks are present at a crime scene, it is not possible to visually determine if those turning tracks represent a full or partial turn of the vehicle. If all of the turns appeared to be shallow this measurement would not warrant calculating inasmuch as it would not be useful to eliminate other vehicles. But when tighter turns of tracks are present, measurements should be obtained from several points to

Calculation of Turning Diameter

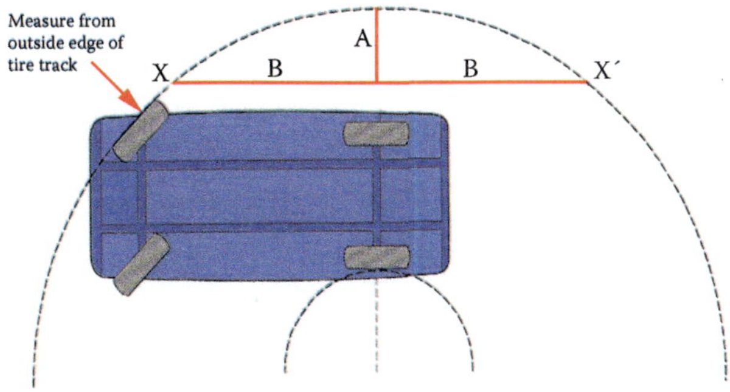

$x - x' = 27$ feet, therefore $B = 13.5$ feet

$A = 10$ feet

$$
\begin{aligned}
\text{Turning Diameter} &= (B^2 \div A) + A \\
&= 13.5^2 \div 10 + 10 \\
&= 182.25 + 10 + 10 \\
&= 18.225 + 10 \\
&= 28.225 \text{ feet}
\end{aligned}
$$

Figure 2.10. Turning diameter is determined by identifying two points on the arc of the outside edge of the outer tire of turning tracks. In this illustration, the vehicle is turning left and the outside edge of the outer (right) tire is used. More than one set of points along the arc should be measured to assure you have found the tightest part of the turn.

ensure that you are capturing the tightest part of the turn. The photograph in Figure 2.11 is one of several general crime scene photographs that document a set of four turning tracks of the perpetrator's vehicle from which a turning diameter measurement could be taken.

Wheelbase

The wheelbase is the distance between the center of the front wheel and the center of the same side rear wheel, as illustrated in Figure 2.12. Vehicles with longer wheelbases, as in Figure 2.13, are noticeably different from vehicles with shorter wheelbases, as shown in Figure 2.14. In most cases, tracks do not provide reliable reference points from which to measure the wheelbase. A close equivalent of the wheelbase is the measurement between the leading edges of the front and rear tires on the same side of the vehicle. Examples of

Figure 2.11. One of several photographs taken of turning tracks at a scene. Measurement of the turning diameter of these tracks will allow for inclusion or exclusion of a suspect vehicle.

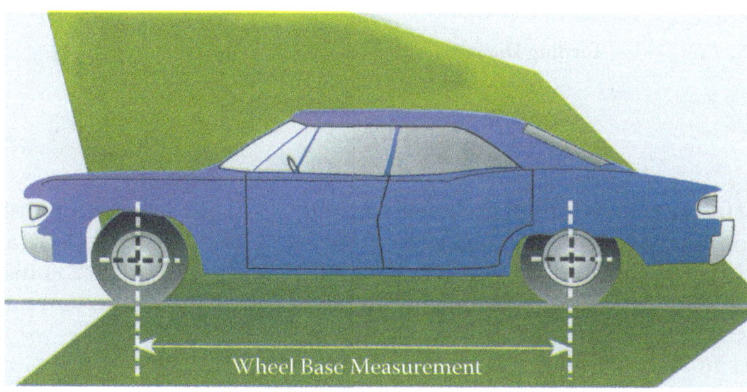

Figure 2.12. The wheelbase of a vehicle is the distance between the center of the front wheel and the center of the rear wheel.

Figure 2.13. An example of a very long wheelbase.

Figure 2.14. An example of a short wheelbase.

scenes where this measurement could be made are depicted in Figures 2.4 and 2.5, where the four tires came to a stop and/or changed direction. When wheelbase measurements are made, they should be made on both sides. A less common opportunity to make this measurement would be in those instances where a car stops in sand, soft soil, or snow long enough to leave four distinct depressions where the bottoms of each tire came to rest. Making a wheelbase measurement in these situations would be from either the center of the depression of the front tire on one side to the rear tire on that side or, if detail permitted, the leading edge measurements as described above. Other methods of making a wheelbase measurement from crime scene tracks have been published but are more difficult, are approximate, and can only be made on a rather pristine set of tracks at the scene.[1, 2]

Rolling Circumference

Rolling circumference is the linear distance traveled in one revolution by an inflated tire under load, as illustrated in Figure 2.15. It is not the same as the measurement of the tire's circumference that is not under load. To measure the rolling circumference of a mounted tire under load, the measurement must be made of one full rotation of the tire. An easy way to calculate this is to apply a spot of paint to the road surface, run the center of the tire over

[1] Bolhouse, R. J. "The Identification of Vehicles from Wheelbase and Tire Stance Measurements." (1984).

[2] Nause, L. A. Forensic Tire Impression Identification. (2001).

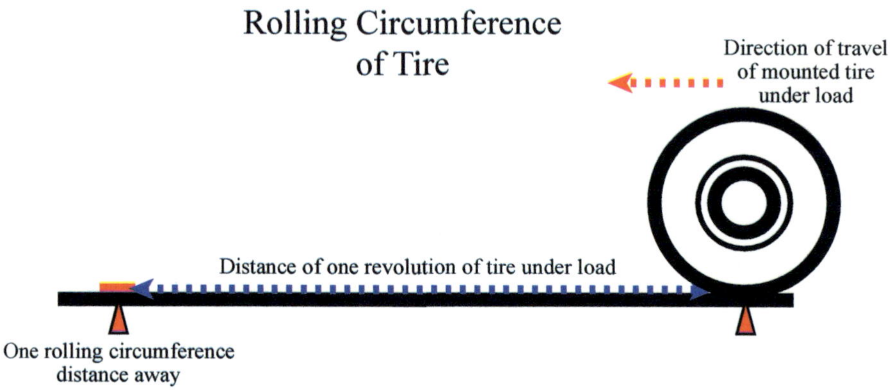

Figure 2.15. Rolling circumference is the distance it takes a mounted tire under load to make one full revolution. It is a shorter measurement than the measurement of the circumference of the unloaded tire. This measurement can be made at scenes when a tire tracks through a substance such as blood or grease and deposits it with each complete revolution.

the paint spot, and continue at least one full rotation until the tire deposits the paint back onto the surface, allowing a measurement between the two spots. Rolling circumference varies with load and inflation. Variations in this measurement will also occur due to various factors, including differences in deflection on a hard surface versus a soft surface. A forensic application of this might occur if a tire runs through a substance, such as blood or grease, and then leaves evidence of that substance each time the tire rolls one full circumference. In cases where this measurement might be required for comparison with crime scene evidence, be sure to not measure the tire circumference of the un-mounted tire, but measure the rolling circumference of the mounted tire under the load of the vehicle. As an example, a tire on a full-size vehicle was determined to have a rolling circumference of 78 inches under load. The same tire, not under the load of the vehicle, had a measured circumference of 81.5 inches. It is also important to note that due to the rounded shoulder profile of many tires, the measured circumference of an unloaded tire will be less on the shoulder than in the center of the tire. In this example, the measured circumference of the center of the unloaded tire was 81.5 inches, and the measured circumference along the shoulder of the unloaded tire was 80.25 inches.

Making Measurements of the Suspect Vehicle

Whenever track measurements are obtained from a scene and need to be compared with a suspect vehicle, they should be compared against measurements made of the actual vehicle itself, rather than relying on the manufacturer's specifications for that vehicle. The following measurements may need to be taken when conducting this examination:

- Track width can be measured by extending a tape measure from the center point of one tire to the center point of the tire on the opposing side. The measurement can also be taken from a set of known tracks prepared with the vehicle.
- Turning diameter can be made by taking the suspect vehicle to a flat area that will record the impressions of the tires, and then making a turn with the steering wheel fully turned in one direction. The diameter can then be measured and calculated as in Figure 2.10.
- Wheelbase can be measured by extending a tape from the center bottom of one tire to the center bottom of the other tire on the same side of the vehicle. The wheels should be positioned straight ahead and both sides should be measured, as they should produce the same measurement.
- Rolling circumference must be measured with the tire on the vehicle under load. A spot of paint can be placed on the center of the tire, or on the road surface. The distance it takes to make one full revolution will constitute the rolling circumference and will be the distance between two spots of the paint.

If after taking track measurements from a suspect vehicle it becomes necessary to remove the tires for examination, the tires should first be permanently identified and marked as to their position on the vehicle. This would include writing on the outside of the tires information that would denote their position, such as left front (LF), right front (RF), left rear (LR), and right rear (RR).

Aftermarket Wheels and Tires

The term *aftermarket wheels* refers to wheels on vehicles that are not OEM equipment. This often includes larger wheels combined with different tire sizes to fit those wheels. In less extreme cases, the wheels may still be able to fit on the stock vehicle. In more extreme cases, the car will need to be elevated or body work will be necessary to accommodate the larger wheel and

Figure 2.16. Aftermarket wheels involve wheel and tire changes that are different from the OEM equipment. All of these will likely change the track measurements.

Figure 2.17. Another example of aftermarket wheels, this Jeep has oversized tires with modified wheels having a large negative offset and widening the track width.

tire packages. Figures 2.16 and 2.17 depict examples of aftermarket wheels. When a vehicle is equipped with aftermarket equipment, that equipment will change the OEM track measurements. This is another reason to use the actual measurements taken from the suspect vehicle itself and not use measurements for that vehicle, as provided through databases or car manufacturers.

Other Track Evidence

Characteristics of the tracks are best observed and interpreted while at the scene to assist in their overall evaluation.

Those who recover tire evidence should be aware of and document other potentially important features with sketches and accompanying general scene photographs. Some of these other features that may be noted and important are:

- Impressions of one vehicle cutting through another impression is proof that vehicle passed through the scene after the other (Figure 2.18).

Figure 2.18. A tire impression that cuts through another can establish which tire made its impression last. This is useful to show the relevance and sequence of tire impressions at crime scenes. In this photograph of several tracks, it is evident which ones were made last as they have cut through and obliterated portions of the tracks that were already present.

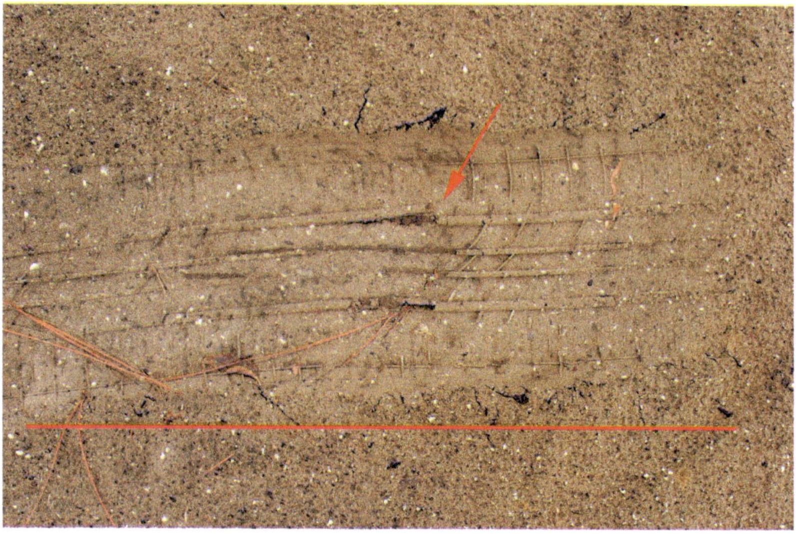

Figure 2.19. Track endings denote a reversal of a vehicle's direction at the scene. In this example where a track ends, the red arrow and baseline show the change of direction of the track of the front tire.

Figure 2.20. One of these impressions is straight (rear tire) and one is not straight (steering tire).

- Areas of a track where there is evidence of the wheel spinning will provide evidence that tire is on the drive axle.
- Tracks that dead end indicate the vehicle stopped and changed direction. Because the front tires steer and are not fixed in a rigid position, tracks that are wobbly or not perfectly straight, particularly on off-road surfaces, can be attributed to the steering tires (Figures 2.19 and 2.20).
- Points of stopping and starting are often evidenced by small changes of direction and/or a change in detail of the tread's impression.
- The presence of shoe impression evidence in areas that relate to the position of the vehicle such as areas where the perpetrator was exiting/entering the vehicle as well as the sequence of whether the shoe impression or tire impression came first (Figures 2.5 and 2.21).

Figure 2.21. Intersection of footwear evidence in combination with tire evidence can be very relevant. Any areas around the vehicle that contain footwear impressions should be documented, including whether the footwear impressions were made prior to or after the tire impressions. In these cases, a more detailed photograph, such as presented here, will clearly document this. See also the footwear impressions in Figure 2.5.

- Tracks that have a weathered appearance may be older tracks and thus not related to the crime (Figure 2.22).
- Single and/or narrow tracks such as those left by bicycles or motorcycles should be documented (Figure 2.23).
- Spinning tire tracks on a road may provide an opportunity to make a track measurement. Note the parallel features of two sets of tracks indicative of both tires spinning and depositing rubber on the road. In some cases at the end of the track, some partial design of the tire may be recorded (Figure 2.24).

Over the years there have been many attempts to analyze rubber samples that have been scraped from tire tracks on the roadway that have resulted from either spinning or braking tires. These attempts have been challenging due to contamination issues, sample sizes available from a particular track and the non-homogenous nature of the tire rubber as blended in the Banbury mixer. A recent study regarding attempts to make these analyses has some success discriminating between compounds of different tire brands. [3]

Figure 2.22. Weathered tracks at crime scenes should be noted and may be relevant or irrelevant, depending on when the crime occurred. In this example, the tracks have almost completely been washed away by rain, evidenced by a raindrop pattern in the soil.

[3] Sarkissian G., "The analysis of tire rubber traces collected after braking incidents using pyrolysis-gas chromatography/mass spectrometry" JFS, September, 2007, vol. 52, No. 5, pp 1050–1056.

Figure 2.23. Bicycle tracks, pictured here, and motorcycle and dirt bike tracks are single impressions and easily distinguished from car and light truck tire impressions.

Figure 2.24. Spinning tire tracks may offer some information about the vehicle, such as rear track width and single versus dual traction. Some limited tread design may also be present along the tracks.

Documenting and Recovering Tire Impression Evidence

3

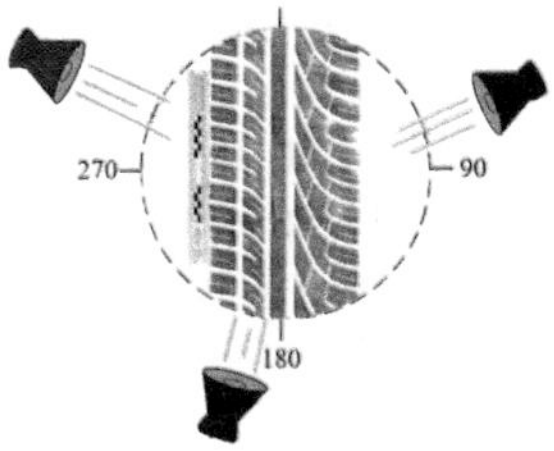

The Crime Scene

Tires leave their impressions over a multitude of surfaces such as snow, dirt roads and shoulders, and other unpaved areas. A tire may also leave a grazing mark of its sidewall or tread against the shirt of a hit-and-run victim or produce a blunt force injury that leaves a contusion that replicates its tread pattern on the skin of the victim's body. At some scenes, tire impressions may be short and isolated. Other scenes may include long impressions of all four tires. The examination of these impressions can place the perpetrator's vehicle at the scene of the crime but, in order to benefit from the full potential of this evidence, these impressions need to be recovered properly and their location and relationship to the crime scene must be properly documented.

The concept that an investigating officer or crime scene technician who has not witnessed the crime but could later use their training, knowledge, skill, patience, fortitude, and insight to locate, recognize, and recover virtually every piece of physical evidence at a crime scene is quite a large expectation. Nevertheless, the attempt to do this is exactly what occurs at crime scenes. With some types of evidence, the task of collection and recovery is quick and easy and the need to collect that evidence is more readily understood. For instance, at a homicide scene, a weapon laying next to the victim is highly visible and its evidentiary value is obvious. In a burglary, specific areas where glass is broken, doors are kicked in, or safes are cracked, or where the robbers have stood or jumped onto counters, are provided greater attention, as it is easily understood the perpetrator was there and may have left fingerprints, shoe prints, or other trace evidence. But tire impression and tire track evidence are often away from the center of the crime scene area and in less conspicuous locations.

In many cases, tire evidence will only be found if the crime scene personnel have a constant awareness of its possible existence and make an aggressive effort to search, locate, document, and recover it. The first officer on the scene must take early action to protect the scene from other vehicular and pedestrian traffic. Along these lines, an officer responding to any crime scene where surface conditions would allow for the retention of tire impressions should immediately preserve that entire area in anticipation of the potential existence of this evidence. I have witnessed crime scenes where this was done very promptly and efficiently. Figure 3.1 is a photograph taken at the perimeter of a scene. The preservation of this area and awareness of the potential tire impressions resulted in the subsequent recovery of significant tire evidence. Unfortunately this is not always the case. But even when the scene is preserved and the presence of tire evidence recognized, the improper, hasty, or sloppy recovery of that evidence can prevent successful examination results. A case in point was one crime scene where numerous tracks of the perpetrators vehicle were in newly fallen snow next to a homicide victim in an empty lot, depicted in Figure 3.2. These tracks provided an opportunity not only to capture good tread impression details of all four tires, but also measure the wheelbase and both front and rear track widths. Figure 3.3 depicts a continuation of this scene where a tight turn of the vehicle provided an opportunity to recover turning diameter measurements. The investigator's limited knowledge of tire evidence, including incorrect measurements of only the front tracks and, later an incorrect assessment and measurement of the perpetrator's vehicle, rendered this evidence essentially useless. Even worse than the above examples are those cases where tire evidence is not even considered at the crime scene but turns out to be an afterthought hours or even days after the crime occurred and long after that evidence has been lost.

Figure 3.1. When a homicide victim was reported found at this scene, officers quickly sealed the entire area off, realizing the potential of tire and footwear impressions.

Figure 3.2. In this case, the perpetrator and homicide victim both exited the vehicle on the passenger side. The perpetrator's returning shoe prints lead to the driver's side. The vehicle had been backed into this area, stopped, and after the homicide, pulled away in a right-hand turn. Although these tracks allow for measurement of the front and rear track width and the wheelbase, none of these measurements were taken.

Figure 3.3. At the same scene as depicted in Figure 3.2, tight turning tracks allowed for the measurement of the turning diameter of the perpetrator's vehicle, which unfortunately was not done.

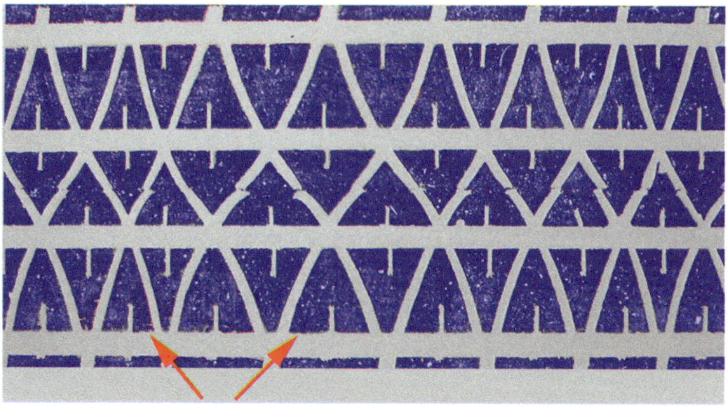

Figure 3.4. Because the size and arrangement of tread blocks vary around the circumference of a tire, it is important to recover as much of its 6- to 8-foot impression as possible.

Putting Tire Impression Recovery in Perspective

A full rotation of a passenger car or light truck tire is approximately 6 to 8 feet in length. Arranged around the circumference of that tire, the numerous tread blocks that comprise the tread design vary in their size and arrangement, as illustrated in Figure 3.4.[1] This means a 6-foot-long tire impression is not simply a repeat of six consecutive 1-foot-long impressions in a row, but is actually a single 6-foot-long impression with continuously changing dimensional features. Further, positioned throughout that tire's long tread are both wear and individual characteristics that contribute to its uniqueness. Thus, recovering a mere 1-foot section of a 6-foot long tire impression would be like recovering 2 inches of a 12-inch shoe impression.

What then is an acceptable method of recovering tire evidence? In cases where the total tire impression runs for 4 feet or less the answer is easy in that the entirety of that impression can and must be recovered through both photography and casting. For scenes having multiple and/or longer impressions, the task of recovering all of the impression evidence soon becomes logistically impossible. Still, the recovery of a sizeable portion of this evidence in the proper way should be made to ensure each tire impression is represented and to significantly increase chances for identification with a tire from the perpetrator's vehicle. There is no simple predetermined answer as to exactly how much of the impression evidence should be recovered in cases involving long lengths of tire impressions. It should be quite obvious in a case involving 25 to 50 feet of impressions of each of the four tires that taking a

[1] This is explained and illustrated in much more detail under the section of Noise Treatment covered in Chapter 7.

few photographs and making one 6-inch cast would be grossly inadequate. The overall quality and quantity of that evidence must be considered at each scene along with the decision as to how much can realistically be recovered. In addition, any track dimensional information present should also be carefully measured and documented.

No one purports to be able to pick the best five out of ten latent fingerprints before they are lifted from a scene and examined. Nor can someone look at five footwear impressions in soil and reliably predict which one will ultimately allow for the strongest examination result. The same is true when trying to assess the value of tire impressions at a scene. This is compounded by the fact that often there are several sets of tire tracks and impressions and, in some cases, there may not be any preliminary information that might suggest which of these, if any, may have been made by the perpetrator's vehicle. A systematic evaluation of these tracks will likely reduce the quantity that need to be recovered, yet the remaining tracks may still constitute a large volume of evidence. In general, the best guidelines regarding how much should be recovered can only be discussed in terms of the minimum amount, which should include photographic documentation and at least one 3-foot cast of each of the potentially important tracks.

Detail Retained in Impressions

When a tire leaves an impression, it transfers its class, wear, and individual characteristics to the substrate. If the substrate is soft sand, soil, mud, or snow, the weight of the vehicle will press these features into the surface in the form of a three-dimensional impression. If the substrate is hard, such as concrete or asphalt, the tire can deposit dirt, dust, mud, or blood in the form of a two-dimensional impression. Like other forms of impression evidence, the direct physical contact of a tire tread against a surface sometimes results in highly detailed impressions, while in other instances the detail retained is poor. A number of factors determine how much detail will be retained. Coarsely grained sand and gravel mixtures are limited by their particle size regarding the degree of detail they can retain. Finely grained sand and soil mixtures and clay soils retain much better detail. Moisture has a large influence on the retention of detail, as shown in Figure 3.5. Dryer soils normally do not retain as much detail as do soils containing moisture; however, excessively wet conditions may also impede some detail retention in other cases. Any contaminants mixed in the substrate, such as stones, sticks, rocks, or debris, will interfere with the reproduction of detail in any impression, as depicted in Figure 3.6. Crime scene technicians and examiners have no control over the amount of detail that is produced in a tire impression at the scene of a crime; however, they do control the search for, preservation, recovery, and documentation of that evidence.

Figure 3.5. A tire impression traveling through wet and dry sand illustrates how moisture can affect the retention of detail.

Figure 3.6. Contaminates that occur naturally in the substrate will often interfere with the retention of detail in those areas.

Recovery of Impression Evidence

The recovery of tire evidence at any particular scene involves a number of specific procedures and techniques. Additional information on the recoery of impression evidence in general can be found through other sources, including *Footwear Impression Evidence: Detection, Recovery and Examina-*

Inset 3.1. General Information for Preserving and Documenting Tire Evidence

- As soon as possible, beginning with the first officer on the scene, visually recognize any potential area in which the perpetrator's vehicle may have left impressions or track evidence.
- Establish an outer perimeter to prevent other vehicles or persons from entering that area.
- Be cognizant that not only tire impressions could be in those areas, but also footwear impressions and other evidence related to the crime.
- If daylight, walk around the perimeter to carefully view the area. Light reflects in different ways and impressions visible from one side of the perimeter may not be clearly visible from the opposite side. If at night, halogen lamps are inexpensive and provide excellent search tools to assist in the detection and recovery of tire impression evidence.
- If other vehicles' tracks are in the area, do not be discouraged or believe that tire evidence is no longer recoverable. Rather, identify those other vehicles and obtain elimination photographs or impressions of their tires. Tires of vehicles having nothing to do with the crime can be eliminated based on design differences, and then a concentrated effort can be made to document and recover the remaining impressions made by the perpetrator's tires. This is the time to attempt to sort out what tracks are relevant to the crime, what tracks can be eliminated, and whether elimination impressions of other vehicles need to be taken.
- Be keen to observe worn or weathered tracks in contrast to fresh tracks; tracks of different types such as dual-wheeled trucks or single-wheel bikes; areas where tracks cut through other tracks; and areas where footwear impressions are associated with tire tracks, indicating the driver exited and reentered the vehicle.
- A scene with only a short impression will be rather simple to approach and recover. A scene encompassing larger areas with multiple tire tracks from several vehicles will be more complex. Depending on the scene and impressions of importance within, create the best plan for recovering the tire evidence.
- Place identifiers next to each impression or item of evidence within the scene to identify their location. Later, these same identifiers should be used in the examination quality photographs and/or casts of those impressions.
- After identifiers are positioned, take additional general crime scene photographs showing the tire impressions with the identifiers.
- After the documentation and general scene photography, take examination quality photographs and cast three-dimensional impressions.

tion,[2] SWGTREAD guidelines,[3] and the International Association for Identification's Recommended Course of Study.[4] Inset 3.1 provides some general considerations useful for preserving and documenting tire impressions.

Original Tire Evidence

Most tire impressions are not recoverable in their original form but must be photographed, cast, or lifted. However, occasionally a tire will leave its impression on victim's clothing or on debris such as wood or paper that it tracked over. In these cases, after photography and documentation at the scene, the original items bearing those impressions should always be recovered. It is likely that forensic photography as well as enhancement techniques later performed in the laboratory might permit for the recovery of even greater detail of the impressions on those items than is possible to recover at the crime scene.

Photographing Tire Evidence at the Crime Scene

Film versus Digital Cameras

A study conducted in 2006 determined that only insignificant and virtually unnoticeable differences were present between images taken with 6 megapixel and 14 megapixel digital single lens reflex (SLR) cameras and with a 35-mm film camera. The study also noted that using a medium format film camera (2.25 inch) did provide noticeably better detail.[5] Regardless of the differences between using a film camera versus a digital camera, professional digital SLR cameras have almost totally replaced traditional film cameras. Nearly every police department has already made the change to digital cameras for general crime scene and examination quality photography. But it is important to emphasize that if a digital camera is used, it should minimally be an 8- to 12-megapixel (preferably higher) professional digital SLR camera with a good quality lens. Further, the maximum file size should always

[2] Bodziak, W. J. Footwear Impression Evidence (2000).
[3] Scientific Working Group on Shoe Print and Tire Tread Evidence (SWGTREAD) guidelines, posted on the IAI Web site http://www.theiai.org/guidelines/swgtread/index.php.
[4] IAI Recommended Course of Study for Footwear and Tire Track Examiners, at IAI website (revised 2006) http://www.theiai.org/publications
[5] Jacobia, J., and Blitzer, H. "Effects of Photographic Technology on Quality of Examination of Footwear Impressions". Journal of Forensic Identification 2007, 57(5) 641–657.

be used. Large capacity storage cards are now relatively inexpensive.[6] If the camera stores the pictures in a JPEG format, the camera should be set at the lowest compression setting. Regardless of whether that camera's file is produced as a JPEG, TIFF, or RAW file, at least one unchanged copy of the original downloaded file should be kept and safely stored. Remember that size and resolution issues are even more critical when photographing larger tire impressions than when photographing shorter shoe impressions, as in the aforementioned study. Whereas on 8- to 12-megapixel digital SLR camera may approach the detail of film of a 12-in. shoe print, photographing larger tire impressions requires overlapping 12-in. photographs to capture the same detail.

General Crime Scene Photographs

General crime scene photographs are taken to photographically document the location of tire impressions, tracks, and other evidence within the overall scene as a supplement to written notes. They are not intended nor are they useful for detailed examinations with tires. Using numbered (1, 2, 3, etc.) or lettered (A, B, C, D, etc.) identifiers of various sizes and colors, placed next to key areas in the crime scene has been practiced for decades. By using these in the photographs, it becomes easier to properly document a crime scene. The use of identifiers positioned next to the impressions, and thus visible in the photographs, provides an easy and accurate way to link the crime scene written notes with the actual evidence that is later recovered through examination quality photography and casting. Figure 3.7 is a composite of a medium-range photograph and a close-range photograph. The medium-range photograph provides a view of three identifiers that mark the location of a tire impression (#5), a shoe impression (#6), and clothing (#7). The close-range general crime scene photograph of the tire impression (#5) does not include a scale because it will not be used for a detailed examination, but it provides additional detail of that item for purposes of recognition and documentation. A subsequent examination quality photograph of this same impression, depicted in Figure 3.8, uses the same identifier, in this case, the numeral 5, which is on a label placed on top of the ruler. When a cast is later taken of this impression, the numeral 5 will be used again, thus linking the general crime scene photographs, the examination quality photographs, and the cast.

The general scene photographs should account for all potentially relevant tracks. Tire tracks, particularly several tracks spanning a large physical area, benefit from being photographed from different sides. The technique of

[6] For example, a 1-gigabyte storage card in an 8.3-megapixel Canon 20D camera, set at an ISO of 100 and at the lowest JPEG compression rate will store 265 JPEG and RAW images.

Figure 3.7. A composite of a general crime scene photograph taken to show the relative locations of a tire impression (5), a shoe impression (6), and clothing (7), and a general crime scene photograph of the impression identified as #5 taken at close range. This close-range photograph is for documentation only and not for examination.

Figure 3.8. An examination quality photograph taken of the impression in Figure 3.8. This type of photograph is taken strictly for examination with a tire from a suspected vehicle. It is taken with the camera on a tripod and always using a scale that has been placed parallel to and at the same level as the bottom of the tire impression.

photographing from several sides and perspectives not only is a more effective way of documenting the tire impressions but also takes advantage of the way natural light reflects off of the impressions from different angles. Figure 3.9A and 3.9B depict an area containing multiple tire impressions photographed from the perimeter on two different sides. More sides and perspectives would be recommended, but for illustration only two are shown here. Note how the reflection of the natural existing light allows for different information in each photograph. Figure 3.9B shows better separation of some of the tracks than does Figure 3.9A. The opposite could be said for some of the other tracks that appear better in 3.9A. At scenes where many close tracks are involved, several photographs from many angles and sides should be taken Walking around the perimeter and initially studing and documenting it in this way will provide an opportunity to possibly eliminate some tracks which will make subsequent recovery easier.

Figure 3.10A depicts a night crime scene where either headlights or flash units were aimed directly at the impressions from the same point of view as the camera. Portions of the tire impressions are washed out and there is no use of oblique light to enhance the impressions. The lighting in this example

A

B

Figure 3.9. Two general crime scene photographs taken from opposing sides illustrate how the reflection of existing light from different angles affects the detail and information seen and photographed. For this reason, the general crime scene photographs of impression areas, particularly with multiple impressions, should be photographed from many sides.

actually made the photographs worse. Figure 3.10B is a night scene where halogen lights on tripods were positioned at oblique angles with their height adjusted to enhance the tire impressions.

When the time comes to actually enter the scene, each track should be assigned at least one identifier and again the general scene should be photographed. This will help ensure that all impressions of potential value at that scene have been accounted for and documented and will enable the best use of additional photographs, taken from different sides and angles. Careful thought should be given to the placement of the identifiers and should include areas of possible interest such as intersections of tracks of different

A

B

Figure 3.10. **A.** A night scene photograph taken with light from the flash of the camera or headlights of a car positioned improperly. The tire impressions are hardly visible because the light was from the same direction as the camera instead of from the side. **B.** Taken with oblique light provided from halogen lights on tripods and clearly identifies the tracks and their relationship. Proper use of portable lights at night allows for both better interpretation and better photographic documentation.

vehicles. Although the importance of the recovery of some of the impressions may be unclear at the time, the best and perhaps only chance of capturing this evidence is during the scene processing. If certain aspects of the tire evidence are not documented and later become a significant issue, sufficient detail will not normally be present in the overall general crime scene photographs to examine or resolve that issue.

Examination Quality Photographs

The term *examination quality photograp*h refers to a photograph taken with the camera positioned directly over the top of the impression for the specific purpose of later using that photograph in a detailed examination with tires from a suspect vehicle. Because they are taken for the specific purpose of examination, each and every one of these photographs must include a linear scale such as a ruler. Unfortunately, a few still advocate using a scale in every other photograph instead of every photograph. I respectfully and strongly disagree with this practice. Examination quality photographs are being taken for one purpose only and that is for a detailed examination that is very reliant on accuracy in size. Any photograph not taken properly with a scale in the picture is of greatly diminished value.

There are many factors to be aware of when taking examination quality photographs of tire impressions. One of the most important factors is recognizing and understanding the need to photographically record the impression in a way that will allow dimensionally accurate natural-sized enlargement to later be prepared. Because most tread designs contain rows of tread blocks arranged around the circumference of the tire, and because these tread blocks are many different sizes and proportions, the difference in size of each of these tread blocks must be accurately recorded. One tread block that is 1.3 inches long may be hard to distinguish from another that is 1.4 inches long unless the photographs were properly taken and can be accurately enlarged to their proper size. A very common mistake made when photographing impression evidence is the failure to position the ruler on the same plane (level) as the bottom of the impression. In the photographs in Inset 3.2 this was done properly. Figure 3.11 depicts an incorrect example where the ruler was placed on the natural ridge of soil, which was at least ½ to 1 inch above the bottom of the impression. If the scale is not positioned accurately on the same plane as the bottom of the impression, enlargements of this photograph to an accurate natural size will not be possible and will prevent the use of this photograph for an accurate dimensional analysis. The reason is simple: Objects more distant from the lens will appear smaller than objects closer to the lens. (Think of standing in the middle of the railroad tracks looking down the tracks. The tracks appear smaller [closer together] as they get farther away.) If the ruler is closer to the lens than the impression,

Figure 3.11. This is an example of incorrectly using a scale. The scale is resting on the edge of the impression at least a ½ to 1 inch higher than the bottom of the impression. This photograph will not be useful in a dimensional analysis with a known tire, because there is no way to make an accurate photographic enlargement of the impression. When the scale is enlarged to its natural size, the tire impression will not be accurately sized.

the photograph can be enlarged so the scale of the ruler is natural size, but the image of the impression, which is farther away, will then be smaller in that photograph than it actually is. When sinking the ruler down to that level of the bottom of the tire impression, position the ruler next to but not in the impression while being careful not to disturb the impression. In some case, you might need to carefully excavate a small amount of soil to achieve this. Figure 3.12 depicts an examination quality photograph of a tire impression. A 3-foot yardstick was carefully recessed into the soil outside and parallel

Figure 3.12. A 3-foot yard stick has been recessed into the ground to the same level (plane) as the bottom of the tire impression. This provides a properly positioned flat and rigid scale that can be used to produce accurate natural size enlargements for later examination with a tire.

to a portion of the long impression. The yardstick provides a straight and rigid 36-inch scale. If a more finely divided scale is preferred, a flat and finely divided ruler can be placed over the yardstick in the areas that each examination quality photograph is taken as in Inset 3.2. Any ruler used should be sufficiently rigid and should be placed in a way to avoid sagging or bending. Metal tapes are not suitable for that reason. Longer rulers, minimally 12 inches or 300 mm, should be used as they allow for easier and more accurate natural size enlargements.

Because tire impressions are larger and longer than shoe impressions, impressions greater than 12 to 14 inches normally cannot be captured on one photograph by most high-end SLR digital cameras while still maintaining the detail necessary for examination. Rather, a series of overlapping photographs must be taken as shown in Inset 3.2. These photographs can later be spliced together to reconstruct the longer impression.

Below is a list of steps and techniques that should be followed closely when taking examination quality photographs.

- Your camera should be a professional quality SLR camera with the capability of interchangeable lenses, manual focus, and aperture priority and a detachable flash unit. The flash unit will be used in a detached position and therefore should either have a minimum 4- to 6-foot extension cord such as the Nikon SC-17 or SC-28 type cords. Cords that only extend to 3 feet are not adequate. Canon does not produce a long extension cord, but does have an excellent wireless SP-E2 speed light transmitter that will activate one or more flash units. A point-and-shoot camera should never be used for this type of photography! Figure 3.13 depicts the use of an SLR camera on a tripod positioned directly over the center of the tire impression. This camera is equipped with a coiled flash extension that permits the flash to be held at a distance of 4 to 6 feet to provide an even distribution of oblique light.
- Select the lens. A fixed focal length lens requires raising or lowering the camera on the tripod to frame the impression properly. The zoom lens allows for more convenient framing of the impression because it can zoom in and out.
- If using a digital SLR camera, always use an ISO 100 equivalent setting. If capturing the pictures in a JPEG image, be sure to set the camera to the lowest compression setting. If using a film camera, use ISO 100 color film. Set the camera on manual focus and adjust the timer as desired. Also set the camera on aperture priority with the appropriate lens position.
- Use a rigid linear ruler with a finely divided scale. The scale should minimally be 12 inches long. Place the scale alongside the length of the section of the impression being photographed. If the impression is

Figure 3.13. A tripod with a camera directly over the impression. A long flash cord or wireless remote flash will permit the proper use of oblique light to add contrast to the photographed impression.

three dimensional, sink the ruler into the soil, sand, or snow adjacent to the impression so it is on the same plane (level) as the bottom of the impression, as depicted in Inset 3.2. When doing this, be careful not to disturb the impression or cause debris to fall into the impression. Never place the ruler or any other object across or in the impression!

- Place the camera on a tripod and position it so the lens is directly over the center of the segment of the impression being photographed. The long axis of the camera frame should run parallel to the length of the tire impression. View the impression and ruler through the lens to ensure you have properly framed the content as depicted in the individual photographs in Inset 3.2. Figure 3.14 depicts an incorrectly framed impression with the long axis of the film plane running at 90 degrees to the impression, wasting a good portion of the image area.
- *Never take examination quality photographs while holding the camera in your hands!* It is simply not possible to take a proper series of detailed, properly illuminated, focused photographs while holding the camera.
- Always focus manually before each exposure. The point of focus should be on the bottom of the impression because this is where the design, wear, and individual characteristics are recorded in the substrate by the tire tread. Trying to take photographs using the automatic focus setting provides unpredictable results and is not recommended. In addition, the automatic focus often does not work well when photo-

Inset 3.2.

Taking overlapping photographs of long tire impressions.

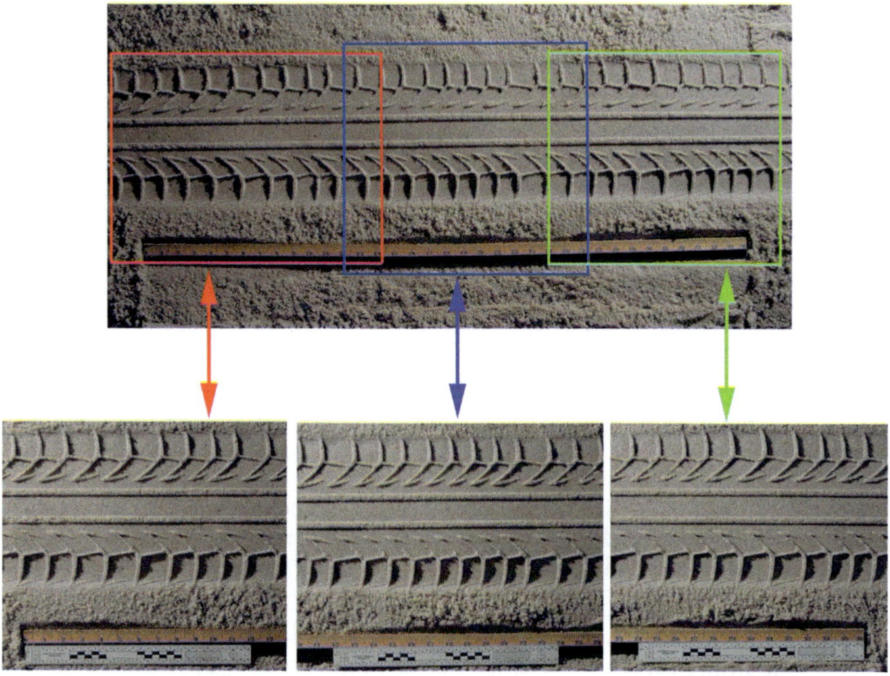

Figure 3.14. This photograph was taken with the long axis of the picture running across the tire impression. This is not an efficient way to maximize the photograph, as a large portion of the photograph is simply waste.

graphing impressions in soil or snow, thus causing the photographer to focus on some other part of the scene such as the ruler. Often when using the auto focus setting to photograph impressions in soil or other textured substrate, you will hear the camera motor running as it is makes unsuccessful attempts to focus. Always focus manually before each and every exposure and focus on the bottom of the impression. This is only way you can be assured that you have done this properly.

- Using the timer to activate the shutter is strongly advisable for a couple reasons. First, it allows the exposure to be made while no physical contact is being made with the camera, thus ensuring the camera is not being moved during the time of exposure. Movement of the camera would blur the photograph. Second, it frees the hands of the photographer and allows him or her to concentrate on positioning the flash to provide oblique light at the proper distance, height, and direction.
- If the impression is 12 to 14 inches or less, it can be photographed in one segment. Simply adjust the camera and lens so the entire impression and ruler fills the frame. If the impression is longer, it must be photographed in overlapping segments, as depicted in Inset 3.2. A good method of taking several sequential photographs of a long impression involves placing a long stationary rigid ruler, such as a yardstick, alongside of the full length of the impression to be photographed. This will not be used as the scale but will simply assist in the later reconstruction of the sequential photographs. It will also provide a platform to assure the scale is on the same plane for each photograph. Place a separate and finely divided scale such as a 300-mm ruler as the scale in each individual exposure. After photographing each segment, advance the scale, tripod, and camera about 10 to 12 inches along the length of the impression, allowing the content of each frame to overlap considerably with the preceding photograph. This should be repeated until the desired length of the impression has been photographed.
- During daylight hours the first photograph taken of each impression segment can be taken with the existing ambient light. Subsequent photographs should employ the use of either an electronic flash or another intense light source to provide oblique light, which will enhance the detail in the photograph. For three-dimensional impressions, the oblique light highlights the raised areas of the impression while allowing the lower areas of the impression to remained in the shadows, thus providing additional contrast. Never take a photograph with the flash mounted on the camera and aimed directly at the impression, as it will reduce contrast and wash out the detail you are trying to capture. Figure 3.15 illustrates the adverse effects of aiming the flash directly at an impression. Compare the contast in Figure 3.15 with the photographs in Inset 3.2.

Figure 3.15. Aiming a flash directly at the impression reduces any contrast. Always detach the flash unit from the camera and use oblique light to maximize the contrast when photographing impression evidence.

- The electronic flash should be set on the TTL (through the lens) setting and, during exposure, should be held at least 4 to 6 feet from the tire impression. This distance allows the light to "even out," thereby avoiding situations where the side of the impression closest to the flash is overexposed in relation to the distant side being underexposed. Figure 3.16 shows an example where the flash was positioned too close to the impression. Also be careful to aim the flash correctly. The flash is being used to create an oblique light source that should be directed evenly across the impression.
- If photographing during the day with bright sunlight or bright ambient light, you must shield the impression from the sun so the flash becomes the dominant light source. This can easily be accomplished with a large black cloth (Figure 3.17). Local fabric stores have many black fabrics. Some fabrics will block out more light than others. Normally a quantity of a good light-blocking black fabric can be obtained for a few dollars. The cloth should extend to the ground, but caution must be used to ensure the cloth does not accidentally drag through the impression, particularly if conditions are windy.
- Oblique light on tire impressions should be directed from three angles. One of these should be directed along the length of the track, since that will be a good angle to detect any tread wear indicators. The other angles should be

Figure 3.16. An incorrectly taken photograph where the flash was either too close to the impression or aimed improperly at the near side of the impression. The result is an overexposure at the near side and an underexposure at the far side. This is why a flash or light source must be positioned 4 to 6 feet away, allowing for the oblique light to even out.

Figure 3.17. The use of a black cloth to block out bright ambient light is necessary. If this is not done, then the oblique light from the flash will be dominated by the existing bright ambient light.

from two positions around the impression. Inset 3.3 provides some basic information about the use of oblique light for impression photography.

- If examination photographs are taken in this prescribed manner, they can be accurately enlarged to their natural size for comparison with a tire. Two or more photographs taken in sequence may also be stitched

Inset 3.3.

Using Oblique Light

Two-Dimensional Impressions

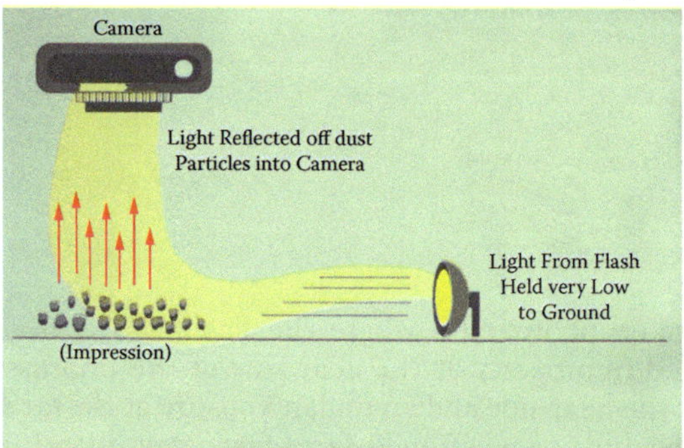

Oblique light that skims the surface will reflect off of dust or residue at 90° and into the camera lens. The light must be held very low, almost grazing the surface.

Three-Dimensional Impressions

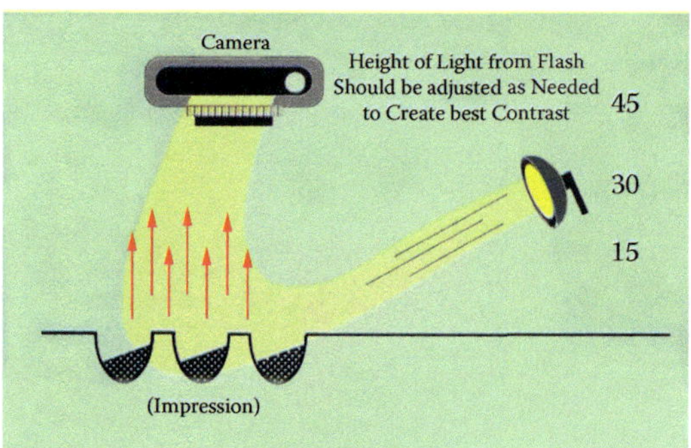

Oblique light creates contrast by shadowing the low areas while illuminating the high areas. The height of the light will be higher with deep impressions and lower with shallow impressions.

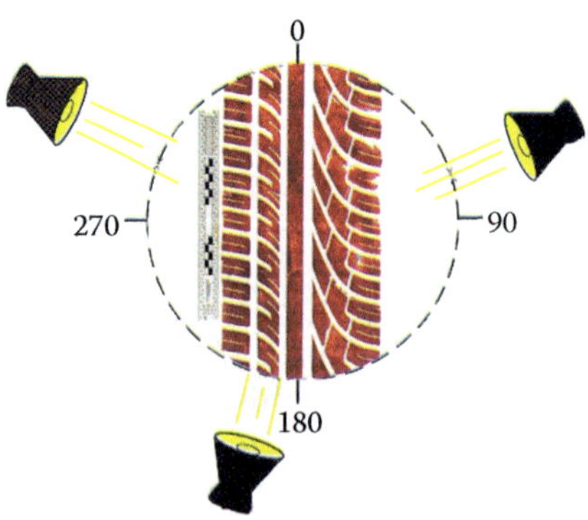

Holding the light at the proper height, photograph the impression with the light from three different positions around the impression.

to create a natural-size reproduction of a greater length of the impression. This has traditionally been done manually in a cut-and-paste fashion when using natural-sized prints made with film. Digitally, it can be done on the computer by using programs such as Adobe Photoshop which allows the photographs to be digitally stitched together, after which the combined image can be printed. Limitations to the digital method may include computer file sizes of combined impressions and the limited size of paper on which a single image can be printed.

Casting Three-Dimensional Impressions

Three-dimensional impressions should always be cast. Casts provide very accurate representations of tire impressions and allow for the recovery of more detailed and size accurate evidence. Whereas photographs are necessary and serve a purpose, they are often accompanied by problems relating to perspective, focus, scale, lighting, depth-of-field, distortion, excessive shadows, and other factors that can limit the examination. With very few exceptions, a three-dimensional cast represents all of the features, dimensions, and details better than a photograph of a three-dimensional impression.

Impressions in soil, sand, mud, and snow can and must be cast. There is really no valid reason not to make a dental stone cast of a three-dimensional impression. To say "the impression was not suitable for casting" is incorrect, and anyone who says this either needs additional training in casting techniques or is making excuses. In most cases the successful casting of a tire impression will result in greater detail and greater examination results. The exception to this may be those cases where the impression was made in coarsely textured materials, such as the typical gravel and sand mix on a road shoulder or on a mixed gravel and soil road. In these cases, the actual detail may be less than captured in a photograph because of the tendency for the coarse surface material to interfere with the detail, but there will still be some detail retained plus the accurate size features of the cast impression will be invaluable.

To make casts of tire impressions, the proper dental stone material and the proper technique are essential. If the impression is only 3 to 4 feet long, the entire impression can and should be cast in one single cast. In the case of longer impressions that logistically cannot be cast in one piece, any cast that is poured should be minimally 3 feet in length. Short casts that are produced with a 2-pound bag of dental stone are normally no greater than 6 to 8 inches in length, usually do not cover the full width of the tread, and do not represent the best way of casting tire evidence. Many departments have 2-pound bags of dental stone premeasured to cast footwear impressions and mistakenly presume that amount is also satisfactory for tire impressions.

Figure 3.18. A 2-pound bag of dental stone will only produce a small cast approximately 6 inches long. This is not the proper way to cast a tire impression. A 3-foot-long tire impression will take anywhere from 12 to 25 pounds of casting material, depending on its depth and width.

Figure 3.18 depicts a typical small cast made from a 2-pound bag of dental stone. Although a small cast is better than no cast at all, the need for casting a longer segment is essential and directly related to the examination results.

It is noted that a single major crime scene involving four to eight 3-foot-long tire casts could easily require between 100 and 200 pounds of dental stone. Because it is not conveniently available in local stores but must be ordered from a dental supply company, an abundant quantity of dental stone should be kept in supply by crime scene units. In order to ensure that adequate casting materials are on hand, I would recommend that any police department that processes crime scenes always keep on hand a minimum of eight 25-pound cartons, or 200 pounds, of dental stone. The other alternative is not having sufficient dental stone at the time it is needed, a situation which will result in the loss of valuable evidence. Dental stone, if purchased in bulk, is not expensive and has an excellent shelf-life, thus will not be wasted. Two hundred pounds of dental stone in 2007 cost $199 total delivered to my office. It is essentially $1 per pound delivered.

Dental Stone Materials

The gypsum industry refers to all gypsum products as "plasters." The term *stone* refers to a harder gypsum product, and the term *dental stone* refers to versions of stones made specifically for the dental industry. Stones and plasters have the same formulation, but are simply processed differently which results in different qualities such as accelerated setting, colors, and the ability to capture finer detail. Plasters and plaster of Paris are inferior and should not be used to cast impression evidence. Dental stone is used worldwide to cast footwear and tire impression evidence. Stones require less water when mixing than conventional plasters and result in harder casts and can therefore endure cleaning without loss of detail. They are made in a variety of colors and compressive strengths. Because there are many forms and qualities of dental stone, those using and ordering dental stone should be aware of some basic qualities such as the powder-to-water ratio and the compressive strength that are essential for casting impression evidence.

The powder-to-water ratio (P:W), sometimes expressed as the water-to-powder ratio (W:P), is determined by the manufacturer for each product. This information is either printed on the box or included inside the box of dental stone purchased from a dental supplier (Figure 3.19). The amount of water in the ratio is known in the gypsum industry as the "consistency" of the product. The amount of powder in the P:W ratio is always 100. A P:W ratio of 100:30 means the product has a consistency of 30. Dental stones commonly range from a consistency of 30 down to 21. Another quality to be aware of is the compressive strength, measured in pounds per square inch (psi). Dental stones used for casting impressions should have a compressive strength of 8,000 psi or higher. The lower the consistency the higher its compressive strength will be. I have had excellent experience with dental stone products that were rated at 8,000 to 9,000 psi.[7] This compressive strength provides sufficient hardness to endure cleaning but still uses enough water to make mixing easy. Dental stone sets up quickly and normally will set up and be ready to recover in 30 minutes, except in very cold weather.[8] Dental stones are sold in different quantities, but the 25-pound cartons are much more portable and manageable as opposed to the awkward 50- or 100-pound portions.

[7] Castone, sold by Dentsply International, and Denstone, sold by Patterson Dental are rated at 8,000 to 9,000 psi and are available in a buff or cream color.

[8] Bodziak, W. J., and Hammer, L. "An Evaluation of Dental Stone, Traxtone and Crime Cast" (2006).

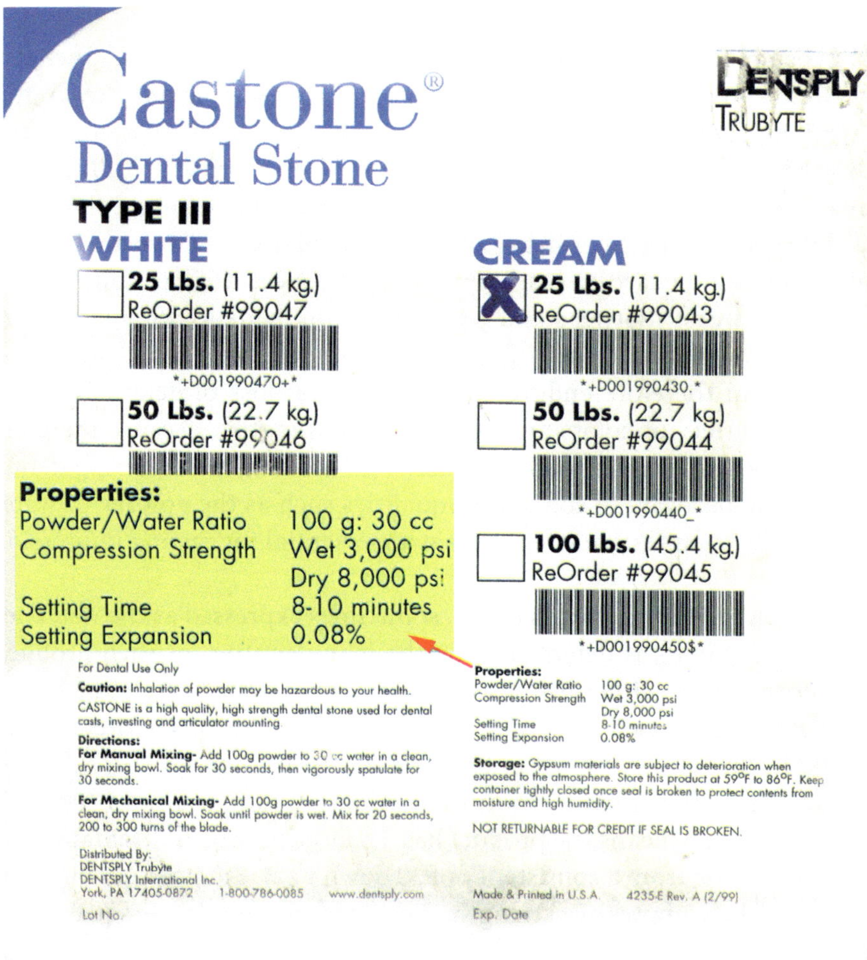

Figure 3.19. Dental stone will come with information either on the box, as shown here, or inside the box. The area enlarged in green shows that this product has a powder-to-water ratio of 100:30, thus a consistency of 30, and has a dry compression strength of 8,000 psi. Dentsply Castone, item 99043 comes in a 25 lb. carton. Available from Dentsply International, 800-877-0020, ext. 54788.

Determining the Powder-to-Water Ratio

Knowing the consistency of the dental stone you are using allows you to figure out how much water is needed per portion of powder. Because the information accompanying the product is often expressed in metric form, a conversion factor can be used to quickly determine the amount of water to be used based on the product's consistency. This factor, .306729, when multiplied with the consistency, will provide the amount of water in ounces for each 2-pound portion of dental stone powder.[9] For instance, the product Castone® has a consistency of 30. Using the conversion factor, 30 × .306729 equals 9.2 ounces of water for every 2 pounds of powder used. Thus, if you need to mix 20 pounds for a large tire cast, that would require 92 ounces of water.

Preparing the Impression for Casting

One advantage of using dental stone is that a full form is not required as a necessity for creating a cast as was the case with the softer plaster products used many years ago. However, casting an impression still requires thought and preparation. If you intend to pour a 3-foot-long cast, more than likely you will need to place something at each end of the tire impression you are casting to prevent the casting material from flowing uncontrollably along the extended impression. Other areas outside of the impression might have topography that requires adjusting to contain the casting material in the impression. Figure 3.20 depicts an impression where, after photography, two

Figure 3.20. A long impression has two flat paint stirrers pressed into the soil to confine the flow of the dental stone.

[9] Bodziak, W. J., Footwear Impression Evidence (2000, p. 78).

paint stirrers have been placed at the ends of the portion of the impression being cast to prevent the flow of casting material beyond that point.

Mixing

Estimate how many pounds of dental stone will be needed for a particular impression based on the length, width, and depth of the impression to be cast and then calculate how much water is needed for that quantity. The estimate will be based on your experience and the length, width, and depth of the tire impression. Regarding an approximate 3-foot-long impression, a very shallow tire impression may only require 8 to 10 pounds of casting powder to fill, whereas a deeper and wider impression may need as much as 25 pounds. As an example, let's say a shallow but wide 3-foot-long impression in soil is estimated to require 14 pounds of dental stone to fill the impression. For the consistency of the dental stone material you are using (30), you calculate that 14 pounds of dental stone will require approximately 64 ounces of water ($7 \times 9.2 = 64.4$ ounces). You would then place that amount of water in a flat-bottom bucket and begin adding dental stone gradually to the water in the bucket while stirring (Figure 3.21). You do not need to weigh the dental stone, but simply add the powder gradually until the mixture has attained a viscosity similar to thin pancake batter. Stir continuously while the powder is being

Figure 3.21. Powder is added gradually to the water in a flat-bottom bucket while it is being stirred.

added to get rid of any lumps. A slight adjustment may have to be made if you believe the mixture is too thin (watery) or too thick (hard to pour). Once all of the powder is added, continue to mix continuously for another 2 to 3 minutes. The additional mixing time is very important to ensure that all the powder has had time to completely absorb the water.

Pouring

Pouring a bucket full of dental stone directly onto the surface of the impression can easily destroy it if proper precautions are not taken. It is therefore important to use a technique that will ensure the dental stone fills the impression without tearing it apart. With some impressions, the natural topography around the impression may permit pouring the dental stone on one side of the impression and allowing it to flow naturally into the impression. A more universal method involves the use of a piece of cardboard to break the force of the dental stone and to help distribute it along the length of the impression. To use this technique, cut a piece of cardboard about 1 foot square. The box top from the dental stone box works quite well. Draw an X in the middle of the cardboard (Figure 3.22). Have an assistant firmly hold the cardboard with both hands so that the edge of the cardboard is about 1 inch above the impression and is lined up with the centerline of the impression, as shown in Figure 3.22. The cardboard should be slightly tilted so the dental stone will slowly flow into the impression. Then pour the dental stone from the bucket

Figure 3.22. A piece of cardboard, like this dental stone box top, can be used to deflect the pressure of the dental stone as it is poured into the impression. The person pouring the dental stone should pour onto the center of the cardboard, where marked with an X.

Figure 3.23. The dental stone is poured onto the center of the cardboard held close to the ground. The cardboard is tilted toward the center of the impression. The person holding the cardboard moves it up and around the impression to ensure the entire impression is filled with dental stone.

onto the X in the center of the cardboard (Figure 3.23). The person with the cardboard can move it slowly to help direct the dental stone to fill the entire impression while the person pouring the dental stone continues to pour onto the center of the cardboard.

Labeling the Cast

All casts should be labeled appropriately before they are removed from the ground. More commonly, those preparing the cast have traditionally scratched their initials and other information onto the back of the cast. This works fine but requires they continue to give this cast some attention until it begins to harden. An alternative method of labeling the cast involves writing the pertinent information on a piece of paper and setting it into the cast instantly after pouring it. Figure 3.24 depicts three common ways to label a cast before it is lifted from the ground: scratching initials and numbers, setting a piece of paper with this information in the cast right after pouring, and

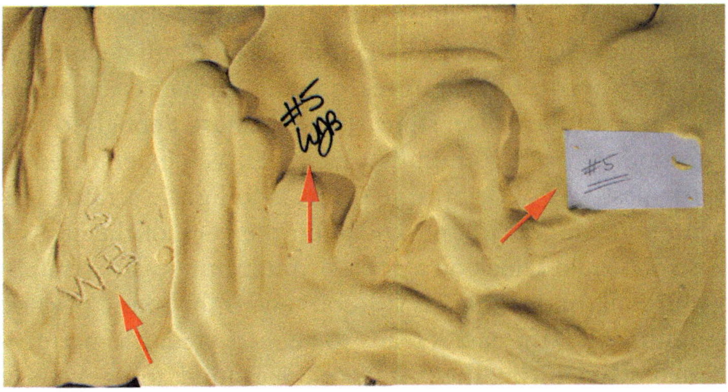

Figure 3.24. The back of this cast has been marked in three different ways: scratching information in the unhardened cast, setting a label with information in the newly poured cast, and writing with a marker on the cast after it sets.

writing directly on the cast with a permanent marker after it has hardened. Any of these methods work fine; however, it should be emphasized that the cast should be identified with these markings and any other pertinent information prior to it being lifted to ensure it is not later mistakenly mislabeled.

Recovering the Cast

Prior to lifting tire casts, the casts should always be photographed to show their relative positions at the scene (Figure 3.25). Should there be any issues

Figure 3.25. It is very important to take general scene photographs of casts of tire impressions before they are lifted. This will document their position relative to the tracks.

later with regard to the relationship of direction and how the tire was mounted on the vehicle, these photographs will serve as important documentation.

At average to warm temperatures, a dental stone cast prepared with a product such as Castone or Denstone should be hard enough to be removed from the ground in about 30 minutes. However, as temperatures and products vary, the best way of determining this is to lightly scratch the back of the cast with your fingernail and knock on the back of the cast with your knuckles as you would knock on a door. If you cannot easily scratch the surface with your nail (indicating it is still soft) and if the sound of knocking on the casts sounds solid, the cast is ready to be recovered. It is permissible and recommended, when lifting the cast from the ground, to use your fingers to rub away the excess soil or sand, as this will only help the cast dry and make it easier to handle. Under no circumstances should you scrape the soil from the cast with any stick or object, nor should you wash the cast or brush it until it has completely dried and hardened for 48 hours.

Drying and Cleaning the Cast

Gypsum products, including dental stone, require more water for mixing than they actually require for complete hydration. Upon setting, the excess water, known in the industry as "free water," must still be dried from the cast, either through a commercial drying process or through evaporation, before that cast completely hardens.[10] Figure 3.26 is a table that illustrates the increase in hardness as the free water evaporates from it.[11] The table indicates that not until over 93% of the water has evaporated does the cast attain its maximum hardness. For tire casts, 48 hours are generally necessary for the excess water within the cast to move to the surface and evaporate. Once dried and hardened, casts made in some soils require little more than a controlled rinse and perhaps a light brushing with a wet brush. Other soils, like clay, are more difficult to clean from a cast's surface. One of the biggest advantages of using dental stone is the fact that once completely dry and hardened, you can immerse the cast back into water without risking any damage. Soaking the cast will soften any stubborn soil on it, during which time you can use a soft brush to assist in its removal. Brushing is best done while the cast is submerged; but if the cast is too large, running a stream of water over it while using the brush is just as successful. Under no circumstances should you use a high-pressure stream of water or a pressure washer, as these will erode detail.

[10] United States Gypsum Company, Drying Plaster Casts, Bulletin No. IG502, Chicago, IL, February 1996.

[11] Ibid.

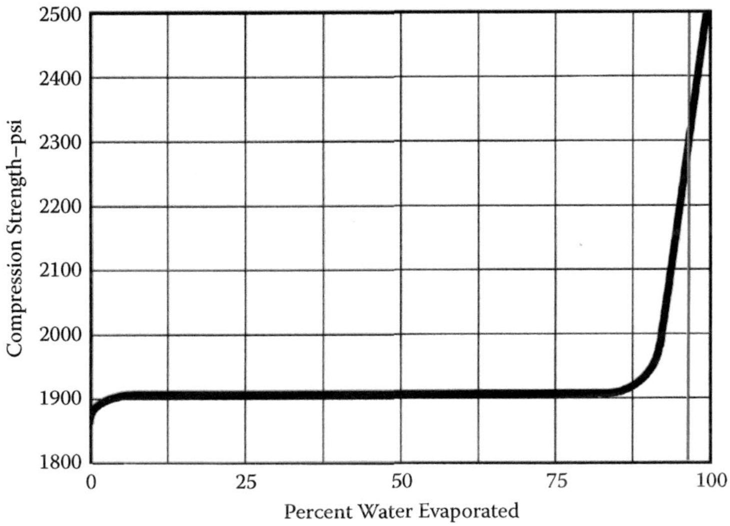

Figure 3.26. This table, provided by US Gypsum, illustrates how a cast only attains its hardness when virtually all (93%) of the free water has been dried from it.

Tire Impressions in Snow

There are many areas where the ground is covered with snow many days of the year. Crime scenes in snow will contain tire impressions of the perpetrator's vehicle in areas that in other weather would not retain impressions. Figures 3.2 and 3.3 are good examples. The recovery of a tire impression in snow, like on other surfaces, must begin with good documentation and general scene photograph eventually followed with examination quality photograph and casts. Because snow is white, obtaining good contrast in the examination quality photographs is more difficult. One technique that helps provide contrast is a careful application of a snow wax or colored spray paint applied at a 45-degree angle so that it grazes the ridges or high areas of the impression. The application should begin far enough away to avoid any chance of damaging the impression with the blast of the aerosol and then slowly and cautiously move closer to the impression during the application. Short bursts of spray seem to be easier to control while doing this and help avoid any damage to the impression from the force of the aerosol. The purpose of this application is not to completely color the impression but rather to simply offer a little bit of color to the high spots of the impression, which in turn will increase the contrast and allow for better photography. This technique can be difficult if not impossible on a breezy day. Figure 3.27 depicts the process of spraying an impression to highlight it. Figure 3.28 shows two different snow waxes available in the United States and a portion of an impression high-

Figure 3.27. Applying a light spray of aerosol snow wax or paint is one way to highlight and increase the contrast when photographing snow impressions. The coloration of a snow impression will rapidly accelerate melting, and any impression colorized should be photographed immediately.

Figure 3.28. There are currently two choices of colorized snow wax, one with a brownish color (Snow Impression Wax) and one with a red color (Snowprint Wax). On the left is a tire impression in snow that has been highlighted with each.

lighted by each.[12] It is noted that once a snow impression is colorized, whether it be with snow wax or paint, the impression will absorb more energy from the sun and the snow will begin to melt, even in subzero temperatures. The very fine detail in the impression will be the first to be lost. Because of this, the impression should be photographed immediately after colorizing it and/or the impression should be protected from the sun in some way from the moment it is colorized, particularly if casting will follow. This can be done by covering the impression with a box or simply having someone cast their shadow over the impression until it is fully recovered.

Although a tire passing over snow easily deforms it, the type of snow as well as any changes that occur to that snow, such as melting and refreezing, are the main factors that determine the detail retained in each impression. Described below are three ways to make a cast of a snow impression. The best recommendation I can make regarding casting in snow is that you obtain prior experience using the various methods and you will then be in a position to determine which method is most suitable at a particular scene, considering the snow quality, the number of impressions, your experience, and the materials available. In addition, understanding the various characteristics of snow will provide further assistance in this choice.[13]

Dry-Casting Snow Impressions

In an article entitled "The Dry-Casting Method: A Reintroduction to a Simple Method for Casting Snow Impressions," Adair and Shaw have taken older reported snow-casting methods and adapted them to use with dental stone.[14] They have given the name of "dry-casting" to this method, which potentially could be the easiest and best overall method available for casting most impressions in snow. With only two additional items, a flour sifter and a spray bottle, along with dental stone, a very good cast can be easily made of impressions in snow in short time. Figures 3.29 through 3.32 depict a demonstration of this process. First a fine layer of about ⅛ inch of dental stone powder is sifted over the impression. A water spray bottle is used to mist water onto the dental stone. If the snow is wet or slushy, the addition of water for the first application of powder may not be necessary as the dental stone powder will quickly absorb the existing moisture from wet snow. Two additional and separate applications of sifted dental stone, each ⅛ inch thick, are then applied. Each application is followed by a light misting of

[12] Snow Print Wax by Armor Forensics and Snow Impression Wax by Sirchie.

[13] Adair, T., Tewes, R., Bellinger, T., and Nicholls, T., "Characteristics of Snow and Their Influence on Casting Methods for Impression Evidence" *Journal of Forensic Identification*, 57(6), 2007, 807–822.

[14] Adair, T., Shaw, R., "The Dry-Casting Method: A reintroduction to a simple method for casting snow impressions" *Journal of Forensic Identification*, 57(6) 2007, 823–831.

Figure 3.29. Using the dry-casting method, three separate layers of dental stone powder, each ⅛-inch deep, are sifted over the impression. If the impression is wet or slushy snow, the powder will absorb the moisture as seen in the photo. If the snow is dry, an application of water sprayed onto the sifted powder is necessary.

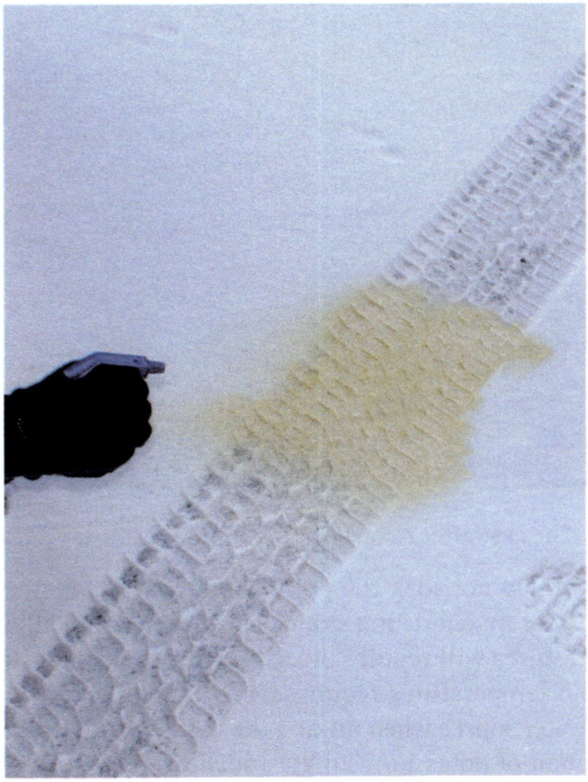

Figure 3.30. Using a spray bottle, a misting of water is applied to each layer of sifted powder as needed.

Figure 3.31. After three layers of sifted dental stone have been applied, a regular mixture of dental stone can then be safely poured over this area to complete the cast.

Figure 3.32. The cast after removal.

water if needed. Do not soak the powder but simply wet it. Next, carefully pour a quantity of mixed dental stone over the shell and allow it to harden. Colder temperatures will require more time for the dental stone to harden. Extremely cold temperatures require a small amount of potassium sulfate added to the water source when mixing the cast.[15] One examiner has found a heaping teaspoon of potassium sulfate added to the mixture works well for this purpose.[16] The potassium sulfate will accelerate the setting of the cast and lower the freezing point of the mixture. The dry-casting process is quick, easy, and inexpensive. It provides reasonably good detail, and, because the initial thin shell generates little or no heat, little or no melting of the snow occurs. Most importantly, most crime scene units are equipped with dental stone and water, and a spray bottle and pastry sifter will only cost a few dollars to obtain.

Snow Print Wax® and Snow Impression Wax

The application of an aerosol snow wax followed with dental stone can also be used to successfully cast impressions in snow[17] . The directions are supplied on the snow wax cans. Whereas logistically a can of snow wax might adequately cover a 12-inch-long footwear impression, the same is not true for an 8-inch-wide by 3-foot-long tire impression. Trying to cast the longer

[15] The potassium sulfate used for this need not be anything more than a fertilizer grade.

[16] Lesley Hammer (Alaska State Crime Laboratory), personal communication, May 31, 2007.

[17] Carlsson, K. "A New Method for Securing Impressions in Snow" *Crime Laboratory Digest* December (1982).

tire impression with snow wax would probably consume four or more cans of wax. After the final coat of wax, dental stone is added to reinforce the wax shell and allow the cast to be lifted. In extremely cold temperatures, potassium sulfate will need to be used in the water mixed with dental stone. This is an expensive technique and difficult to use for large tire impressions.

Casting Snow Impressions with Sulfur

Sulfur has always been one of the better methods to cast snow impressions, although there is added time involved. Nevertheless, for those highly detailed dry snow impressions, the best chance of recovering the finest detail will be with sulfur. The sulfur, obtained either in powder or prill form, must first be melted. This can be done using an electric hotplate and a 2- or 3-quart pan. An electric heating source is much safer than a gas stove. Sulfur is flammable and heating improperly with a gas flame could be dangerous. Thicker metal pans will retain the heat better and seem to be more efficient at melting the sulfur than thinner and less expensive pans. A quantity of sulfur is first added to the pan (Figure 3.33). Heat is applied slowly as the dry sulfur is stirred; a wooden paint stirrer works well. As the sulfur begins to melt, it will clump together (Figure 3.34). Continue heating and stirring continuously and eventually all the sulfur will melt (Figure 3.35). This process requires your full

Figure 3.33. A quantity of powdered or prill sulfur is added to a pan.

Figure 3.34. The pan is placed on to a hot plate and slowly heated to melt the sulfur. As the sulfur begins to melt, it will clump around the unmelted sulfur.

Figure 3.35. Eventually all of the sulfur will melt. Additional sulfur can then be added until the quantity needed is melted.

attention, for if you allow the sulfur to get too hot, it will change into an irreversible syrupy brown mass and will be ruined. During this process, as the sulfur melts, additional sulfur will need to be added and melted until the necessary quantity is reached. In the case of a footwear impression, 4 pounds of sulfur will be sufficient, but in the case of a tire impression, more may be required. Once the sulfur is melted, the heat can be turned off and it can be allowed to cool (Figure 3.36). Stirring must continue during this phase to ensure that the entire amount of sulfur stays at the same temperature. As the sulfur cools, yellow crystals will form around the edge of the pot. This is normal and cannot be avoided. When crystals begin to form in the liquid portion it will become cloudy, a signal that the sulfur is nearing its crystallization temperature and is ready to pour. It may be necessary to use two paint stirrers or other materials to create a place for the sulfur to be poured and directed into the impression (Figure 3.37). After the pouring begins, it may be necessary to move the pan to further distribute the sulfur so as to cover the entire impression. In this method, as the sulfur strikes the snow, it is cooled and hardens instantly, initially creating a shell that captures the detail of the snow impression. Figure 3.38 shows the cast just after pouring. The lighter yellow areas have cooled, but the darker areas are still very hot.

Figure 3.36. The heat is turned off and the sulfur is allowed to cool, stirring occasionally to maintain an even temperature. When the temperature of the sulfur lowers back to its melting point, it will begin to form crystals and will appear cloudy, as pictured here.

Figure 3.37. The sulfur must be poured steadily without interruption. The formation of a pathway outside of the impression that can direct the flow of the sulfur into the impression is recommended. Creating a chute with two paint stirrers or using other methods to direct the flow is usually necessary. Here the sulfur is first poured outside the impression area but is directed into the impression.

Figure 3.38. The sulfur cast after pouring. The sulfur will harden the instant it touches the snow, immediately capturing the detail of the impression. Areas of the sulfur on top will remain hot for a while until it completely cools and solidifies. A sulfur cast is extremely brittle and fragile. After it cools, a thin coat of dental stone over the back of it will help stabilize it and allow it to be preserved. When applying the dental stone, do not let any flow over the edges of the cast, as the dental stone will flow beneath the cast, undercutting it and covering the detail.

Lifting Tire Impressions

Although most tire impressions left at crime scenes are those retained in soil, sand, mud, and snow, there are occasions when a tire may leave its impression on a two-dimensional surface. These surfaces could include asphalt, concrete, clothing, paper, or other debris in the road that might retain a two-dimensional impression. In some of these instances, particularly when the surface containing the impression cannot be taken to the laboratory, lifting the impression may be another method of enhancing and/or recovering that impression after it is photographed.

Lifting an impression involves the transfer of the impression from one surface to a new surface. The objective of this transfer is to create better contrast and/or to enable an actual recovery of the impression. Lifts, like casts, provide the actual life-size evidence and potentially more detail than obtainable in a photograph. Dry dust or residue impressions left on clothing, paper, or other items can be lifted with conventional lifting techniques and devices such as electrostatic lifters, as well as gelatin or adhesive lifters. For those not familiar with lifting materials and methods, these techniques are adequately described in the literature.[18,19] Figure 3.39 is a photograph of an electrostatic lift of a tire impression from paper.

In some cases a tire will leave its impression on a road surface. This may be formed when a vehicle with a wet tire parks and the moisture over the dirty tire drains onto and around the contact patch of the tire, drying in that position before the vehicle is again moved. A tire impression may also occur on concrete, as a tire will occasionally transfer its black impression (Figure 3.40). It is possible to lift impressions like these by using dental stone.[20] To make a dental stone lift, prepare the impression by surrounding it on all sides with a 2-inch-wide strip of sticky duct tape. Place the duct tape within a ½ inch of the impression. Do not use any release agent during this technique! Application of a release agent on the impression that you are attempting to lift will prevent its ability to be lifted. Prepare a normal mix of dental stone and pour it over the impression, letting the dental stone extend onto portions of the duct tape. When the dental stone has hardened, pull up the tape to assist in lifting the cast. The cast should release from the surface. It should be noted that this technique is not fail-safe. Some concrete surfaces are highly textured and may not release the dental stone cast. If the cast will not lift by pulling up on the tape, place the tip of a large chisel-edged screwdriver at the junction of a thicker edge of the cast and the ground, hold the screwdriver at a 45-degree angle, and tap it lightly with a hammer. This will normally pop

[18]Bodziak, W. J. Footwear Impression Evidence (2000).
[19]SWGTREAD
[20]Geller, J. "Casting on Road Surfaces" (1990).

Figure 3.39. An electrostatic lift of a tire impression.

the cast loose. It is noted that this technique may not always work depending on the surface and conditions; however, attempting this additional technique is the last step in recovery, and thus any added detail that is realized through this technique will be more than otherwise would have been recovered.

Contusions

Blunt-force injuries that result when sufficient force is rapidly applied to the skin can cause micro-bursting of the blood vessels beneath the skin and result in replication of the object that created the force, such as a tire. The resulting discoloration of the areas where the blood vessels have ruptured allows for its visualization. Figure 3.41 depicts a contusion across the head of a victim. As the tire and its considerable weight pressed the tread design against the skin, blood was forced from areas of greater pressure, directly beneath the tread blocks, to the areas of lesser pressure such as grooves and sipes and the edges of designed areas. Blood forced into those areas will cause

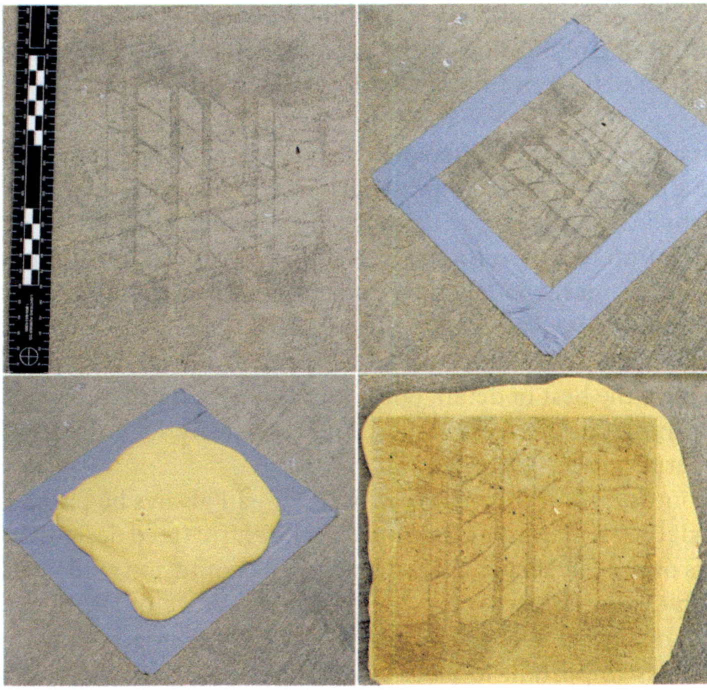

Figure 3.40. Dental stone can be used to lift residue prints of tires on concrete and other surfaces. In this series of photographs, the tire impression *(top left)* is surrounded with duct tape *(top right)* and a mixture of dental stone is applied over both. Once set, the removal of the tape will help release the dental stone cast from the surface. The impression will be recorded on the cast.

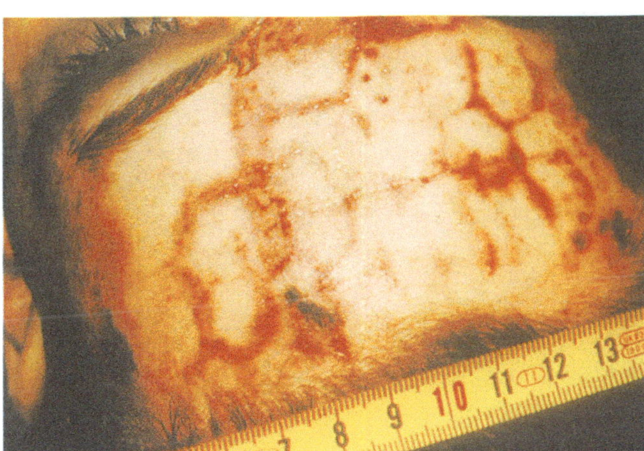

Figure 3.41 A blunt-force pattern injury (contusion) caused by a tire on a hit-and-run victim.

the tiny blood vessels to burst, leaving blood beneath the skin in those areas and providing the replication of the grooves and edges of the design. More about blunt-force pattern injuries is addressed in forensic medical literature and in other texts.[21]

When a tire runs over a person, there is a considerable chance that tire will leave a dust or residue impressions on the victim and/or clothing. In addition, the victim may be lying over top of the tire impression or the tire may have run up to and across the victim while in that position. In either case, important impression evidence adjacent and beneath the body should be considered. Figure 3.42 depicts a rape and homicide case where the tire ran over the victim. The impression, as seen in this photograph, does not appear to have the best of detail, but it was cast with dental stone, contained numerous individual characteristics, and was easily identified with a tire from the perpetrator's vehicle.

Tire contusions on the victim, if present, will always be partial impressions in that they will never fully represent the entire tread design. They often encompass only a few inches or less. Recovering contusion evidence through photography is not an easy task due to the curvature of the body and the sometimes mixed presence of blood or dirt. When photographing the contusions, it is very important to place a scale as close to the contusion and on the same plane as the contusion as possible. To complicate the recovery of this evidence, protocol usually restricts crime scene technicians from moving victims at the scene, meaning it may not initially be possible to take the

Figure 3.42. A tire impression in soil just before the tire ran across the homicide victim. The impression was cast and identified.

[21] Bodziak, W. J. Footwear Impression Evidence (2000).

best or the most complete photographs of contusions or tire evidence on the victim. Additionally, contusions that may be beneath the victim's clothing or on other parts of the victim's body that are not evident until the victim is removed may not be recoverable at the scene. Proceeding to the autopsy or hospital to take additional photographs is necessary. Not only will there be a better opportunity to fully examine the victim, but contusions often change in coloration during the hours after they are inflicted, possibly providing additional detail. In addition, the contusion will often be photographed better after the autopsy cleaning of the victim. The inside and outside of the clothing should also be examined for tire impressions using high-intensity light and an alternative light source.

Known Exemplars of Tires for Elimination and Examination

4

General Information

Known exemplars are also referred to as known tire impressions or inked tire impressions. There are two occasions to either document a tire design or take known exemplars of tires. The first relates to those tires from vehicles that are categorized as "elimination vehicles." The second pertains to tires from a vehicle that, as a result of the investigation, is believed to possibly have caused the questioned tire impressions during the commission of the crime.

Known exemplars play an extremely vital role in both the investigative and the examination process. Records of elimination tires allow for documentation of the tire designs of vehicles present at the scene but which are known not to be involved in the crime. These provide the means to eliminate those vehicles and their impressions based on tread design. In those cases, the actual tire is normally not needed. On the other hand, in the case of any suspect vehicle(s), it is essential to both have the actual tires as well as to make full circumference impressions of the tire(s) for a detailed examination. The full circumference impressions act as a tool to assist in the comparison of the actual tire with the impression. This more detailed tire impression examination involves not only the tread design, but the tread dimension, wear, and individual characteristics of the tire.

Documenting Tires From Elimination Vehicles

Elimination vehicles include police and emergency vehicles as well as other vehicles, such as the victim's vehicle, that may have caused impressions in the crime scene area before, during, or subsequent to the time that area was preserved. When the scene is processed, several tire impressions of those or other vehicles may be present, in addition to those of the perpetrator's vehicle. In these cases it becomes necessary to sort out which impressions belong to the perpetrator's vehicle and which impressions were simply present for other but innocent reasons. This evaluation is relatively easy at some scenes, but for those involving numerous tire tracks it can be complex and can take a structured effort on the part of the crime scene recovery team. It should be noted that this process of elimination is one that is best performed while at the crime scene. It becomes much more difficult and usually not possible to do this effectively weeks later simply through the examination of general crime scene photographs. Rather, an aggressive effort at the scene with sufficient notes and photographs to document the tire impressions and make records of elimination vehicles is the best and most effective method.

As part of this effort, those at the crime scene should be able to observe or recognize certain detail. For instance, some tracks may be obviously older and almost faded away and thus not significant, while others may be fresh in their appearance and warrant the focus of additional attention. Tracks that cut across others can instantly prove that one vehicle left impressions after the vehicle whose tracks it cut through. Newly fallen snow or a recent rain may assist in differentiating older tracks from the most recent tracks. Smaller single tracks may be those of a motorcycle, bicycle, or all-terrain vehicle. But in those cases where many otherwise equal and fresh tracks are present within the crime scene area, it becomes necessary to take other steps to eliminate as many as possible by learning what vehicle they came from. This would include the visual examination of vehicles present at the scene, including emergency vehicles, to see if the tires of those vehicles correspond with any of the tracks. Once done, the focus can then be on the recovery of those remaining impressions that may have been produced by the perpetrator's vehicle. Because tires come in hundreds of different designs[1] the likelihood that a police or emergency vehicle or other vehicles that innocently drove through that area would coincidentally have a tire design identical to those on the perpetrator's vehicle is very minimal. For that reason, the documentation of tires of elimination vehicles need only be in the form of a digital photograph or partial recording of the tire design accompanied by the information of which vehicle they came from and the name, style, and size of the tire. They do not need to be extensive, full-circumference impressions like those later described as necessary for a full tire examination.

Some methods of documenting "elimination tires" are set forth below.

Photographs of the Tread Design

Good digital photographs of the tread designs of the tires on the vehicle are sufficient for elimination purposes. Because it is likely a digital camera will already be at the scene, no additional equipment will be necessary. Documen-

[1] The Tread Design Guide, published annually by Garfield Productions in Boca Raton, FL, depicts thousands of tire designs

tation should accompany or be included in that photograph that would indicate the identity of the vehicle the tire was on, the position(s) that tire design represents, as well as the manufacturer, brand, and size of the tires. This method is quick and confirmable because digital photographs are instantly displayed on the camera. Another advantage of taking a digital photograph is that it can be used in all situations, including wet or snow-covered tires and in situations where the vehicle cannot be moved. Figures 4.1 and 4.2 depict two digital photographs of tread designs recovered for elimination purposes. A scale is not needed in these elimination photographs because the elimination is being made based on the design alone.

White Adhesive Lift of Tire Design

White adhesive will remove the dirty residue that covers the tread surface of dry tires and can provide a reasonably good recording of the tire design. It is a quick method that is not messy and does not require moving the vehicle. It is not practical in wet or snowy conditions. To make the elimination print, a white adhesive or white gelatin lifter, is simply pressed against the full width of a portion of the tire tread, as shown in Figure 4.3.[2] When removed, a clear

Figure 4.1. A digital photograph of an elimination tire packed with snow. It would be difficult to make an actual impression of this tire using ink or powder. The digital photograph is quick and confirmable.

[2] The Tread Design Guide, published annually by Garfield Productions in Boca Raton, FL, depicts thousands of tire designs

Figure 4.2. A digital photograph, taken with information included in the photograph about the identity of the tire of a vehicle, is a quick and easy way to document the tread designs of elimination vehicles.

Figure 4.3. Pressing a white adhesive lift against a tire tread will provide an elimination record of a tire design. The vehicle information can be written right on the lift. On the right is the lift, turned around to show the tire design.

protective cover sheet is placed over it to preserve the design information. The vehicle, tire information, and position on the vehicle can be written directly on the back of the lift. This is a very quick and simple method to recover elimination prints. A white adhesive or gelatin lift should be used, as clear adhesive lifts provide little contrast.

Identicator® Inkless Method and Materials

The Treadprint™ materials[3] provide the means to take quick elimination prints but are only usable in dry conditions and only if the vehicle can be moved. The applicator pad can be used to apply the solution to a small segment of the tire and then the tire can be moved across a small segment of the specially treated Identicator board. This method and product, pictured in Figure 4.4, is discussed later in this chapter. The information about the tire and vehicle can be written directly adjacent to the impression.

Figure 4.4. Using the Identicator Treadprint kit to obtain a known impression. The examiner uses the applicator to coat the tire with a special solution. The coated tire then leaves a detailed black impression on the treated chart board.

[3] Armor Forensic sells many forms of inkless impression materials, including the Treadprint materials for tire impressions. See www.armorforensics.com regarding TP-16.

Other Methods

Any other method that is capable of either photographically or otherwise recording a small portion of a tire tread, accompanied by the information of the tire and vehicle that it was on, is satisfactory for the purposes of documenting elimination vehicles.

Known Exemplar Impressions of a Suspect Vehicle

During the investigation, certain tire impressions will remain in question, i.e., they cannot be accounted for, thus they possibly originated from the perpetrator's vehicle. Those impressions will need to be compared with the tires of any suspect vehicle. At the onset of that examination, if those tires are determined to be a different design, then elimination of those tires can be made and full circumference detailed known impressions of those tires will not be needed. However, in those cases where the suspect's vehicle tires are similar in design to the crime scene impressions, a more detailed examination must follow and will require the actual tires as well as detailed known impressions of those tires taken in a prescribed manner. Before removing any tires from the suspect vehicle, the positions those tires occupied such as left front (LF), right front (RF), left rear (LR), and right rear (RR) should be marked on the outside of the respective tires with a permanent type marker.

Many examiners prepare known exemplars of a tire and then conduct the entire examination comparing the exemplar with the crime scene impression. This is not correct. The final examination should be between the crime scene impression and the actual tire, where the maximum amount of detail is contained and where individual characteristics can best be evaluated. Although some of the examination is performed with the known exemplar impressions, they are primarily used to help the examiner locate the exact area(s) of the tire(s) that potentially could have made the crime scene impression. Once located, that specific area of the tire's tread can then be compared directly against the crime scene cast or photograph. Thus, when selecting a method to prepare the known impressions, it is not important to be concerned if the impressions contain the maximum amount of detail, but only that they contain sufficient detail and accuracy to serve their purpose, i.e., to locate the position(s) on the tire that potentially could have left the crime scene impression.

Known impressions also demonstrate how the tire leaves its impression, document the tread design and dimensional features and condition of wear, assist in the location of individual features present on the tire, and provide demonstrable proof of the examination results either as part of the report and/or as testimony in court. It should be restated that in cases where the tire's design appears to be the same as the crime scene impression and a full forensic examination is conducted, the actual tire is necessary during the examination. To conduct a forensic tire examination using inked impressions only and without the actual tire is incorrect methodology.[4] The entire process of making the full-circumference impression with the actual tire and then having that tire to complete the examination should be the responsibility of the forensic examiner. Having a crime scene technician or investigator attempt to make impressions of tires so the tires can then be released is improper and will not allow for the full and proper forensic examination between that tire and the crime scene impressions.

There is more than one method that can be used to produce full-circumference known tire impressions as set forth below.

General Instructions

Taking detailed full-circumference tire impressions is an involved process that normally requires a minimum of three persons. In part, this is because it is recommended that the vehicle be pushed across the film or board when recording the impressions, but several people are also necessary to carry out the many tasks that are part of this process. The final goal is to acquire two accurate full-circumference impressions of each tire.

In some cases, when the examiner has access to the seized suspect vehicle, the tires will already be mounted and ready for impressions. This is convenient, but if the suspect vehicle is no longer available or only the tires were seized it is not imperative to make the impressions using the suspect vehicle. Rather, the tires can be mounted on a similar vehicle that uses that tire size. The exact amount of air pressure is not critical, but you should ensure the tire is inflated to the approximate recommended pressure. If they must be mounted on a compatible vehicle, you may wish to mount them two at a time on the respective sides of the rear axle, as making impressions on a nonturning axle is easier to control. Please note that proper and accurate tire impressions *cannot be made* by rolling a tire by hand, as the dimensions and totality of the resulting impressions will be significantly different from those made on a vehicle under load.

Full-circumference impressions are necessary for a couple reasons. First, on most passenger and light truck tires, the size of the tire's individual tread blocks and their arranged sequence vary around the circumference of the tire, as shown in Figure 3.4. Thus, if you only had a portion of the tire's full circumference, there is a good chance that particular section of tread blocks would not correspond with the portion recovered from the crime scene. Second, remember that only

[4] There are occasionally unfortunate cases where impressions were taken and the tires released before any examination. In cases where for some reason a tire is not available but an impression has been taken, a limited examination may still be possible.

one segment of the tire could actually have produced the crime scene impression. Not having a full-circumference known exemplar may fail to include that same segment and would therefore adversely affect the examination results including the location of important wear and individual characteristics.

It is very important to note that these two full-circumference impressions should be made with the starting point on one impression offset approximately 180 degrees to the other impression. The importance of this is illustrated in the drawing in Figure 4.5. In that drawing, the long impressions represent the two known impressions, offset by approximately 180 degrees or one-half rotation. The crime scene impression is the short dark impression. If only one known impression were obtained or if both of the known impressions were identical and like the one on top, then the corresponding portion that matches the crime scene impression would be interrupted by the end of the impression. This might prevent the examiner from being able to match the crime scene impression to that impression. The second known impression on the bottom includes the area of the entire crime scene impression. The importance of this is explained more thoroughly in Chapter 7.

General Materials

Materials that are needed for this process depend on the precise process that is used. However, the following will be needed for practically all of the methods:

- A fairly smooth concrete or asphalt surface where you will make your impressions. A large indoor garage is preferable; however, this procedure can be done outside if dry and not windy. The ground in the pathway where the tire will roll during the making of the impression should also be swept to eliminate any gravel or debris that might puncture the impression materials.

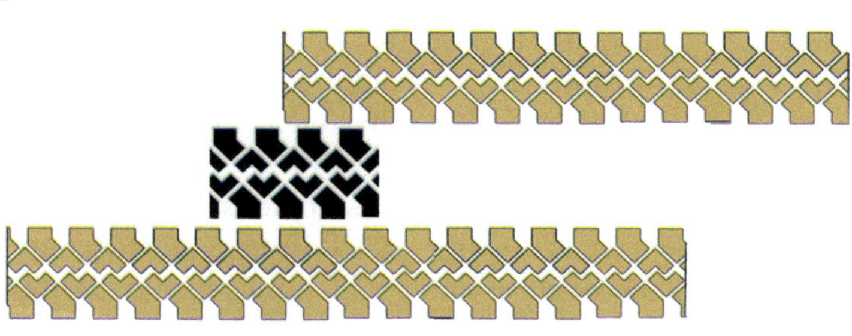

Figure 4.5. This drawing represents two full-circumference tire impressions on the top and bottom, offset by 180 degrees, as well as a short crime scene impression. Note that only the bottom impression represents the full crime scene impression. If only the top full-circumference known impression was prepared, it would be difficult to associate the specific pitch sequence of the crime scene impression with this tire.

- A length of approximately 50 feet of paper should be laid over the surface being used. The purpose of this is to prevent the tire, once inked, from picking up dirt and grit from the raw road surface. Brown contractor paper is thick and excellent for this purpose. It is available at hardware stores. Brown Kraft wrapping paper or white butcher paper comes in rolls in 2½ to 3 foot widths and can also be used. Either is suitable for this purpose, but the durability of a thicker paper works better.
- Duct tape is used to hold the paper onto the road surface as well as to tape segments of the chart board together.
- A pair of heavy work gloves can be used to wipe the dust and dirt from the tire tread surface and can also be used whenever handling the tires.
- Scissors and markers.
- A supply of chart board. Chart board is a solid board used to mount pictures and for other graphic arts needs. It may also be referred to as illustration board or art board. It can be found in art supply stores in a variety of thicknesses and qualities. The board that will be used as a backing for the impression needs to be laminated on only one side. The board that is used for the ink board can be used repeatedly for several impressions as long as it does not de-laminate. Thus, if possible, use a thicker chart board with lamination on both sides for the ink board. Chart board typically comes in 30 × 40 inches and most art stores can cut it lengthwise into two 15 × 40-inch pieces. The two 15 × 40-inch pieces can then be taped together with duct tape to produce a piece of chart board that is now 15 × 80 inches in length. (Caution: Never use foam core board because it will wrinkle under the tire pressure and will not work for this procedure.)
- Oil-based printer's ink is needed when using the ink methods. An excellent ink is a black Speedball oil-base block printing ink. It comes in 2.5 oz. tubes and is available at graphic art stores.[5] It will be workable long enought to make several impressios but will dry overnight. Fingerprint ink is not suitable because it dries too fast. Water-based inks should not be used because they are incapable of retaining crisp detail.
- Wet media film is a general term for a clear film that comes in rolls and that has been treated to receive ink on its surface. This film normally is made in wide rolls around 40 inches wide, but when ordering, it can be cut into more usable 12- to 13-inch widths for tire impressions.[6]

[5] Speedball Oil Based Block Print can be found for sale at graphic art stores or on the internet.

[6] Wed Media Film must be ordered from Grafix Plastics, 800-447-2349, ext. 128. Wet Media Duralar or Aceate, in thicknesses of .004 or .005 is needed. The film will come in long rolls and can be ordered already cut in widths of 12–13 inches..

- Petroleum jelly such as Vaseline®, black magnetic fingerprint powder, and clear acrylic spray.

Note that the tires must be dry when full-circumference impressions are obtained.

Methods

Inked Impressions on Clear Wet Media Film[7]

It is my opinion that this method provides the examiner with the best full-circumference known standard for the purpose of making tire comparisons, particularly for locating the area(s) of a tire that corresponds in tread design and tread dimension. It provides a continuous and high-contrast inked impression on a clear film that can then be used as an overlay to allow direct comparison with the questioned impression.

1. Tape down a long length of heavy brown paper to cover approximately 50 feet of surface, as shown in Figure 4.6. This paper serves to provide

Figure 4.6. A 50-foot section of brown contractor paper has been taped to the ground to provide a clean surface. The vehicle will then be positioned at one end of the paper.

[7] Bodziak, W. J. "Some Methods for Taking Two-dimensional Comparison Standards of Tires" (1996).

a clean working surface. The paper should be taped to the ground with duct tape. If this is done in an interior garage, less taping is necessary. Exterior locations, particularly on a breezy day, may require complete taping around the entire perimeter.

2. Position the vehicle with the tire on the paper so it is in line with the direction of the paper and the tire to be printed is near the end of the paper.
3. With work gloves on your hands, lightly rub the tire's surface to remove loose grit and dirt. This is a very important step in this process that should not be overlooked. Do not remove any rocks firmly set in the sipes or grooves. You will need to advance the vehicle forward 2 to 3 feet to complete this process.
4. Measure the circumference of the tire, as shown in Figure 4.7A. Tire circumferences for most cars and light trucks will usually range somewhere between 6 and 8 feet. Larger truck tires may have even greater circumferences. You will need to know this measurement so you can prepare the proper lengths of both the ink and impression boards in order to ensure you have sufficient lengths to receive a full-circumference impression. I would suggest you always make this board about 4 inches longer than the actual tire circumference to simply provide a safety margin to ensure you get a full-circumference impression.
5. Measure the distance between the front and rear tires, as shown in Figure 4.7B. In most cases, this distance will be longer than the tire circumference. If the vehicle has a tire circumference that is greater than the distance between the front and rear tires, then logistical problems will be encountered because the section lengths of board necessary to record a full-circumference impression will not fit in between the front and rear tires. Figure 4.8 depicts a jeep that had this problem and required hinging a small portion of chart board at the end to allow the full continuous circumference of the tire to be inked. A similar chart board arrangement will need to be made to receive the inked impression that the tire will produce.
6. Once the necessary measurement of the chart board is known, assemble with duct tape the sections of chart board to create the desired lengths as illustrated in Figure 4.9. One of these lengths of board will be needed for the ink board and one will be needed to hold the clear film. Remember, both should be about 4 inches longer than the circumference of the tire that is being recorded. Thus, if the tire circumference is 76 inches, the total chart board length should be 4 inches longer, or 80 inches long, if the distance between the tires allows. This will ensure there is plenty of room for a full-circumference impression.
7. A spatula or paint stirrer and heavy-duty fingerprint roller, like those shown in Figure 4.10A, will assist with spreading the ink. The spatula or paint stirrer can be used to spread the ink across a few areas of the

A

B

Figure 4.7. The circumference around the tire **(A)** and the distance between the front and rear tires **(B)** must be measured to determine how long a full-circumference impression is and thus how long the chart board segments must be. In most cars, the tire circumference is less than the wheelbase (distance between the tires), thus the inked board will easily fit between the front and rear tires.

Figure 4.8. This vehicle has tires with a large circumference but a relatively short wheelbase and therefore requires the length of chart board for both the ink and film to have a hinged section at the end (arrow) so it can fit between the tires. As the vehicle moves forward, the hinged area is lowered. This will have to be done for both the inked board and the clear film that receives the impression in order to obtain full circumference impressions.

Figure 4.9. The chart board on the left is thicker and is laminated with white board on both sides. The less expensive chart board on the right is laminated on only one side with a colored nonlaminated side. Both can be used successfully. Duct tape is used on the backside to piece together the required length needed.

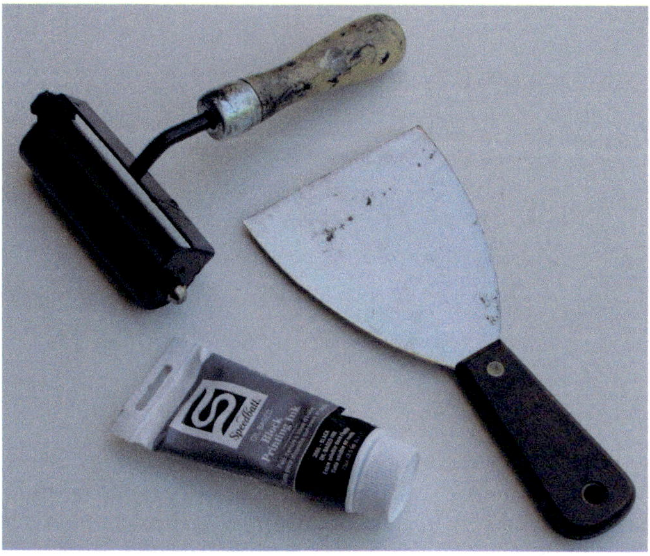

A

B

Figure 4.10. **A.** Printers ink that dries in 2 to 4 hours, a spatula or a paint stirrer, and a sturdy ink roller are used to prepare the inked board. **B.** The spatula or paint stirrer is used to initially apply some ink and spread it across areas of the chart board.

Figure 4.10C. Then the roller is used to complete the application of a thin coating of ink across the entire board surface.

chart board (Figure 4.10B). A fingerprint roller is then used to spread the ink further until the chart board is covered with a thin and even coating of ink (Figure 4.10C). The amount of ink should be sufficient to cover the white chart board but should not be too thick because it will fill in small cuts, sipes, and other characteristics and will obliterate or conceal other details. In addition, too much ink will result in the ink being pressed out to the edges of the tread blocks possibly enlarging their actual size. Too much ink will also increase the ink's drying time. On the other hand, too little ink will result in very light and/or incomplete impressions. Adjustments in the amount of ink may have to be made after the first impression is made.

8. Cut and tape a piece of clear wet media film to the second section of chart board (Figure 4.11). Place two small pieces of duct tape on each end to prevent the film from sticking to and wrapping around the tire. Make sure the board is on a flat surface when the film is taped to it to ensure the film is flat against the chart board and there are no air pockets.
9. Place the inked board in front of the rear tire and line it up so when the vehicle is moved forward the tire will roll across its surface. Notice in Figure 4.11 the inked board has been placed between the rear and front tires and the chart board containing the clear media film is in a position to be moved in between the rear and front tires as the vehicle is moved forward. It is necessary to push the vehicle when making the impres-

Figure 4.11. The inked board is placed between the front and rear tires so the rear tire will roll straight down and across the center of the inked surface. The other chart board, identified with the red arrow, has a piece of clear media film taped to it. As the vehicle moves forward, it must be slipped between the front and rear tires so the inked rear tire will deposit the inked impression across it.

Figure 4.12. As the vehicle moves forward from the inked board onto the media film, it will leave its full-circumference impression.

sions, so you need to have at least three persons on hand to complete this procedure. Pushing the vehicle will ensure the tire does not spin or slip when moving across the ink board. Avoid stopping the vehicle with the brakes because this may also cause a slip in the impression. Instead, stop the vehicle by pushing in the opposite direction.

10. As the vehicle moves across the media film attached to the chart board, it will leave its inked impression on the film, as shown in Figure 4.12.
11. Continue to push the vehicle until it completes the impression and let it continue onto a scrap piece of chart board covered with a scrap piece of film (Figure 4.13). This is important to have and use because the inked tire will bond to the paper or chart board if it rests on it for too long, and that will interfere with subsequent impressions.
12. After each impression is made, but *before removing that impression*, write on the media film with a marker: (1) the tire brand and line of tire; (2) what that tire's position was on the suspect vehicle, i.e., right rear,

Figure 4.13. The tire should come to rest on a piece of scrap chart board covered with a piece of scrap film. If the tire covered with ink rests on the brown paper or uncovered chart board, the paper from those items will quickly and permanently adhere to the tire's surface and interfere with any subsequent impressions as well as the examination.

left front, etc.; (3) tire size; (4) indicate the outside of tire when making impression; (5) an arrow indicating the direction relative to the front of the vehicle; (6) the date the impression was made; and (7) any other information, such as your initials, case number, and other important information (Figure 4.14).

13. Examine the inked impression to see if there was too much ink or not enough ink. Adjust the ink on the ink board if needed.
14. Run the fingerprint roller over the ink board to smooth out the prior impression on it. Repeat the entire process for a second impression of the same tire. *Be sure to start the second impression of each tire half way around the tire at a different location,* for reasons illustrated in Figure 4.5.
15. When all the impressions have been made for a tire, you may want to consider driving on that tire for a half mile or so to remove the ink; otherwise, handling of the tire during the examination may be messy.
16. The inked impressions should be secured until thoroughly dry! This may take anywhere from 2 to 4 hours; but to be safe and ensure that the ink is totally dry, overnight drying is recommended. Once dried they can be rolled up and easily stored (Figure 4.15).

This method provides two detailed inked impressions for each tire having a high degree of contrast on a clear surface. They will be used as full-circumference first-generation transparencies during the forensic examination.

Inked Impressions on White Board

A few examiners still prefer black inked impressions on white chart board itself rather than on the clear film. To obtain this type of impression, the same procedure as above can be followed but simply without the clear film taped to the chart board. Instead, the impression will be recorded directly onto the white chart board. Disadvantages of this method are that this impression cannot be used directly as an original transparent overlay, the storage of the chart board takes up considerably more space, and quantities of chart board must be purchased and prepared.

Powdered Impressions on Clear Wet Media Film

Another method uses petroleum jelly and black magnetic fingerprint powder. Petroleum jelly comes in many brands but is known to most as Vaseline and has excellent qualities for this purpose. Whereas many ask if silicon spray on a rag or sponge, or other methods, can be used, I have found the petroleum jelly to work best. Both aerosol sprays and products with a thinner viscosity have inherent problems, are difficult to apply evenly, and may cause streaks.

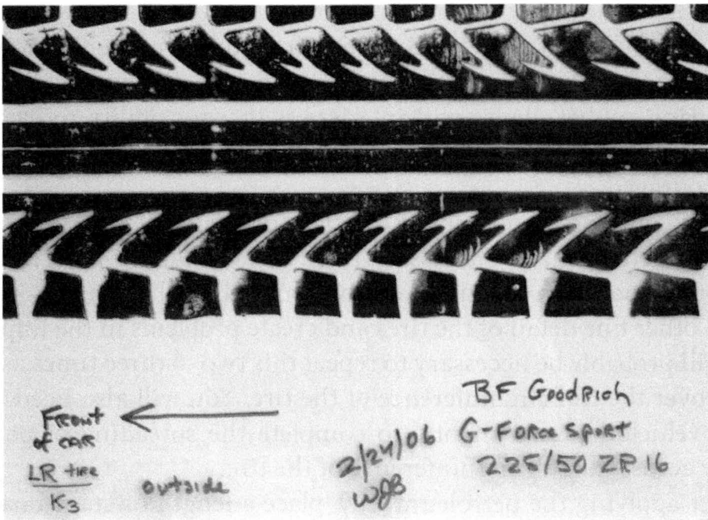

Figure 4.14. The appropriate information should be placed on the actual impression prior to its removal. This would minimally include the tire brand and size, position the tire came from on the suspect vehicle, direction and date taken, which side of the impression was the outside of the tire, investigator's initials, and the like.

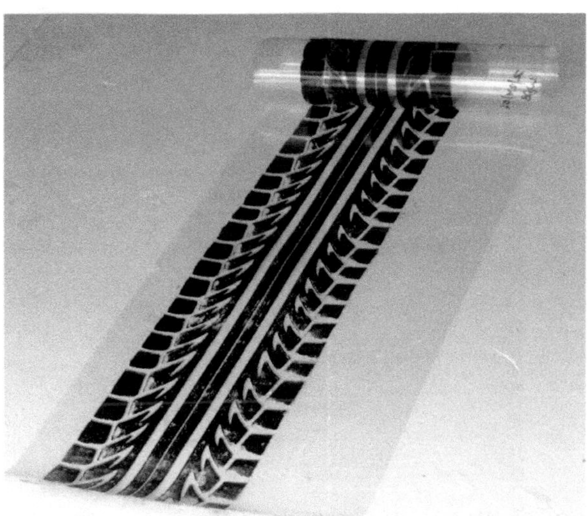

Figure 4.15. Once the ink is dry, the impression on the film can be rolled up for storage.

1. As before, prepare the paper, position the vehicle, and dust off the tires.
2. Take a small dab of petroleum jelly in your bare hands (Figure 4.16) and rub your hands together until the material is evenly distributed. Wearing rubber gloves will interfere with your ability to evenly distribute the petroleum jelly across the surface of the tire and is strongly discouraged.
3. Using your bare hands, rub the surface of the tire to spread a very thin film of petroleum jelly across the tread surface (Figure 4.17). Be sure not to apply too much because excessive amounts will fill in the sipes, cuts, and other fine detail of the tires and create problems in the impression. It will probably be necessary to repeat this two to three times as needed to cover the full circumference of the tire. You will also need to move the vehicle forward slightly to complete the spreading of petroleum jelly across the full circumference of the tire.
4. After applying the petroleum jelly, place a length of chart board with the clear media film taped over it in front of the tire you wish to print.
5. Roll the vehicle over the chart board or film. This will leave a very thin and clear petroleum jelly impression on the film (Figure 4.18).
6. Mark the impression as before to indicate the vehicle, brand, line of tire, etc.

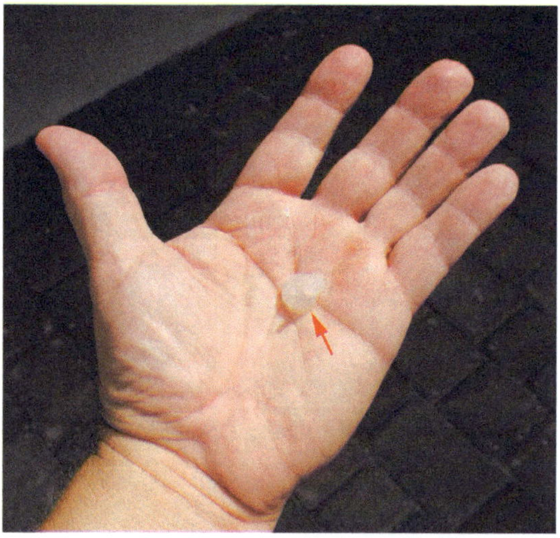

Figure 4.16. A small dab of petroleum jelly is applied to the hands, which are then rubbed together to allow for a thin and controlled application. This small amount of petroleum jelly, repeated three times, is all that is needed to adequately coat the full circumference of the tire. Too much petroleum jelly will fill sipes, cuts, and other important detail and will not allow for a suitable known standard. Using gloves for this is not recommended.

Figure 4.17. The petroleum jelly is applied evenly and with bare hands to the tread surface. This may have to be done in two or three parts to cover the entire tire circumference.

7. Then dust the impression with black magnetic fingerprint powder. A highly detailed impression will be developed (Figure 4.19). Remove any excess powder, first with the magna brush and then by tilting the chart or film and tapping it on its side to let any remaining loose powder fall off.
8. Apply two to three light coatings of a fast-drying clear acrylic spray over the impression. This will fix the impression and keep it from smearing.
9. Repeat the process, making sure that you offset the second impression half way around the tire from the first starting point. You will normally not need to re-apply additional petroleum jelly for the second impression.

This method, if properly done, actually provides better detail than the inked methods. However, the powdering and spraying that is necessary to develop and preserve the impression later interferes with that detail and the ability to see through the clear film when using it as an overlay, and the resulting amount of contrast is not as great as with the darker black printing ink. Consequently, when impressions obtained this way are placed over a cast or photographed impressions during the examination, they may not provide

Figure 4.18. The tire leaves a very thin deposition of petroleum jelly on the clear film, seen at the arrow.

as much contrast as the inked impressions on clear film. Figure 4.20 shows a small segment of an inked impression and a small segment of a Vaseline and black powder impression, both from the same tire and on clear film. Although both are adequate for the examination, the difference in contrast is significant. Most examiners prefer the black ink on wet media film method.

Powdered Impressions on White Board

For those examiners who prefer a black inked impression on white board rather than on a clear surface, the above procedure using petroleum jelly and black magnetic powder can be followed but without the clear film taped to the chart board. Instead, the impression will be recorded directly onto the white chart board. The impression will still have to be developed with powder, then sprayed or protected with a clear film to prevent if from smearing.

Treadprint

The Identicator materials have been used to obtain highly detailed known shoe impressions for many years. The Identicator Treadprint kit consists of

Figure 4.19. Black magnetic fingerprint powder is applied to the petroleum jelly impression on the clear film while it is still taped to the chart board. The chart board will be placed on its side and tapped to remove the excess powder. Two to three light coats of a fast-drying glossy acrylic spray will then be applied to protect the impression and prevent it from smearing.

Figure 4.20. On the left is the darker inked impression on clear film, which provides more contrast and which is the more preferred method. On the right is the petroleum jelly impression on clear film, which has been treated with black fingerprint powder and then sprayed with a fixative. It provides excellent detail but does not provide as much contrast. Note that both are more than sufficient for the examination and the choice is controlled by personal preference and other factors.

an applicator pad and 16 tread panels, each 10 × 24 inches.[8] The panels have been treated with a special solution that will turn black on contact with the solution in the applicator pad. Instructions are provided with the Treadprint kit, but in brief are as follows:

1. Clean dirt and debris from the tire as described above. It will be necessary to clean the contact area of the tread after the procedure begins.
2. Tape sections of the Treadprint panels (treated board) as needed to accommodate the circumference of the tire.
3. Position the Treadprint panels in front of the tire.
4. Using the treated applicator pad, thoroughly wipe the surface of the tire to cover it with a coating of the pad's solution.
5. Move the vehicle so the tire rolls over the Treadprint panel. The solution on the tire will cause a reaction with the treated board, resulting in an ink-quality impression on the board.
6. Stop the vehicle and clean the portion of the tire that was contacting the ground. Wipe the surface of this area with the tread applicator pad and continue rolling the vehicle to complete the impression.
7. Mark the appropriate information on the panel as discussed prior.

This method works well and is suitable if all that is desired is a black-on-white impression. The chart board provided is rather narrow, so it would not be possible to use for extra-wide tires. It cannot be used with clear media film to provide a clear transparent impression. See Figure 4.4, which shows an examiner using the applicator pad to apply a coating on the tire. As the tire runs over the treated panels, it leaves its impression.

Additional Techniques

Some examiners like to mark the tire in segments, as depicted in Figure 4.21. If this is done, those same segment identifiers can be marked during the impression-making process (Figure 4.22). This is convenient during the examination because the portion of the known impression can rapidly be linked to the part of the tire that made it. Making inked impressions already involves many steps, and any additional step, such as marking segments on the inked exemplar as the vehicle is moving, will likely take an extra person. It should be emphasized that the tire must continue rolling and should not stop during the impression-making process. This makes the marking of those segments somewhat difficult. If you do choose to do this, priority should be given to making a continuous rolling full-circumference impression, and the segment marking should be of secondary importance. If the tire

[8] See www.Identicatorinc.com and www.ForensicSource.com

Figure 4.21. Tire segments can be marked on the tire with tape or a china marker.

has been labeled with segment markings "A" through "H" only one or two of these need to be marked as the impression is laid down. This will make it easy to associate the impression with the exact position on the tire from which it came.

Dual Tire Assemblies

Occasionally a vehicle with a dual tire assembly will be involved in a crime and leave its tracks at the scene. Dual tire assemblies are sets of two tires, mounted side by side on two separate wheels but locked in that position. Because the two tires, including any noise treatment, tread wear indicators and other features, are locked in a fixed position relative to each other, a set of dual tire tracks left by these tires can potentially retain that information as well. Because the relationship of these tires is of extreme importance, full-circumference known impressions should be made of both tires simultaneously, thus capturing the relationship of how they are mounted. The only way

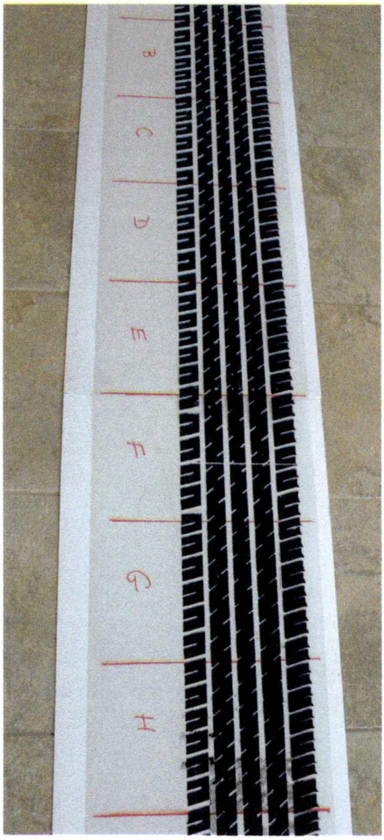

Figure 4.22. An inked impression on clear film over chart board with segment markings that correspond with the marked segments depicted in Figure 4.21 and that were placed on it as it was being made

to capture this is to ensure the tires are still on the actual vehicle. Once they are removed and dismounted from the wheels, the relationship of tread information those tires left at the scene and the potential of that evidence will be lost.

Key Points

- Elimination photographs or prints of nonsuspect vehicles should be made at the crime scene to assist in focusing on the tire tracks of the perpetrator.
- When a suspect vehicle is located and the tires are seized for examination, the positions those tires occupy on that vehicle should be marked on the tires, particularly if those tires are to be removed.
- Two continuous and offset full-circumference known impressions made in one of the above described ways will be obtained to make a full and thorough examination.
- The proper inks or powder and other materials are essential to provide impressions with sufficient contrast and comparative features.
- Essential information should be recorded on each impression prior to it being removed to ensure the accuracy of that information.
- Making known impressions is a function that should be performed by the examiner at the time of the examination. It is necessary to have these impressions and the tire when comparing a tire with a questioned impression.
- Test impressions cannot be made by rolling the tires by hand. They must be made either on the suspect vehicle from which they came or on a comparable vehicle.

Tire Manufacturing[1]

5

Designing a Tire

Tires were originally designed by tire engineers and draftsmen who painstakingly created a blueprint for a tread pattern from which a prototype tire was made. That tire was then tested on a track. Tire designs that performed well were then manufactured. If it did not perform well, that design went back to the drawing board. Today, tire designs are created on very elaborate computer systems using what is called finite element analysis. Finite element analysis consists of a computer model of a material or design, or combination of both, that can then be stressed and analyzed for specific results. In other words, the computer is able to provide accurate predictions of the tire's qualities and performance under a variety of conditions. Using this computer, the tire engineer can make modifications, each time seeing instantly how that modification might improve the design. Figure 5.1 depicts part of a tire design during the design and development stages. Once the design is completed, tire prototypes are produced, and although they are still track tested, the use of this sophisticated design technology now permits manufacturers to produce tires and tread designs whose performance far exceeds that of the tires of prior years.

[1] Special appreciation to Mark Thomas, Principal Cure Development Engineer, and Tony Brinkman, Principal Tire Analysis Engineer, both of the Cooper Tire and Rubber Company, for their technical assistance and guidance in writing a large portion of this chapter.

Figure 5.1. Tires are designed on modern computer systems that can immediately predict performance parameters and reduce design development time.

Tire Mold Types

There are two types of tire molds. One is a known as a "shell" or "two-piece" mold; the other is a "segmented mold." The two-piece mold consists of a top half and a bottom half. Each half contains one sidewall and half of the tread design. Figure 5.2A illustrates this top and bottom half arrangement. Figure 5.2B depicts a two-piece mold in a factory. The two mold halves will close around the green tire during the tire curing process. The point at which the two halves meet or join together is known as the "parting line." Although the two halves fit precisely together during the tire curing process, the extreme pressures exerted internally on the tire cause some rubber to seep into the very narrow gap between these two halves along this parting line. In the industry, this small amount of escaped rubber at the parting line is known as "flash." As a result, the area where the two halves join will be clearly visible on the newly molded tire at or near the center of the tread pattern and oriented in a circumferential direction around the tire. The rubber flash at

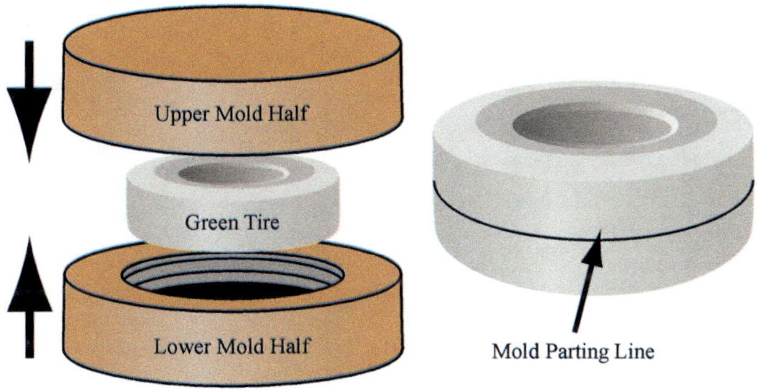

Figure 5.2A. A two-piece mold, known as a shell mold, consists of a top and bottom, each containing a sidewall ring and half of the full-circle tread design. The area where the molds meet, and where some flash is present after cure, is known as the mold parting line.

Figure 5.2B. A shell mold. The arrow points to the green tire just placed in the mold. Note that it contains no tread design. The tread design ring of the upper half of the mold is visible. The green tire is sitting on top of the bottom mold half.

the parting line on a new tire produced in a two-piece mold is depicted in Figure 5.2C. In worn tires the parting line may remain easily visible on some tires while on others it may be difficult to find, particularly if the center rib

Figure 5.2C. The mold parting line of a shell mold (red arrow). The white arrow denotes the ventless seams where air escapes during mold cure. These seams end at the mold parting line on a shell molded tire.

is solid. Two-piece molds are lower in cost and usually are manufactured for tires having less-sophisticated construction and simple tread patterns.

The segmented mold (Figure 5.3A) is composed of a full circle of several, usually eight or more, tread segments and two sidewall plates. The tread segments open and close like pieces of a pie. As the tire curing process begins, the segments are drawn inward, around and into the tread portion of the green tire. Concurrently, each sidewall plate, one on the top and one on the bottom, form and shape the sidewalls of the tire. When the cure is com-

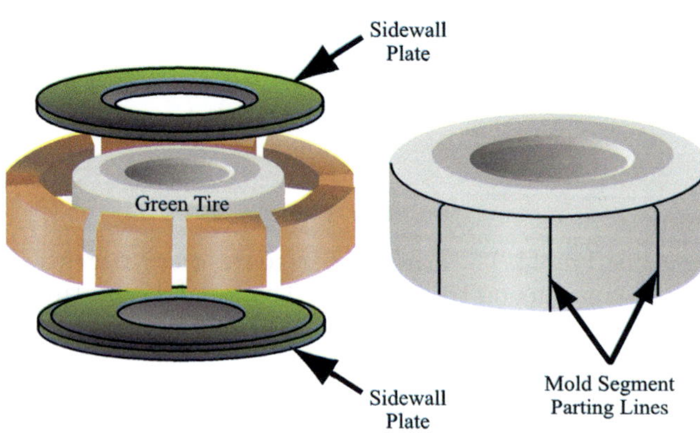

Figure 5.3A. A segmented mold consists of several segments that open and close around the tire. Between each of the segments, the finished tire will contain some flash where the segment mold parting lines are. The sidewall plates are mounted separately.

Figure 5.3B. A segmented mold. The green tire (arrow) is sitting on the sidewall. Above, the open segmented mold is about to be lowered over the green tire. The other sidewall plate is above the segments.

plete, the segments move outward to release the cured tire from the mold. Each segment only includes a portion of the tread length in a circumferential direction; however, they do include the full width of the tread pattern. A segmented mold is depicted in Figure 5.3B. At each location where the segments meet or join one another, there will be visible segment parting lines across the tread pattern of the cured tire. During the tire curing process, and as with two-piece molds, a slight amount of rubber may be forced into the very narrow clearances between the segment ends, resulting in flash that defines these segment parting lines. Depending on how the mold was made, the segment parting lines may extend in a straight line across the tread or, instead, may be a curved or even an irregular line, which may or may not follow the pitch of the design across the tread surface. Figure 5.3C depicts a parting line across the tread surface of a tire molded in a segmented mold. Segmented molds are higher in cost than are the two-piece type, but they do provide certain advantages for manufacturing today's more technically sophisticated tires.

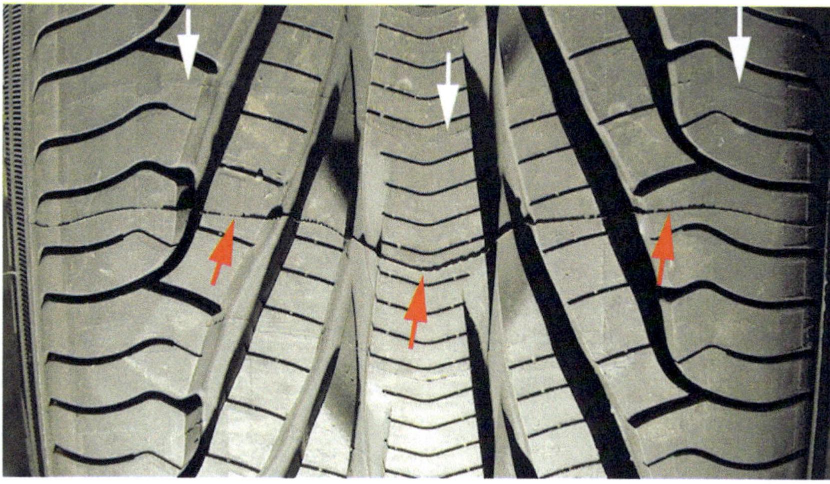

Figure 5.3C. A segment parting line is clearly visible (red arrows) as are smaller vent lines (white arrows). Notice the vent lines also cross the entire tread in the segmented mold.

Mold-Making Methods

Two primary methods of producing the tread portion of molds have been in use for many years. They can be divided into the cast process and the engraved or milled process. Molds are the origin of the design and dimensional class characteristics of tires. When molds are made, they each have a part number or mold number. Factories normally produce a series of molds in each particular design and size tire. These originate either from the same original plaster carving (cast molds) or from the same computer program (engraved molds). The mold numbers will be different for each mold so that any tire made could be traced back to that particular mold, if necessary. If a particular mold's designation was 33456, and 10 identical molds were made with the same design and dimensional designation, the numbers on each tire mold (and tire) might be designated 33456-1, 33456-2, and so forth. New tires made from any of these related molds will be essentially indistinguishable from one another, unless, of course, a sipe blade becomes bent or broken, mold parts become slightly misaligned, or some other damage occurs. An infrequent exception to this would be situations where perhaps four molds were made by one contractor and the following year another contractor produced six more molds. Another exception might be where additional molds were made by the original contractor but perhaps with some modification or improvement. In these exceptions, it would be possible to have mold numbers in the same series, i.e., 33456, but with some variation between them.

Cast Molds

The cast method of producing multiple tread rings from a carved model is a long, multistep procedure. The process allows multiple plaster copies (casts), with varying pitch sequences, to be reproduced from the same one or two original carved models. Carved models are built by creating colored layers of plaster, built one upon another with precise thicknesses and curvatures across the tread profile. Figure 5.4 shows the various colors of plaster at different depths on the right and on the left, the carved design which extends down to the various depths as gauged by the colored plasters. Once the plaster has cured, an expert carver then uses a detailed tread design drawing and, assisted by the different colors at different depths, literally hand carves the tread design into this plaster section. Through a series of casting procedures, a green cast is produced from this carved model. The green cast is a positive image of the tire design and will have sipe blades set into it (Figure 5.5). An intermediary cast is made from the green cast. From these, white plaster casts can be poured. These white plaster models are then carefully and precisely trimmed to length and assembled into a full circle on a heavy steel plate. These assemblies are then placed in ovens for several hours to remove all moisture (Figure 5.6). At the foundry, a combination of metal and sand copes are built around each of these assemblies to contain the molten aluminum alloy as it is poured into the cope and around the plaster "rings," creating a cast tread ring. When they cool, the plaster and cope material is broken away from the newly formed tread ring. The tread ring is pressure

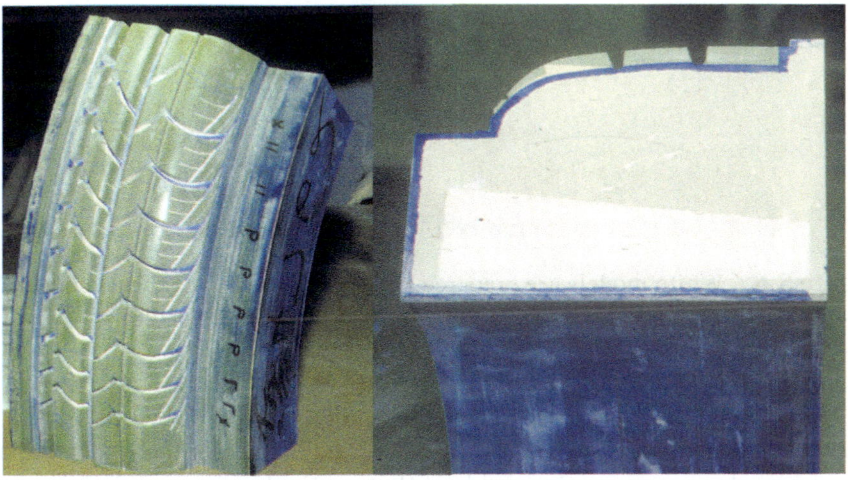

Figure 5.4. On the left is a carved portion of a tire design. The artist uses the different depths of the colored plaster as a guide for how deep to carve the design. On the right is the profile of a section showing how the colored plaster is used to gauge the depth of the design.

Figure 5.5. A model of tread design after insertion of the sipe blades.

Figure 5.6. White models are prepared from the master. It is these models the molten aluminum will be poured around to produce the tread rings.

cleaned to remove any remaining plaster or other materials (Figure 5.7). It is then placed on equipment that can test and adjust its exact size and diameter to ensure it meets the required tolerances. Using this technique, manufacturers can produce as many tire molds of that particular size and design as are needed, all with nearly indistinguishable features, and all from one or two original carvings.

Figure 5.7. Two tread rings, each of one half of the tread design for a shell mold.

Engraved Molds

Some tire tread molds are engraved in a process where the design is milled, or machined, into a section of metal, usually aluminum or steel. This process was used for making the first tire molds more than 100 years ago and had been the dominant method until the casting process was refined in the 1960s and 1970s. Historically, it has been a highly skilled and labor-intensive process, requiring unique equipment and tools. Since the late 1980s, and the development of computer-assisted design and manufacture (CAD-CAM) the engraving process has experienced tremendous improvements in accuracy and manufacturing efficiency through the application of computer technology and sophisticated 5- and 6-axis machining centers. Today's tire molds of a given size and design that are made with this process are essentially identical, with tires from these being indistinguishable from one another except for the mold identification that may be found on the tires' sidewalls.

Mold Finishing

Two sidewall plates must be made for each tire mold, whether it be a clamshell mold or segmented mold. When producing the sidewall plates, there is a lot of lettering that must be created into or onto these. Historically, and until recently, all the sidewall lettering was hand stamped into the metal sidewalls of the molds. This was done by a highly skilled craftsman using a hammer and very hard steel stamps. Each stamp has a letter, numeral, or symbol engraved on one end. This stamp, usually a "square rod," several inches in length, is held against the mold sidewall and pounded to the prescribed depth into the metal, one letter or number at a time. Engraving was developed for some of these items when, in the 1960s, large, raised white lettering on tire sidewalls became popular. Hand-operated pantograph engraving machines were used for this until the late 1980s. It was then that, much like tread engraving, the evolving computer technology was applied to sidewall engraving. Today, virtually all the designs, lettering, and technical information found on a tire's sidewalls originated with very high-tech engraving machines cutting these features into the molds' sidewalls.

If the tread wear indicators were not already included in the tread design such as they might be in an engraved mold, they must be added during mold finishing. These can be stamped into the design. The exact positioning of the tread wear indicators and the style of these may vary from one tire mold to another when added by hand.

In some tire molds, hundreds of tiny vent holes must be individually drilled through the tread surface to allow for the release of air during the mold cure process. These vent holes allow for the air in the mold to escape. Once the air escapes, rubber fills these holes. If the manufacturer does not remove these small protrusions of rubber they will be visible on new tires (Figure 5.8). Any of these small pieces of rubber that are on the tread surface will quickly wear off as soon as the tire is used on a vehicle.

Ventless Molds

In recent years, tire mold makers have created another way to release air from between the surface of the tire and the interior of the mold during the curing process. This does two things: it eliminates the drilling of hundreds of vent holes through the tread portion of the mold, and the lack of extruded rubber vents on the tire surface enhances its appearance.

This method utilizes a "ventless" tire mold, which is composed of interconnecting pieces of design, with the interface of the pitches often serving as a vent line. In other words, the tire mold is made in a puzzle-like fashion with each approximate pitch of design comprising the pieces of the puz-

Figure 5.8. Tread molds traditionally had hundreds of vent holes drilled into the tread surface to allow for the air trapped between the green tire and the mold surface to escape. This resulted in tiny projections of rubber (arrow), simply known as vent hole rubber. With newer ventless molds, this vent hold rubber will only be found on the sidewall areas.

zle. These fit together and create the tread design. The interface surfaces of these pieces are made to fit together so precisely that air can escape through the almost microscopic spaces between them but, ideally, the rubber cannot. Although there may be many variations of how this is achieved, one method involves an aluminum pour casting in which each pitch is separated by voids. Then each pitch is cut from the aluminum casting and reassembled pitch by pitch along the interior of a tire mold to create the tread portion of the mold. The venting is achieved at the pitch line formed where each of the pitches intersect as described above. In the finished tire each pitch length is defined by the presence of the vent separation in the mold and the subsequent raised, fine line of rubber, and occasionally, a small amount of flash that may seep through the small void along these interfaces. Vent holes will still be drilled in the sidewall plates to vent air from those areas.

In some cases, the flash or defined vent lines from these "ventless"-type molds may also be evident in the crime scene impression. Figure 5.2C depicts a tire produced in a clamshell mold with the ventless seams. Note how the divisions stop at the mold parting line in the center of the tire where the shell mold halves join. Figure 5.3C depicts a tire produced in a segmented mold with ventless seams. The seams in the segmented mold run across the full tread width and actually curve as does the heavier segment line division.

Tire Manufacturing

Most people have little idea how the modern radial tire is manufactured. Once they have seen how a tire is made, they are amazed at the technology and effort needed to produce one. For forensic examiners, a general understanding of how tires are manufactured assists in the evaluation of class characteristics and also provides some knowledge to help evaluate other questions that might arise during the examination of tire evidence. The tire industry is a very competitive industry, and tires cannot be reverse engineered. Therefore, tire companies are extremely protective of their rubber compounds and ingredients, manufacturing methods, and many other core trade secrets they possess. It is therefore becoming more difficult to find a tire manufacturer that will provide examiners a tour of their production facilities. This chapter cannot take the place of a good detailed tour of a tire manufacturing facility, but it does introduce the reader to some basic information about tire manufacturing.

Tire Components

In each factory tire manufacturers use rubber, fabric, and steel to produce the various components of the modern radial tire. Many different rubber compounds are produced from a variety of raw ingredients in order to produce specific behaviors and performance characteristics needed for the tread, sidewall, and other rubber components. Rubber-coated textile fabrics such as nylon, polyester, or rayon are used in the plies of the tire and will be placed under tension while coated with rubber. Steel cords will be used in the belts of the tire as well as steel wires in the beads. In the end, approximately 20 components are included in the building of a tire. The following is a brief and simplified description of some of the more basic tire components.

Inner Liner The inner liner, sometimes referred to as simply the liner, is the innermost component of the tire. It is usually composed of a special halobutyl rubber compound that creates an effective barrier against water and moisture penetration into the body of the tire, while holding the pressurized air within the tire. The liner is the first component applied during the building process. During mold cure, a bladder will exert pressure against the liner to force the green tire against the tire mold. As this happens, the pattern of the bladder will be transferred to the inner liner. When you look on the inside of an unmounted tire, the manufacturer's distinct bladder pattern is visible (Figure 5.9). These patterns are important in providing an escape route for air that becomes trapped between the tire and the curing bladder during the mold cure process. In the first World Trade Center bombing, these liner patterns were useful in helping reconstruct the tire fragments of different brand tires.

Figure 5.9. The bladder presses the green tire against the mold surfaces during mold cure. The bladder contains a design that is transferred to the green tire and can be seen in any unmounted finished molded tire. Different manufacturers use different patterns.

Beads The beads of the tire are rubber-insulated, multistrand hoops of very strong steel wire, around which the body ply cords are wrapped. In the finished tire/wheel assembly, the beads keep a tire locked firmly in place around the bead seats of the wheel rim, providing an air-tight seal, while also transmitting the driver's inputs to the rest of the tire. Figure 5.10 depicts a supply of beads ready to be used in tire production.

Figure 5.10. A supply of beads ready to be taken to the tire builder. The beads on each side of the tire resist centrifugal forces and help hold the tire on the rim.

Apex An apex is a specially formulated triangular rubber wedge that is used to provide a stiffness transition from the rigid steel bead area to the thinner, flexible sidewall of the tire. An apex is applied around the outer face of each bead hoop.

Ply One or more composite layers of twisted fibers of polyester, rayon, or nylon, coated with rubber, designed to provide strength to the tire while maintaining its resilient flexibility. For the typical passenger or light truck tire, two plies are placed over the inner liner, wrapped around the bead, locking the bead into place. The inner liner plies, and beads form the tire carcass.

Sidewall Rubber The sidewalls of the tire are composed of special rubber compounds designed to protect the sides of the tire and to withstand the stresses of flexing within a tire. Additionally, the white sidewall, or white-lettered sidewall, is designed to resist scuffing and yellowing. The sidewall rubber will acquire raised and indented lettering and a unique tire identification number during mold cure. Figure 5.11 shows the sidewall as the extruding machine applies a thin black layer of rubber to protect the white rubber portion throughout the manufacturing processes. During the final finishing process, the white sidewall or raised white letters of the sidewall will become exposed as the thin black layer of rubber will be buffed off to expose the white rubber, and a colored protective paint will be applied prior to storage or shipping.

Belts The belt of the radial tire is composed of thousands of individually guided steel wire cables, rubber encased, and then cut at a bias angle. Typically, passenger and light truck tires will contain two belts, with the belt wires of one belt laid in an opposing angle to the other belt. This "fishnet" effect provides rigidity to the tread so that tire forces that occur during normal rolling, cornering, acceleration, and handling maneuvers do not cause abnormally high tread wear rates and/or loss of contact and loss of traction. Secondarily, the steel belts provide increased strength and puncture resistance in the tire crown.

Overlays In the case of high-performance and ultra-high-performance passenger tires, as well as higher speed rated light truck tires, rubber-coated nylon, rayon, or other textile fabrics may be applied circumferentially around the tire as narrow strips or as an overlay ply (slightly wider than the widest belt) overtop of the topmost steel belt component. The overlay component restricts the centrifugal growth of the tire's shoulder regions during high-speed testing, allowing the tire to satisfactorily perform at speeds well in excess of 100 mph.

Tread The tread portion of the tire consists of special rubbers that are extruded through die plates that shape the profile to specified dimensions

Figure 5.11. Sidewall rubber with the black-and-white portions. A strip of black extruded rubber is being applied to cover the white areas. Later, if the tire is meant to have raised white lettering or a white stripe, the black protecting cover is ground away.

required for the tire. The tread compound ingredients will vary greatly between tires in order to optimize various performance characteristics for different tire designs. For example, different ingredients may be used to optimize rolling resistance and wet traction, in comparison with a tread rubber designed to optimize dry traction and tread wear. During mold cure, the tread pattern with its many design elements, grooves, sipes, and other specific detailed features will be implanted into the tread component.

Building the Tire

The first-stage building machine consists of a collapsible multisegment steel building drum mounted on a horizontal shaft driven by an electric motor (Figure 5.12). The tire is assembled on the building drum by a skilled tire builder. The builder applies the inner liner to the building drum, wrapping

Figure 5.12. A tire building drum that allows for the components of the tire from the liner to the tread to be added as it revolves. In this way the tire is built into the green tire, which is then taken to the mold for cure.

the inner liner once around the outside of the building drum as it turns, cutting the inner liner to length, and overlapping the beginning edge with the ending edge to complete the inner liner. The builder then applies the first ply to the building drum, wrapping the ply once around the building drum and inner liner, overlapping the beginning edge with the ending edge to complete the ply. He turns the edges of the ply down over the ends of the drum, then operates the machine to set one bead assembly against ply 1 at each open end of the drum.

A bladder then inflates and forces the ply at each end out around the bead assemblies and presses these "turn-ups" against the ply and the drum. The builder then applies the second ply to the building drum, wrapping the ply once around the building drum atop the turn-ups, tearing the ply cut to the length between cords, overlapping the beginning edge with the ending edge to complete the ply. He then applies an anti-chafing strip atop the ply 2 at each end of the drum. The builder applies the sidewalls around the ply and anti-chafing strips and presses the overlapping ends tightly over the beginning edges. The builder operates the machine to operate a pair of pneumatically loaded metal wheels, which press the sidewalls against the anti-chafing strips, plies, and inner liner that are pressed against the building drum to compact the assembly and force out any air remaining between the components of the assembly. He then operates the machine to turn the edges of ply 2 and the anti-chafing strips snugly around the bead assembly toward the inner surface of the drum. A simple illustration of this is provided in

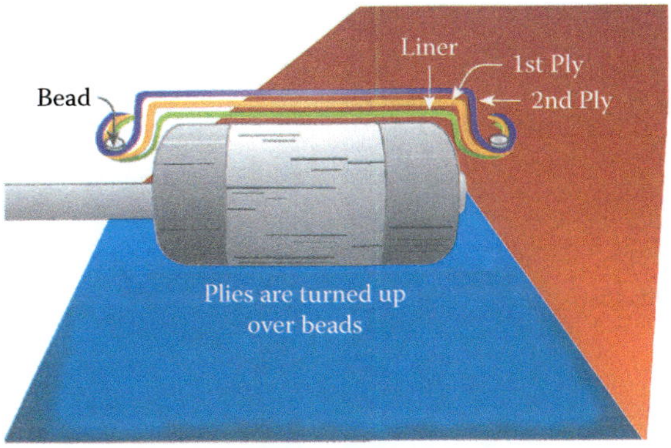

Figure 5.13. An illustration of how the liner and plies are turned over the beads to form the initial carcass of the tire during tire building.

Figure 5.13. The builder operates the machine to collapse the drum, slides the "first-stage" tire off the drum, and inspects it inside and outside.

The first-stage tire is then transported to a second machine, where it is expanded by pressure, and its shape is changed from cylindrical to toroidal (doughnut) shape. At this machine, the builder applies the first belt to a building drum, wrapping the belt one time around the building drum, and cutting it to length to complete the belt. He repeats this operation, alternating the cord angle direction, for belt 2. The builder then applies the tread rubber around the belts and presses the cut ends together.

This belt and tread assembly is then transferred onto the expanded first-stage tire. The builder then operates the machine to activate the pneumatically loaded wheels known as "stitchers," which press the tread and belts against the first-stage tire to compact the assembly and to force out any air between components of the assembly. The builder operates the machine to collapse the inflation rings, slides the "green" unvulcanized tire off the rings, and inspects it inside and outside. The green tire is not the exact shape as a finished tire. Green tires are included in Figures 5.2B and 5.3B.

Molding and Curing

The green tire then goes to the curing press containing the tire mold where the tire is placed over an inflatable rubber bladder, illustrated in Figure 5.14. The curing press encloses the tire in the two halves of a metal mold, which is the complementary form of the vulcanized (cured) tire. The rubber diaphragm forces the tire against the tire mold where the tread rubber is formed to match the ribs and grooves of the mold, and the sidewall rubber is formed to match the shape, lettering, and profile of the sidewall portions of the tire mold. The

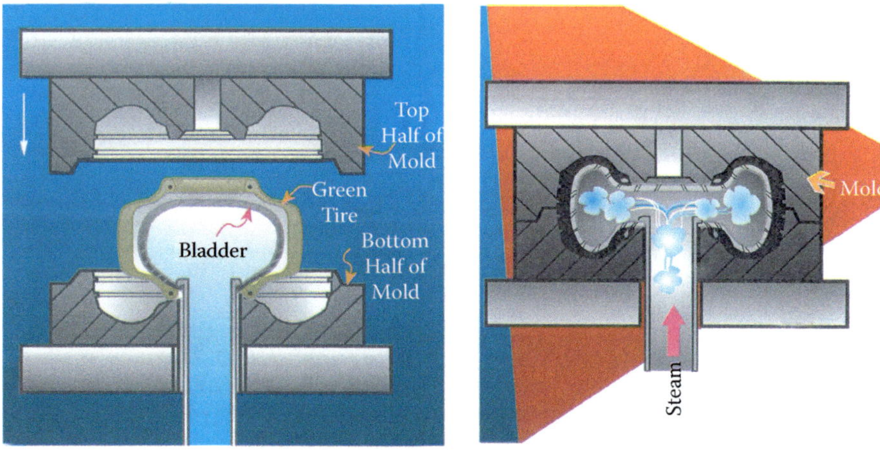

Figure 5.14. The green tire is placed in the mold. As the mold closes, a bladder is inflated and forces the green tire against the sidewall and tread design of the mold surfaces. Steam heat and pressure within the mold cure the tire as the design is implanted to it.

bead area of the green tire is formed to match the mold bead rings and rim flange contours, which will permit the cured (vulcanized) tire to properly fit against the bead seat of the vehicle wheel. This forming and molding is done by the steam pressure inside the rubber diaphragm at pressures that can be over 200 pounds per square inch. The curing of the rubber compounds is accomplished by the heat of the mold halves, which are heated continually by either electric- or steam-heated platens in the vulcanizing machine and by the heat from the steam inside the rubber diaphragm. The rubber compounds throughout the tire are chemically and physically changed during curing from a stiff plastic consistency to a semirigid elastic form. During curing, the various green rubber components are linked chemically and physically, as the shorter rubber molecules are linked into very long, polymerized chain-line molecules. Molecules in adjacent plies, tread, etc. are linked together across the interfacing surfaces when curing is complete. The tire is held in the curing press for a specified length of time at specified internal pressure and temperature and at specified external temperature. At the end of the curing period, the internal pressure is released, the mold is opened, and the tire is removed from the machine. Figure 5.15 depicts a cutaway view of a few of the components within the finished radial tire.

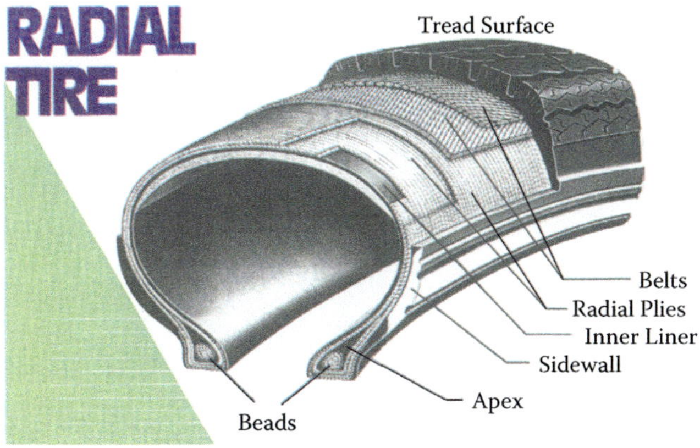

Figure 5.15. A radial tire cutaway showing the various components exposed after the tire has been made.

Final Finishing and Quality Control

Once the tire is released from the mold, it will go through additional quality control steps, including one process that will inflate the tire and measure the uniformity as the tire is rotated against a dynamometer. Further finishing steps may include buffing the sidewall, checking the tire for proper balance, trimming off mold flash and rubber vents, and sorting and labeling the tire. The tire is then warehoused until shipped.

Retreaded Tires[1]

6

Retreading Defined

Retreading is a process where the remaining worn tread of a tire is removed by buffing, after which the original tire casing receives a new tread. The term *retreading* is the popular and common term used today, but it has also been called recapping and remolding. Many millions of tires are retreaded each year in the United States. School buses, long- and short-haul delivery trucks, postal vehicles, dump trucks, racing cars, city buses, emergency vehicles, military vehicles, and airplanes are among some of those using retreaded tires. In 2006, approximately 17.6 million retread tires were sold in North America, the majority of which were medium truck tires found on 18 wheelers.[2] Tires can be retread more than once as long as the casing remains in good condition. Tires on local short-delivery vehicles wear much faster and thus are often retreaded many times over the life of the tire casing, while tires on trucks traveling longer distances wear longer and are retreaded fewer times. Retreading passenger tires was once common in the United States but is now almost nonexistent.

How Tires Are Retreaded

In general, there are two methods of retreading a tire: the pre-cure method and the mold-cure method. The pre-cure method involves the application of a segment of new pre-cured tread over the original tire casing. It is a more flexible method for retreading a variety of sizes and the most common method of retreading. Mold cure involves the application of strips of raw rubber to the prepared tire casing, after which the tire is placed into a mold where the tread

[1] Personal communications with Paul Gage (Goodyear Tire & Rubber Company), May 16, 2007; Marvin Bozarth, Tire Industry Consultants, Shelbyville, KY, May 18, 2007; and Harvey Brodsky, Managing Director, Tire Retread Information Bureau, Pacific Grove, CA, February 13, 2007.

[2] "2006 Fact Sheet for Retreaded Tires," Tire Retread Information Bureau, 900 Weldon Grove, Pacific Grove, CA (www.retread.org).

design is formed and cured. It provides a cleaner and new tire look but represents a much smaller portion of the retread market. Regardless of which of these methods are used, the tire is first inspected and prepared in the same way.

Tire Inspection

Tire casings are acquired from tire dealers, vehicle owners, or other sources. Prior to retreading or remolding, each tire must first be inspected. The tire is first inspected visually on both the inside and outside surfaces. Then, the tire is placed on an inspection machine like the one in Figure 6.1 to further help locate holes, nails, debris, and any other defects that are not as visually obvious or that are hidden within the tire casing. If these defects are repairable and the overall tire casing passes inspection, the tire can be retreaded. If the tire casing cannot be repaired or is otherwise considered unsafe, the tire is rejected. Next, any remaining tread on the tire must be removed through a high-speed buffing process. A buffing machine like the one depicted in Figure 6.2 will accurately remove the proper amount of old

Figure 6.1. This inspection machine will help locate holes, nails, and defects that have occurred to the tire during its use.

Figure 6.2. A tire on a buffing machine. The buffing machine removes the old rubber and ensures the tire surface is properly round.

rubber while also truing the tire to a precise diameter and shape. The buffing process also allows for further inspection of the casing. After buffing, the tire is ready to receive the new tread, either through the attachment of a segment of pre-cured tread rubber already containing the tread design or through the mold cure process.

Pre-Cure Method

The pre-cure method involves the use of pre-molded tread stock that is shipped to the retread facility in large rolls. After the old tire carcass is inspected and buffed, a thin but very soft and sticky gum rubber is applied around the newly buffed tire casing (Figure 6.3). The gum rubber helps bond the pre-cure tread material to the carcass. Figure 6.4 shows the new tread rubber, which is then applied from the roll to the tire carcass. The tread rubber will be cut and spliced to fit tightly around the full circumference of the tire (Figure 6.5). The area where the beginning and end of the new tread rubber meet is known in the industry as the splice. At the splice, extra gum rubber will be used to help bond that area. Figure 6.6 shows the fitting of one end of the tread rubber to the other. In addition, staples will be used to hold that area together until the curing process bonds the new rubber together. In some factories, plastic staples,

Figure 6.3. A thin layer of gum rubber has been applied around the newly prepared tire casing.

Figure 6.4. The pre-cured tread stock is fed from the roll in the foreground to the tire casing in the background. The gum rubber will cause the pre-cured tread to temporarily stick to the tire until it is cured.

Figure 6.5. The tire revolves as the pre-cure tread stock covers the old casing. The machinery presses the new stock firmly against the casing.

Figure 6.6. The layer of gum rubber runs around the tire casing and is the dark thin material seen here between the new tread stock and the old casing. The operator will often add some additional gum rubber to go between the splice joint.

Figure 6.7. Numerous plastic staples have been used to temporarily hold the splice joint together until the tire is cured in the autoclave. The staples remain in the tread and represent additional individual features. Note the misalignment of the tread design and the extra melted gum rubber that has filled the splice area, both indicated at one point with the arrow.

as shown in Figure 6.7, are used and they will melt into the tread rubber when vulcanized. In other factories metal staples are used. Because these staples are quickly and randomly applied, their precise positions on the tread surface are random. The holes these staples create will remain in the tread, and evidence of them may be included in a tire impression. The splice joint is also normally very noticeable because in most instances the design at one end will not match perfectly with the design at the other end. In addition, any extra gum rubber in the splice area can partially fill grooves and uneven areas and will be obvious. An example of a retreaded tire, after some wear, is depicted in Figure 6.8 and shows a typical unmatched and uneven splice joint. Next, a wicking cloth, which is much like a piece of cheese cloth (Figure 6.9), will be laid across the splice and stapled into place. A rubber envelope will then be placed around the tire, and the tire will be moved into an autoclave where regulated heat and pressure will bond the new tread to the old carcass. While in the autoclave, that envelope will help exert pressure against the tread to help bond it to the carcass. That pressure will also cause the transfer of the wicking cloth pattern to the edge of that tire. Figure 6.10 shows a tire within the envelope being removed from the autoclave. Figure 6.11 shows an area near the splice where the wicking cloth pattern has been pressed into the rubber. After removal from the autoclave, the tire will be removed from the envelope and will head to the finishing area, where it will receive a final inspection and painting (Figure 6.12). The painting of the sidewall to match the new and dark black tread is mainly for aesthetics but also covers up the writing that has been placed on the sides of the tires as they work their way through the retreading process.

Figure 6.8. A worn retread with the typical mismatch of the design at the splice joint.

Figure 6.9. The wicking cloth is applied and stapled over the spliced area.

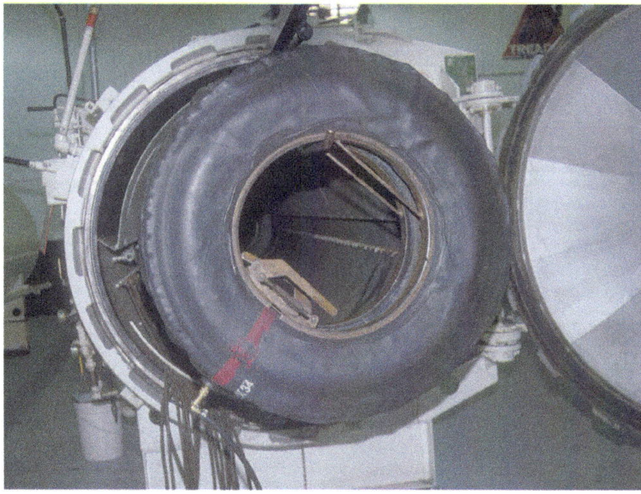

Figure 6.10. The tire is covered with a rubber envelope, which will help create a differential in pressure and will help press the pre-cured tread against the casing until cured in the autoclave. This tire is being removed from the autoclave, the envelope will be removed, and the tire will go to the finishing department.

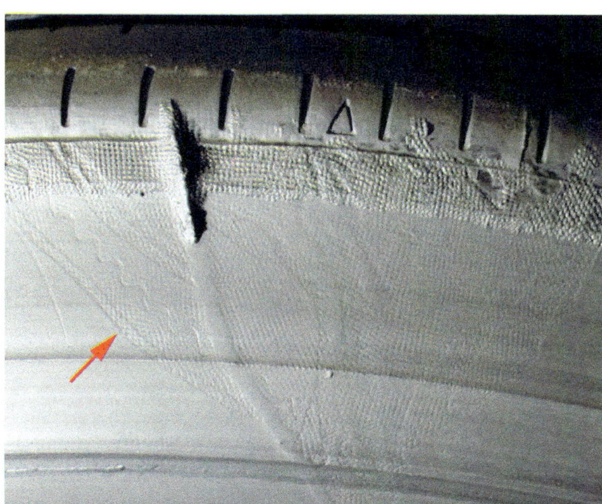

Figure 6.11. The arrows point to the transferred texture of the wicking cloth, which is placed over the splice in the pre-mold process.

Figure 6.12. The retread process will end with the tire receiving a coat of protective paint. This is mainly for aesthetic reasons, to make the sidewall tire rubber appear new and the same color as the darker new tread but also to cover the writing that is typically placed on the sidewalls as they go through the retread process.

Pre-Cure Tread Design Stock

Tread stock for the pre-cure method comes from many manufacturers in many designs. Companies like Bandag, Goodyear, Michelin, and Oliver are among the largest producers of the pre-cure tread stock. Pre-cured tread stock will sometimes have the manufacturer's name and/or corporate symbol molded on its edge or on the actual tread. Figure 6.13 depicts the side of a retreaded tire that used Goodyear pre-cured retread stock. Pre-cured tread stock normally does not incorporate noise treatment, as much of this tread stock is for medium-sized tractor trailers and other vehicles that either are noisy, travel at lower speeds, or operate in off-road situations. Some pre-cure tread stock does include tread wear indicators, and some have raised areas in the grooves to reduce stone holds. Some retread designs are intentionally produced to be very similar to OEM tire designs.

Figure 6.13. Pre-cured stock will often contain molded information on the edge such as 22/32nds, Goodyear, and TMX, which can be associated with the source of the retread stock. Other stock will have lettering or information on the actual tread surface. Both examples are seen here.

Ring Tread Process

There is a modified pre-cure process that was developed in Italy by Marangoni, known as the Ring Tread process. This process is also used by Goodyear and is known as the Goodyear Unicircle process. Both involve pre-cured tread material made in a continuous seamless circle. This tread is stretched around the tire carcass and therefore will not contain a splice. It will still need to have a wicking cloth so those features may be present on the tire. This process is more expensive and so far is a small part of the pre-cure market.

Mold Cure Method

The mold cure method in the retread industry involves the same inspection and repair process. If the tire carcass passes the inspection, the remaining tread design will be buffed away as in the pre-cure method. Using one of several methods, uncured tread rubber will be applied over the crown surface of the newly buffed casing. The tire is then placed into a mold where the tread design will be transferred from the mold to that new rubber and it will leave the mold like a new tire. The mold cure process requires a considerable investment because there must be molding equipment for each size and design of tire, thus the mold cure method is not as common as the pre-cure process.

Segmented Mold Cure

The vast majority of the mold cure method involves the use of a five- to six-piece segmented mold. Different equipment at different retreaders will vary. As with any segmented mold, the points where the segments join will have a trace of rubber flash.

Solid Tread Ring Mold Cure

Another mold cure method, used mainly for bias tires, employs a solid tread ring with variable shoulder plates. If the solid tread ring is truly one piece and has no seams, there will not be flash across the molded tread surface like from a normal segmented mold; but there will be flash at the segment points on the shoulders. However, sometimes solid tread rings are actually made in sections and pinned together, and although they are now technically one piece, the points at which they were joined will still provide some segment flash at those points in the finished tire.

Bead-to-Bead Mold Cure

In a special mold cure method known as bead-to-bead retreading, the sidewalls will also be buffed and new rubber will be applied over the sidewall areas as well. In this version of the mold cure method, new sidewall lettering and an entire new brand name will be molded into the sidewall. Bead-to-bead retreading is conducted at only two plants in North America, thus represents a very small percentage of the mold cure retreaded tires.

Retread DOTR Number

As with new tires, the U.S. Department of Transportation requires a series of numbers and letters be placed on the sidewall of a retreaded tire. The Department of Transportation Retread number, known as the DOTR number, identifies the tire as a retread and provides information about who retreaded it and when it was retreaded. The retread number will be on the sidewall of the tire, normally next to the original DOT number.[3] It may or may not be pre-

[3] In bead-to-bead retreading, all the original lettering, including the original DOT number, will be removed or covered over.

R	LWM	4706
Indicates Retread Tire	Retreader's Code Numbers	Date of Manufacture 47 = 47th week 06 = 2006

Figure 6.14. The DOTR retread tire number may begin with DOTR, "R", or simply with the retreader's code number. Each retreader's code, in this example "LWM," is assigned to a specific retreading facility. The four digits at the end denote the week and year the tire was retread.

LUY	CAVE SPRINGS RECAPPERS	HWY 264 W	CAVE SPRINGS, AR
LVA	GRIFFIN RADIAL TIRE, INC	2375 UNIVERSITY AVE W	SAINT PAUL, MN
LVC	*JOSEPH F LOY TIRE SERVICE, INC	1657 SAW MILL RUN BLVD	PITTSBURGH, PA
LVD	YOST'S, INC	RD # 1 - BOX 10A	BENTON, PA
LVE	McCUBBIN RECAP	297 BUFFALO ST	GOWANDA, NY
LVF	*DUKES TIRE CO	2291 LOUISVILLE AVE	MONROE, LA
LVJ	*TURNER TIRE & TEXACO SERVICE	HWY 67	PFAFFTOWN, NC
LVK	O B NUZUM TIRE SERVICE, INC	830 CALIFORNIA AVE	BAKERSFIELD, CA
LVL	*EASTERN TIRE CO, INC	1105 N POINT RD	BALTIMORE, MD
LVN	LOWRYS TIRE CENTER	HWY 909	CHESTER, SC
LVP	MARLBORO TIRE SERVICE, INC	401 HWY 15 BYPASS	BENNETTSVILLE, SC
LVV	*SUTHERLAND TIRE	PO BOX 515	JONESBURO, TN
LVW	*SHETRON'S TIRE SERVICE	145 WEST ORANGE ST	SHIPPENSBURG, PA
LVX	AIKEN BLACK TIRE SERVICE, INC	PO BOX 1605	HICKORY, NC
LWC	*HARTFORD RECAPPING SERVICE	46 JOHNSON ST N	HARTFORD, WI
LWD	*CARL'S MOTOR SALES	MAIN ST	CALLICOON, NY
LWE	*HARMONY TIRE & RECAPPING CO	PO BOX 4	HARMONY, NC
LWF	LONE WOLF TIRE	RT 2 - BOX 245-A	GRUNDY, VA
LWH	*J & D TIRE CO	1026 BOONVILLE ST N	SPRINGFIELD, MO
LWJ	*RICHEY'S ASSOCIATED TIRE CENTER	PO BOX 367	BINGEN, WA
LWK	*STOWELL TIRE CO	206 ROSE ST	ABILENE, TX
LWM	AMERICAN RETREADING, INC	HWY 1 S	ROCKINGHAM, NC

* **Discontinued Code**

62

Figure 6.15. A portion of a page from the publication *Who Retreads Tires* that shows the retread code "LMW" is listed to American Retreading Inc., Highway 1 S, Rockingham, NC.

fixed by the letters "DOTR" or "R." Figure 6.14 depicts the information contained in the retread number, and Figure 6.15 is a portion of a page listing the retreader's code.[4] It is noted that although the major retreaders abide by this requirement, I have seen tires where this number was either never placed on the sidewall or was possibly scuffed off. Thus, the absence of a DOTR number does not necessarily prove the tire is not a retread. Figure 6.16 depicts the retread numbers on an old tire that has been retreaded at least three times. The most recent number is "KEB 247" indicating it was retreaded at the Goodyear Tire and Rubber Company, Cranberry Township, Pennsylvania during the 24th week of 1997. Notice that its original DOT number is still

[4] This page is from Who Retreads Tires, published by Tire Guides, Inc., Boca Raton, Florida. This source book is further discussed in Chapter 12.

present. Figure 6.17 depicts retread number "RPYY3705RS" branded into the side of the tire. The first "R" stands for retread, the "PYY" indicates it was retread at Keen's Tire Shop, Brunswick, Georgia, the "3705" indicates it was retread during the 37th week of 2005, and the "RS" stands for retread stock.

Figure 6.16. A tire that has been retreaded three times. The most recent number "KEB 247" indicates it was retread at the Goodyear Tire and Rubber Company, Cranberry Township, Pennsylvania (KEB), during the 24th week of 1997 (247). Three-digit date codes were used prior to 2000. Four-digit date codes have been used since 2000, an example of which is in Figure 6.17. The original DOT number is still on this tire sidewall.

Figure 6.17. This retread number, RPYY3705RS, has been branded into the sidewall of the tire. It denotes it is a retreaded tire (R) that was retread at Keen's Tire Shop, Brunswick, Georgia (PYY) during the 37th week of 2005 (3705) using retread stock (RS)

Determining Whether a Tire Is Retreaded

As a forensic examiner, it is important when examining each tire that you know if it is a retread or if it is an original tire. When a tire is retreaded with the pre-cure method and with most of the mold cure methods, the original sidewall name and style (e.g., Goodyear Wrangler), and the original DOT number of the tire should still be present on the sidewall. Only the bead-to-bead mold cure method will replace the sidewall names and other information. Below are clues that will indicate the tire is a retread.

Splice

In the pre-cure method, the splice runs entirely across the tread, and when the ends of the new tread stock are not perfectly matched, the splice is easily detected (Figure 6.7 and Figure 6.8). In addition, gum rubber used to help bond the tread at this location will likely be present in excess in the grooves on each side of the splice. Note that the Goodyear Unicircle and Marangoni methods of applying continuous circles of pre-cured tread do not involve a splice.

Wicking Cloth

The presence of the impression of the wicking cloth on the edge of the tire, as shown in Figure 6.11 and Figure 6.18, is proof the tire has been retreaded.

Irregular Edge Bond Filling

When edge irregularities are present, rubber can be used to fill gaps or holes. This creates an irregular edge quality, as illustrated in Figure 6.18.

Lettering on Edges of Tread Stock

Some of the pre-cure tread stock contains very fine lettering on the edge or tread of that stock (Figure 6.13). This will often indicate the manufacturer of the pre-cure stock, such as Goodyear, Michelin, or Bandag. It might also include a corporate symbol and other information relating to the retread stock. Note that some new tires are molding this information on their tires as well.

Variations in Coloring

Seeing a difference in the coloration of a darker tread and a lighter colored sidewall is not a reliable method of determining the tire has been retreaded.

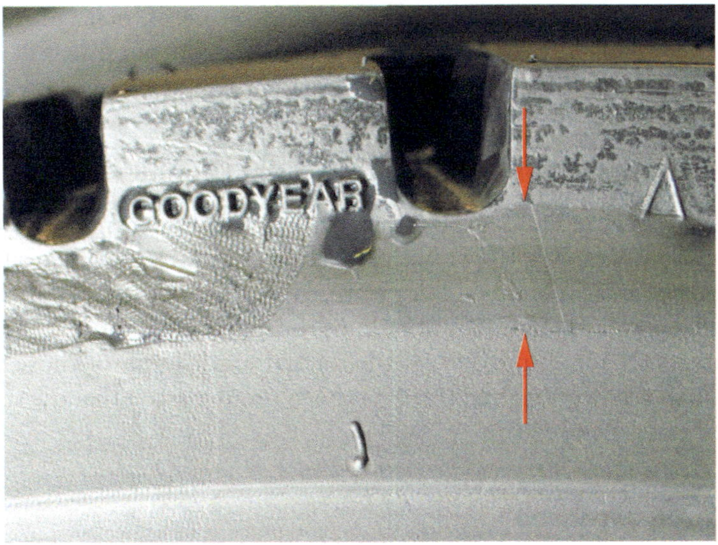

Figure 6.18. In the procure process, it is sometimes necessary to use extra rubber to fill in the irregular edges between the new tread and the sidewall. This extra rubber, seen between the two arrows, is not uniform and in some cases is fairly obvious, thus providing evidence of the retread process.

Tires that are retreaded with the pre-cure and mold cure methods receive a coating of paint in the finishing department, not only so the new darker tread rubber will match the sidewall color, which due to exposure to the elements, has become a lighter gray over time, but to cover up all the writing that had been placed on the sidewall as it worked its way through the retreading process. It may be possible, with ultraviolet light, to actually see the writing through the layer of paint, if the tire is a retread. Failure to see this writing does not mean it is not a retread.

Correlation of Tread Design and Sidewall Information

Compare the manufacturer and brand information indicated on the sidewall with the actual tread design on the tire. Because the sidewall of the pre-cure and mold cure retreaded tires, with the exception of the bead-to-bead mold cure process, will still have the original manufacturer's name and the original style, you can look up that particular tire design in the *Tread Design Guide* or *Tread Assistant* and see if the current tread pattern corresponds with the original tread pattern. Note that in some cases, retreaded designs are very similar but not exactly the same as the original tire design.

Also if you are examining several tires from one vehicle, you may find that some or all of the tires have the same tread design, but different sidewall names. This is very likely a situation where the tires have been retreaded.

Close Examination of the Interface at the Shoulder

Many new tires have molded letters, texture, or tread wear indicator symbols along the shoulder of the tire very close to the tread surface. When a tire's old tread is buffed away to prepare it for retreading, many times that buffing partially eliminates a portion, but not all, of those features. Close examination of this area will sometimes reveal the partial eradication of those features and establish that the original tread has been removed and that the tire being examined is a retreaded tire.

Mold Cured Tires

Those tires that are retreaded during a mold cure process will not contain the telltale signs found in the pre-cure process, such as the irregular splice, evidence of a wicking cloth, etc. The DOTR number will be the main clue to look for. This may be branded into the sidewall, but may also be a smaller version actually molded into the edge of the new tread shoulder. Another reliable method of determining if a tire was retreaded in the mold cure process would be the close-up examination of both edges of the shoulders at the point where the tire was buffed, as described above, to see evidence of any partial eradication of prior molded numbers, symbols, or texture changes. There also may be some possible clues that these tires have been retreaded, as indicated above in the discussion on the mold cure processes.

Forensic Significance of Crime Scene Impressions Made by Retread Tires

Retread tires comprise a much smaller portion of the tire population than new tires, thus associating a vehicle with retread tires to a crime scene can have added significance simply because they are not as common, i.e., their precise design is not on as many vehicles. Further, most retreads are made using the pre-cure method wherein the replacement tread is wrapped around the tire carcass, resulting in a very noticeable and unique splice joint. This splice joint, accompanying staple marks, and mismatched tread design at the splice are individual characteristics that are often retained in impressions a retreaded tire leaves.

Regrooving

Regrooving is not a retreading or remolding process. A regrooved tire is a used tire that has had its original tread pattern deepened by manually cutting the existing grooves deeper or by cutting a new pattern of grooves into the remaining tread rubber. It is a process that is often used only to get a few more miles out of the life of a tire. It often results in preventing retreading, particularly if it the grooves are cut too close to the casing. Because regrooving is mainly preformed freehand with a cutting tool, it can result in a unique pattern, particularly if the tire is already bald and the regrooving must involve the creation of new grooves. Regrooving too deep on a tire that is already bald is not legal but occasionally seen. The National Highway Traffic Safety Administration has advised tire dealers that regrooving is permitted only under strict federal standards and only on tires that are labeled "Regroovable" on both sidewalls by the manufacturer.[5] Figures 6.19 and 6.20 depict some characteristics found on a regrooved tire and show the considerable unevenness along the groove structure as well as numerous individual features around and within the grooves.

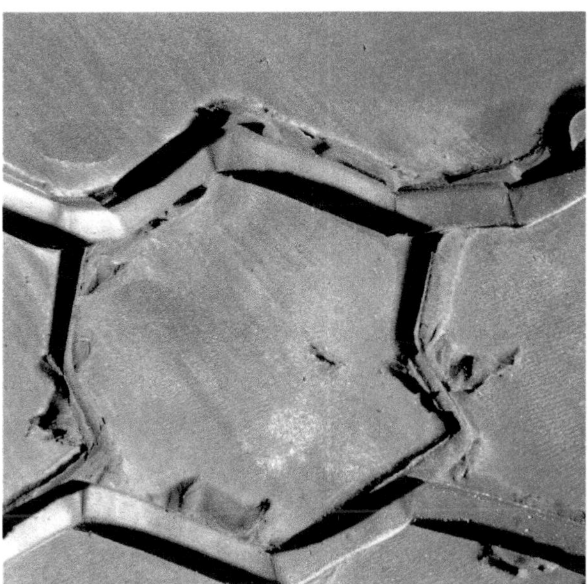

Figure 6.19. A small section of a regrooved tire shows the uneven grooving as well as many areas where the existing tread was marred, producing a large number of individual characteristics.

[5] Regrooving Truck Tires, news release dated August 1998, made by the Tire Retread Information Bulletin.

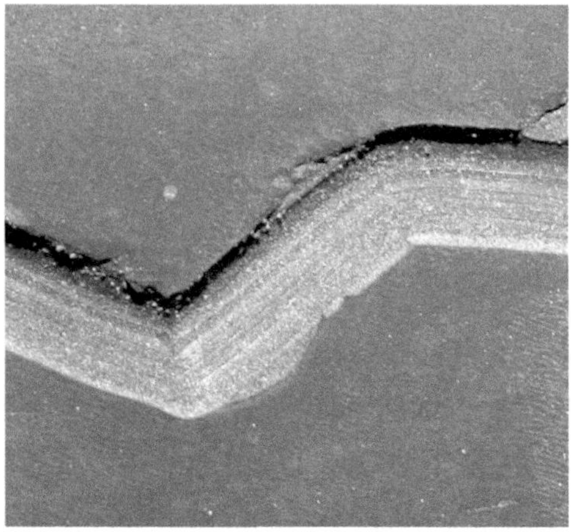

Figure 6.20. A closer view of the newly cut grooves of a regrooved tire showing the unevenness of the groove structure.

Tread Design and Dimension

7

Tire Parameters Affect Design

In the early 1900s when Harvey Firestone produced his tread design consisting of the words "Non-Skid" placed repeatedly at an angle across the tread surface (Figure 1.7A and Figure 7.1A), the design was not just added to the surface after the tire was made, but was actually engraved in the mold and thus was an actual molded design.[1] Other tire manufacturers also changed to molded tread designs, as illustrated in the Goodyear diamond design in Figure 1.7B. A few early tire designs are featured in Figure 7.1A–F. As cars and roads improved and speed limits increased, tire science and technology continued to evolve with the automobile. Today's car and truck tires last for a longer period of time and travel at much higher speeds in both wet and dry conditions. The variety of vehicle types and uses demand a large selection of tire designs and sizes to provide tires whose qualities and performance are suited for different vehicles and uses.

When designing a tire, tire engineers consider not only basic tire performance characteristics—that is, the ability to stop, start, and turn on all kinds of wet and dry surfaces; quick, responsive maneuverability; and the tire's durability—but well over 100 additional tire performance parameters.[2] These additional parameters can include, for example, tread wear, rolling resistance, impact resistance, stone retention, groove wander, ride, skid resistance, noise, water evacuation, cut and tear resistance, footprint size, cornering stability, and steering response. Tire engineers cannot produce the one single tire and tread design that maximizes all of these performance parameters. Instead, they make trade-offs to reach a tire that has the correct balance of parameters that is desirable for a particular purpose. For instance, a winter tire, designed

[1] Lief, A. The Firestone Story (1951, p. 51).
[2] Kovac, F. J. Tire Technology (1978).

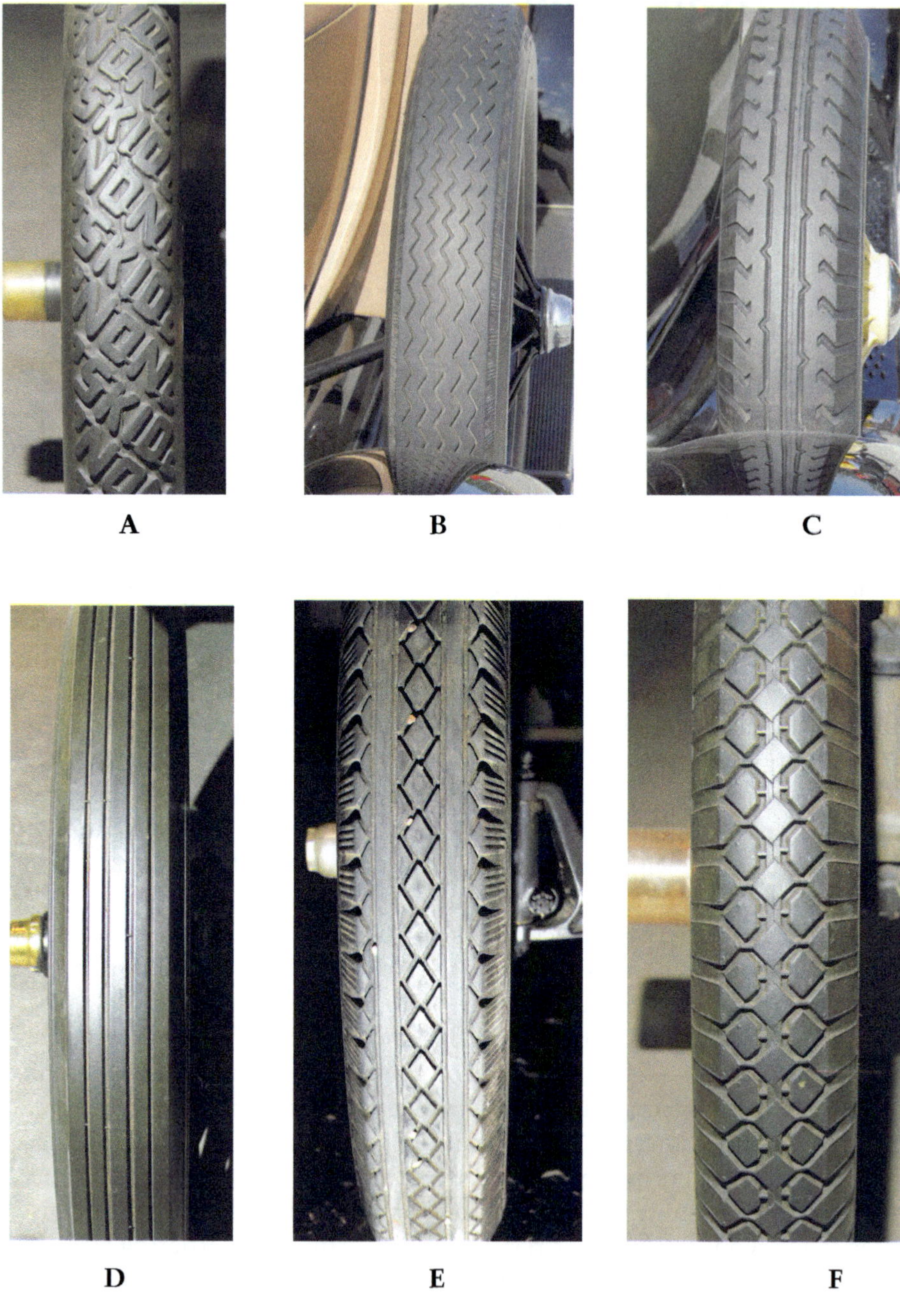

Figure 7.1A–F. Early tire designs like the Firestone Non-Skid design (A) were developed to reduce skidding.

for a passenger vehicle that will drive on wet, dry, ice, and snow-covered roads, must have deep grooves and lateral slots to dig through the snow but also have enough rubber in contact with the road surfaces to provide traction on dry roads. Likewise, a tire designed for a luxury vehicle may provide more cushioning and a softer ride, but that tire will likely be less responsive than a super high-performance tire when traveling at high speed around a winding road. All tire designs, however, must fit into what the tire industry calls the "window of acceptability." Whereas some parameters might excel in a certain tire, all parameters must still meet minimum standards within that window of acceptability on any tire that is designed.

Tread Design

Tread Design Terminology

Some basic terminology as it relates to tread design is set forth in the following pages.

Tread Blocks The term *tread block* is an industry term that refers to the individual tread elements that are arranged circumferentially around most tires to compose the tread design. Figure 7.2 and Figure 7.3 depict examples of tread blocks. While "block" might suggest a simple square shape, many asymmetrical or directional tread patterns (Figure 7.3) feature very different and unique shapes. Passenger tire tread blocks tend to be smaller than those on truck tires. The very large, open tread blocks found on the shoulders of off-road, all-terrain, agricultural, and many construction tires are often referred to as lugs.

Pitch Length The term *pitch length* refers to the circumferential length allotted for each tread block. Tire manufacturers design pitch lengths from a position within a tread block to the corresponding position in the next tread block. An example of this is provided in a drawing of a section of a tire blueprint depicted in Figure 7.4. In this drawing, the three pitch lengths for this design are noted as 1, 2, and 3. The lines on the drawing that divide one pitch length from another pass through the center of the actual design elements. Figure 7.5 illustrates another design with four tread blocks of different sizes. The pitch length is measured from the pitch dividing lines, beginning at a point within one tread block and ending at the same point in the next tread block. The blueprint for a tire design would show the lines that define the pitch length, as illustrated in Figures 7.4 and 7.5.

Pitch Sequence The term *pitch sequence* is a term manufacturers use to describe the order or arrangement of the various pitch lengths around the circumference of a tire. The blueprint of each tire will state this pitch

Figure 7.2. Two tire designs with more conventional tread blocks.

Figure 7.3. Tread blocks from two designs: the top one from a directional design tire and the bottom one from an asymmetrical design tire.

sequence. An example of a pitch sequence from a blueprint is provided in Figure 7.6.

Noise Treatment Noise treatment is a phrase used by tire manufacturers. It refers to the use of varied pitch lengths arranged around the circumference of a tire in a particular pitch sequence for the purpose of reducing noise. This is discussed in more detail later in this chapter.

Ribs Tread ribs are the rows of solid rubber or rows of tread blocks separated by major tread grooves that run circumferentially around the tire. Manufacturers will generally describe a tread pattern by the number of tread ribs in the pattern; for instance, a five-rib design would feature two outermost rows, two inner rows, and one center row of tread blocks and contain four major circumferential grooves. Tread patterns may contain solid rib designs with no defined tread blocks; ribs composed of tread blocks separated by

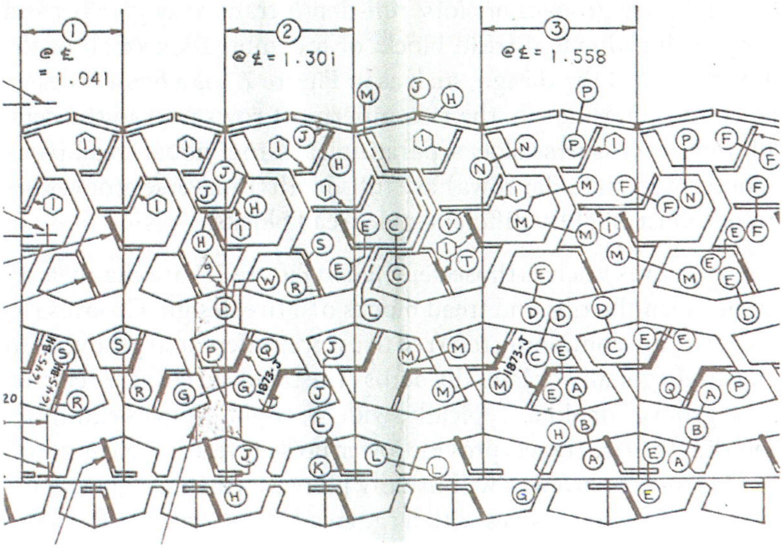

Figure 7.4. A portion of an older blueprint showing how the designer of a tire would divide the pitch lengths.

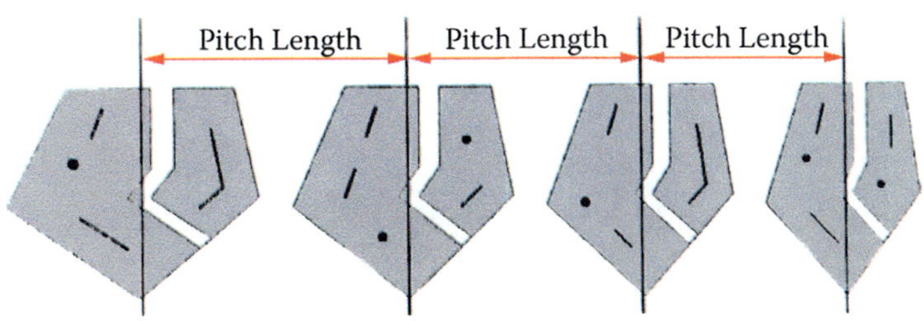

Figure 7.5. An illustration of a three tread block sizes and how the pitch length divisions run.

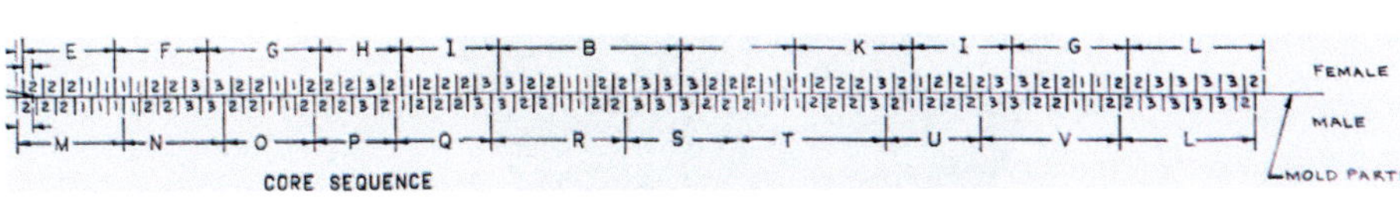

Figure 7.6. An example of a pitch sequence from a blueprint. This will be on each blueprint of a tire design and will define the mixed arrangement of pitch lengths on both sides of the tire.

shallow, transverse grooves or slots; full-depth transverse grooves and slots separating each individual tread block; or a combination of all of these. A typical symmetrical tire design, such as in Figure 7.7, is a five-rib design, featuring a solid centerline rib, the two innermost rows next to the center rib have full-depth transverse slots separating each individual tread block, and the two outermost shoulder rows have full-depth transverse grooves between their more robust, slightly different style tread blocks.

Grooves Grooves, such as those depicted in Figure 7.7, are channels or voids that run between the ribs and tread blocks of a tire design. Grooves running around the tire are commonly referred to as circumferential grooves. Grooves that can run diagonally or laterally across the tread surface are referred to as transverse grooves or slots. Typically, wide, straight grooves running in the direction that the tire travels provide lower noise levels as well as good water removal. Transverse grooves will usually increase traction but also increase noise levels. Very wide grooves with large tread blocks, such as found on mud tires and off-road tires, provide for improved grip on soft surfaces (snow, silt, sand, and mud, for instance) and provide self-cleaning (throwing mud from between tread blocks in an off-road tire, for instance) but will also increase noise. Grooves on some tires are tapered, i.e., the groove bottom is narrower than the top, so as the tire wears down, the width of the groove will decrease.

Figure 7.7. A symmetrical tire design. This design has two shoulder ribs (1); a solid center rib (2) with two divided inner ribs in between; circumferential grooves (3); lateral grooves or slots (4); and sipes (5).

Sipes In the footwear industry, siping involves cutting thin cuts or slits across a rubber surface to improve traction on wet surface. Siping was invented and patented by John Sipe in the 1920s when he cut small slits across his boots to keep from slipping.[3] Depicted in Figure 7.7, tire sipes in a new tire are not cut into the tread but are molded into the tread blocks during the mold cure process, thus making them part of the overall tread design. Sipes are included in tread designs to allow for movement and flexibility along the edges of the tread blocks and provide more traction edges to increase traction in snow, ice, mud, and on wet road surfaces. Les Schwab, a large private tire company with stores in the western U.S., offers a siping service which utilizes a special machine to add sipes to new or used tires. Other tire stores also offer this service. Additional information about sipes and how they change as a tire wears is provided in Chapter 8.

Tread Design Categories

The term *tread design* or *tread pattern* refers to the features and arrangement of tread blocks and/or ribs of various shapes, separated by grooves and covering the portion of the tire that makes contact with the road. The specific tread design of a tire in a forensic comparison also takes into account the pitch sizes, pitch sequence, and tread wear indicators. To clarify this, take the example of Goodyear's Integrity line of tires depicted in Figure 7.8. Generally speaking, the tread pattern of the Integrity tires, from the smallest 13-inch tire to the largest 17-inch tire, will be similar. But each different tire size in the Integrity group of tires will have its own set of tread block sizes, groove widths, overall tread widths, and other very specific detailed features that make each size of this tire a variation of that design. For the same reasons, the dimensional characteristics determined from a tire impression made by a particular tire size will be different for each of those tire sizes.

Tread patterns can generally be divided into three design categories: those with the conventional non-directional symmetrical tread design, those with a directional tread design, and those with an asymmetrical tread design. These are further described below.

Non-Directional Symmetrical Tread Design

Non-directional symmetrically designed tires are designed to rotate in either direction without loss in performance. The tread will appear the same no matter which direction you view it from. Today these are still the most common design category. The tires depicted in Figures 7.7 and 7.8 are non-directional symmetrical tread designs.

[3] Wikipedia, "Siping," http://en.wikipedia.org/wiki/Siping.

Figure 7.8. A non-directional symmetrical center rib tire design with a mixture of tread block sizes.

Directional Tread Design

Tires with a directional tread pattern are designed to provide optimal traction and handling performance when rotating in a specific direction. Figure 7.9 is an example of a directional tire. To gain full benefit of these directional tread patterns, tire manufacturers mold information on the sidewalls of the tire, indicating the proper direction of rotation. Arrows and/or words will indicate the proper rotation direction identifying how the tire should be placed. Figure 7.10 is a close-up view of the sidewall of a directional tire showing the arrows that indicate how that tire should rotate. Many directional tire manufacturers now produce both sidewalls cosmetically the same, either black or with a band of white rubber on each side so this tire can be mounted either way. In these cases, the tire manufacturer may also include the term “LEFT” on the bottom half of the mold and “RIGHT” on the top half of the mold to make it clear how to mount the tire. In this way if the tire is dismounted from the wheel, flipped over, and remounted, it can be moved to the other side of the vehicle and still maintain its designed direction of rotation. Because the industry recommends that tires be rotated about the vehicle at periodic mileage intervals throughout a tire’s life, this provides an opportunity to do so, with a directional tire.

Figure 7.9. A directional tread design. This tire is made to perform best when operating in the direction indicated by arrows on its sidewall.

Figure 7.10. Symbols and words will denote the direction of rotation for directional tread designs.

Asymmetric Tread Design

An asymmetrical tire design is one whose opposite sides of its tread pattern are not identical. Figure 7.11 depicts an asymmetrical tread design like the one featured on the cover of this book. Asymmetrical tires are sometimes referred to as uneven tire designs. Asymmetrical tires were designed to improve handling and reduce noise. They are not a directional design and thus can rotate in either direction. These tires are interchangeable on any position of the vehicle.

Other Categories or Types of Tread Design

Non-directional symmetrical, directional, and asymmetrical tread designs all can include other features or types of tread design, often described separately as follows.

Rib and Center Rib Tires

Rib tires are more traditional tire designs that contain circumferential rows of tread blocks divided by circumferential grooves. Those having an odd number of ribs will have a center rib. Radial construction has allowed for tire manufacturers to create more aggressive tire designs with more transverse grooves and sipes. Modern radial passenger tire designs featuring

Figure 7.11. An asymmetrical tread design. This design can still be interchanged on any position of the vehicle.

these more aggressive rib patterns usually are mud and snow (M + S) rated and described as all-season, aggressive rib, center aggressive rib, or continuous center rib tires. The Goodyear Integrity (Figure 7.8) can be described as an all-season aggressive rib with continuous center rib design.

Block Design

In general, block design tires are composed of an arrangement of tread blocks in a more scattered arrangement, as opposed to rows of tread blocks arranged circumferentially around the tire. Figure 7.12 is an example of a block design tire.

All-Terrain and Off-Road Tires

Designed for trucks and SUVs to withstand more rugged off-road conditions and perform better over muddy terrains and rocky surfaces, all-terrain and off-road tires have a larger, more coarse tread, are noisy, wear out more quickly, and are less suited for highway driving. An example of an off-road tire on a pickup truck is depicted in Figure 7.13.

Motorcycle Tires

The most common motorcycle tires contain tread designs that extend around the shoulder of the tire to provide good water removal and traction during

Figure 7.12. A block tread design.

Figure 7.13. An off-road tire design.

Figure 7.14. A motorcycle tire does not need varied pitch sizes, as it is not concerned with noise.

cornering (Figure 7.14). They typically do not have noise treatment because a quiet tire on a noisy motorcycle is not a concern. Some designs are also produced for larger motorcycles that are similar to passenger tires, and others have specific knobby designs produced for dirt bikes and off-road racing.

Snow Tires

Years ago, snow tires had noisy designs that appeared more like a block tire design. They were normally placed on the rear wheels of a vehicle during the winter months as they were made primarily for driving in the snow. The winter tires made today for driving in snow are made of new rubber compounds that can perform well not only on ice and snow but also in dry, wet, or slushy driving conditions. Their modern designs do not appear much different from regular tires. An example of a newer snow tire is depicted in Figure 7.15.

High-Performance Tires

Performance tire designs are generally wider and lower in profile, have a higher speed rating, and are primarily produced for sport cars and some luxury cars. They are designed for speed, acceleration, braking, and cornering, but their softer tread compounds mean they will wear more quickly. An example of a high performance tire is depicted in Figure 7.16. Note this tire

Figure 7.15. Modern snow tires look like ordinary tires but have special rubber compounds that make them perform better in icy conditions.

Figure 7.16. A high-performance tire with a directional tread design.

has a directional tread design and several arrows molded on its sidewall to indicate the mounting direction.

Agriculture and Construction Tires

These are tires designed specifically for off-road conditions encountered by farm and construction equipment. Figure 7.17 is an example of a construction tire design.

Figure 7.17. A construction tire design.

All-Season Tires

All-season tires, also known as mud and snow rated tires (M + S), are any tires that are rated as suitable for driving year round and provide a good balance of traction in dry, wet, and snowy conditions. Most, if not all, are aggressive-design passenger tires like the Goodyear Integrity tire in Figure 7.8.

Spare Tires

A spare tire can be a full-size fifth tire of the same size and design as the other four OEM tires. For space-saving reasons, many vehicles come with smaller spare tires, sometimes referred to as donut tires (Figure 7.18). These smaller spare tires are only intended to provide a way for the vehicle to get to a repair shop where the full-size tire can be repaired or replaced. Some versions of these smaller spare tires, to save even more room, come deflated and collapsed and are supplied with a pump to inflate them when they are needed.

Self-Sealing Tires

Self-sealing tires are designed to automatically repair most punctures instantly and permanently. These are regular tires with standard tire construction with the addition of an extra lining inside the tire containing a puncture sealant under the tread area.

Figure 7.18. A donut spare tire marked "TEMPORARY USE ONLY."

Run Flat Tires or Self-Supporting Tires

Run flat tires are also regular tire designs that feature a stiffer internal construction that is capable of temporarily carrying the weight of the vehicle, even after the tire has lost all air pressure.

Implement Tires

Implement tires include a broad category, including tires used on items such as wheel barrels, lawn equipment, wagons, agricultural equipment, and other similar items.

Bicycle Tires

Bicycle tire construction also incorporates beads but contains fewer components. These tires rely on an inner tube to hold the air. Their tread does not incorporate tread wear indicators, noise treatment, or varied pitch sizes.

Tread Dimension

Tread dimension refers to the dimensional features of the tire tread including the physical sizes of the tread blocks and their arrangement around the tire. Circumferentially, the pitch lengths and/or the pitch sequence of the tread blocks around a tire will change from one tire size to the next. Tread dimension also includes the dimensions across the width of the tread surface. Tread widths are related to the section width of the tire, indicated in the tire size designation. The wider a tire of a particular design, the wider the tread blocks within it will be. Tread dimensions are transferred along with the tread design in the impression the tire leaves.

Accuracy of Tread Dimensions in Impressions

It would be nice if all tire impressions left at crime scenes were always perfect representations of the sizes of the tires that made them. Although this does occur more often than not, it is also possible, frequent, and normal for there to be slight variations in the physical dimensions. This means that a tire may leave its impression at a crime scene, and later, when that impression is compared with a known impression of that tire, the physical dimensions may not match perfectly. If they do not match perfectly, the examiner must decide whether the dimension of the impression is off slightly due to one of several reasons, whether the tire did not make the impression, or whether the impression simply did not retain sufficient detail to determine either.

Factors in Dimensional Evaluation

Inadequate Known Exemplars

In instances where a tire impression is left at a scene by a tire having varied pitch sizes, it is imperative that two staggered sets of known impressions representing the full circumference of the tire be obtained as described in Chapter 4. If an 18-inch-long crime scene impression is being examined, and the examiner only has a partial impression of the tire, it is more likely than not that the pitch sequence and tread block dimensions will not correspond, even if that tire actually made the crime scene impression. This occurs all too often when an examiner does not understand the concept of varied pitch sizes and the necessity of obtaining full-circumference impressions of the tires. On other occasions, impressions of tires and not the tires themselves are submitted for examination, and these impressions are likely to be partial and/or improperly taken. Although examiners should always have the tire(s) and make their own known impressions, sometimes due to reasons beyond their control they are faced with this limitation. In these cases, it is unlikely the examiner will be able to properly evaluate the tread dimension. In the case of inadequate known standards, the proper answer may not be that the dimension of the tire and impression are different, but simply that there was insufficient information to evaluate the full dimensional aspects of the impression due to the fact that the examiner did not have the tire.

Tires with Tread Blocks of One Size (No Noise Treatment)

In instances where a partial tire impression is made by a tire having tread blocks of one size around the tire, many areas of the tire could potentially have left the impression. In these cases, the size of the tread blocks can be examined and if they correspond then that the tire possibly made the impression as well as other tires having those same design and dimension. If they do not correspond, then this may be because it was a different size tire. Virtually all passenger and light truck tires incorporate varied tread block sizes; however, medium-sized truck tires, off-road tires, most retreadeded tires, motorcycle tires, and bicycle tires, usually do not.

Impressions with Limited Size or Detail

When an impression is very short or partial, or when an impression is simply limited in detail so that the tread blocks are not distinct, there may not be sufficient quantity and quality of the impression to make a full or accurate dimensional analysis.

Changes in Tire Inflation

Changes in tire inflation will change the size of the tire footprint and thus will also change the rolling circumference of the tire. However, these changes are minor. In one instance, using a Mazda Miata, the author measured the lengths of the same exact portions of its tire impression at 30 psi at 34 inches, at 20 psi at 33 15/16 inches, and at 10 psi at 33 13/16 inches. The length of the impression made by the 34-inch section was only reduced by 3/16 inch when the pressure was reduced to 10 psi. Although measurable, this is not likely to make any significant difference during an examination.[4]

Improperly Photographed Impressions

If the examination involves a photographed tire impression, many things can affect the dimensional accuracy of that photograph. If the camera's film plane (back) is not perfectly parallel to the impression, then the photograph will have a perspective problem that can affect the ability to accurately enlarge the photograph of the impression to its natural size. This type of problem usually occurs due to errors in photographic procedure. Another problem commonly encountered occurs when the scale (ruler) is not placed on the same exact plane (level) as the bottom of a three-dimensional tire impression or when the ruler is resting on the ground at an angle. If the ruler is not on the same plane and parallel with the bottom of the impression, an accurate enlargement will not be possible. Photographic procedural errors often result in limited examination results. Casts can resolve these problems, but unfortunately some impressions are only photographically recorded and thus the examination must rely on those photographs alone.

Saturated and Spongy Substrates

Heavy soils that are saturated with water or that are composed of materials like peat may give them a spongy quality that results in a rebound effect after the tire leaves an impression. In soft loose soils, the tire may compress the soil to different degrees along the length of the impression and/or may also be slipping while laying down the impression. Although these are not common occurrences, I have encountered these problems, and they can result in a misrepresentation of the size features of the tire.

Footprint or Contact Patch

A tire that is not under load is round. When that tire is placed on a vehicle under load, the portion of the tire having contact with the road surface flattens. This flattening is known as deflection. This flattened area is known as the tire's footprint or contact patch. Strictly defined, the tire footprint is the contact area of a tire against a flat hard surface under load, whereas a contact patch is the actual area of the tread in contact with any road surface under

[4] Lower tire pressure will slightly decrease the rolling length or distance per revolution, thus will record greater mileage on the odometer. Mark Thomas (Cooper Tire), personal communication, April 25, 2001.

any condition, whether it be in soft soil or on a road surface during cornering at high speeds. The contact patch will increase linearly as tire inflation decreases or load increases. It is also important to understand that the dimensions of the tread differ in the contact patch from the same respective area of the tire when not under load. This means the tread dimensions reflected in a tire impression will not be the same as the dimensions of an unloaded tire. This is why known impressions must be made under load.

Deflection

Deflection was discussed and defined in Chapter 1 and illustrated in Figures 1.4 and 1.5. The shape and size of the contact patch for the same tire can differ depending on the surface it is on due to differences in deflection. The contact patch of a properly inflated tire on soft soil is longer than that tire's contact patch on a hard surface. This is because when the tire sinks into the soil the differences in deflection create a longer impression of the same area of the tire's tread. The deeper the tire sinks into the substrate, the larger the impression.[5] One explanation is that on soft road surfaces, the contact patch will be increased because the contact patch is shifted much farther forward than it is on paved surfaces. The softer the soil, the larger and farther forward will be the contact patch (Figure 7.19).[6]

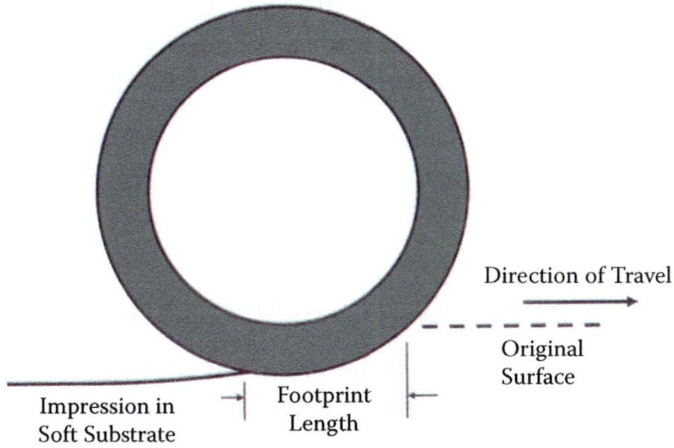

Figure 7.19. The contact patch is longer when a tire sinks into the substrate due to differences in deflection.

[5] Larry Shelton (Goodyear Tire & Rubber Company), personal communication, April 17, 2007.

[6] Mark Thomas (Cooper Tire), personal communication, April 25, 2001.

Forensic Significance of Deflection

If a tire leaves a larger contact patch on a soft surface, such as soil, in contrast to leaving a smaller contact patch on a hard surface, such as used to take known inked impressions, the forensic examiner must be aware of this possibility and how it could affect the evaluation of that evidence. I first saw repetitive examples of this when teaching tire examination classes. In each class, we would produce some impressions in shallow soil and some in deeper soil, and the known inked impressions would be prepared on a hard surface. Over numerous classes, without exception, there would be minor discrepancies between the deeper impressions and the known impressions of the tire. The impressions made in deeper soil would always be larger than those made on a hard surface. In a controlled demonstration of this, I made two 3-foot-long impressions of a tire, one in loose soil ¾ inch deep, and one in loose soil 4 inches deep. I then made an inked impression on a hard surface of the same exact portion of the tire and compared that impression with casts of the two impressions in soil. The differences in deflection between these surfaces resulted in the shallow soil impression being ¼ inch longer than the inked impression over the 36 inches and the deeper impression being ¾ inch longer over the 36 inches than the inked hard surface impression.[7] If not aware of this normal variation of tire impressions left on different substrates, the examiner would encounter difficulty in locating the proper area of the tire that left the impression and could even erroneously eliminate the tire as the possible source of that impression. More is discussed about ways to evaluate this in Chapter 10.

Noise Treatment

Introduction to Noise Treatment and Pitch Length

From the first automobiles through the 1950s, car speeds were slow compared with the high speed limits of our interstate highways today. In addition, the sound integrity features of those early automobiles were inferior. Engine and other roadway noises that passed into these vehicles dominated any noise that a tire produced. Eventually, improved roads and automotive technology allowed cars to travel at greater speeds, while at the same time those cars were produced with more airtight and sound-insulated passenger compartments. Tire noise became an increasingly important issue, and tire manufacturers began designing tires in ways to reduce the noise they generate.

[7] Bodziak, W. J. "Tire Impression Variables: Variations in Tire Deflection on Soft versus Hard Road Surfaces" presented at the IAI Annual Educational Conference, Danvers, MA, 2003.

Noise is produced by a tire due to several causes. One cause is the interaction of the tire with the particular road surface. When driving from one road surface to another at high speed, such as from an asphalt highway surface across a short bridge having a concrete surface, you can hear the change in tire noise. Another source of tire noise is generated by air that is trapped and compressed between the tread pattern and the surface of the road which then rapidly escapes. And another source is the noise generated by the tire design itself, as the individual tread blocks pound against the road surface like a hammer, vibrating and emitting sounds of a specific pitch. In general, smaller tread blocks generate higher pitched sounds, whereas larger blocks generate lower pitched sounds. If the lengths and spacing of all tread blocks around the tire are the same size, the sounds produced by the tire consist of repetitive emissions of the same frequency or pitch, thus producing a very noticeable noise. This noise is often described as a whine or hum. However, if different tread block sizes are used in a mixed arrangement around the tire, the sounds created will tend to cancel each other out, producing less noise.

Figure 7.20 is a simple drawing of a zigzag design to illustrate pitch length. The design remains the same, except as the pitch length gets longer, the design is elongated circumferentially. If a tire has only one single pitch length, all its tread blocks will be the same size. When designing a tire, the tire engineer will normally incorporate three or four different pitch lengths as well as their placement in a mixed arrangement, known as the pitch sequence, as one way of reducing tire noise. This is referred to in the tire industry as noise treatment. The point height in this drawing refers to the width that design occupies. Widths of tread blocks remain the same around the tire.

Today's tire designs are created on elaborate computers that not only have the ability to develop new tires designs quickly, but during the design phase can analyze and predict the noise that tire will produce, thus helping design a tire that is quieter while it is still on the drawing board. Virtually all

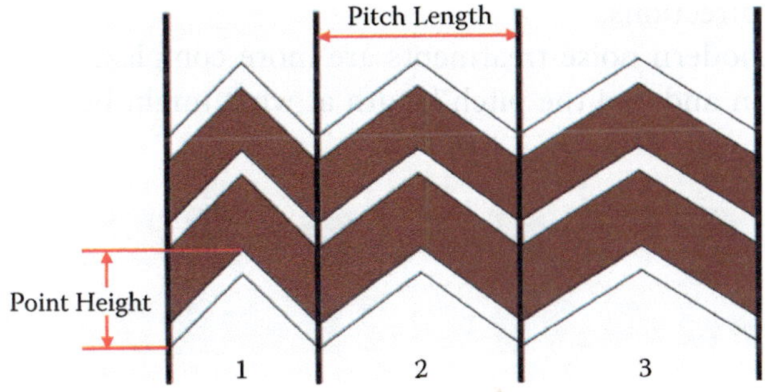

Figure 7.20. The pitch length is the circumferential length allotted for each tread block. The point height is the width that design occupies.

passenger and light truck tires produced today have noise treatment incorporated in their designs.

Evolution of Noise Treatment

Noise treatment did not appear overnight but evolved over years. In its earliest applications, tire manufacturers mixed up tread block pitch lengths by simply arranging them in a simple 1-2-3 pitch sequence (Figure 7.21). In other words, the tire would have three different-sized tread blocks and they would repeat in the simple sequence of 123123123123 and so on around the tire's entire circumference. In this early example, the pitch lengths and tread block sizes were essentially the same, and visually on a tire design it was very easy to distinguish which tread block represented each size. When a tire with this simple pitch sequence laid its impression down, the continued repetition of the 1-2-3 sequence was not very useful for helping to associate a crime scene impression to a particular portion of a tire. This was because the entire tire contained the same repeating 1-2-3 sequence. Any crime scene impression would have that same sequence and thus could have been produced by any area around the entire circumference of that tire. In fact, if the tire was running in the opposite direction, the sequence would be the same, so an examination would have to consider the tire running in both directions as well (Figure 7.22).

Tire manufacturers began mixing the sequence in a more random manner, such as 1233112312312331123123 and so on. This is illustrated in the top portion of Figure 7.23. Notice that in this example, although the pitch lengths are mixed, there is still some repetition of the sequence. For example, in the bottom of Figure 7.23, a crime scene impression with that pitch sequence could have originated from more than one section of that tire. Again, these older pitch arrangements would leave the same pitch sequence regardless of their direction, so the examination would also have to consider the tire running in both directions.

Today's modern noise treatments are more complex. The tire designer does not begin and end the pitch length at what might be described as the

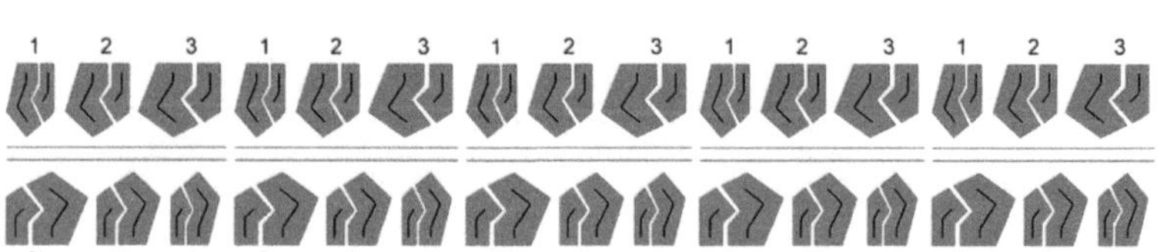

Figure 7.21. A simple 1-2-3 pitch sequence, very typical of tires with early noise treatment.

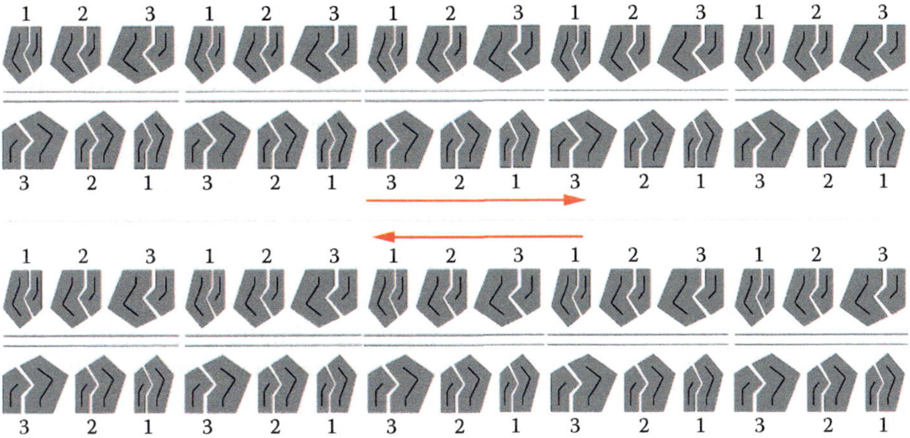

Figure 7.22 Tires with the 1-2-3 sequence running in both directions were duplicated on each side so they had to be examined in both directions around the full circumference of each tire.

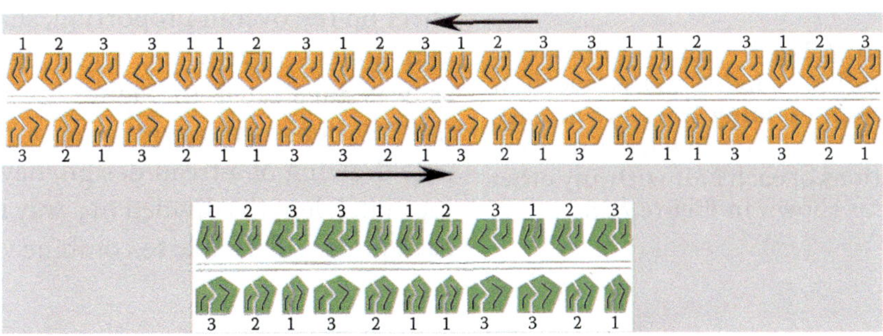

Figure 7.23. A more random mixture of the 1-2-3 pitch lengths *(top)* reduces the number of possible locations around the tire that could have left a crime scene impression *(bottom)*.

visual beginning and ending of a tread block. Rather, on a computer the designers create pitch sizes that begin and end at a location within the tread block known as the pitch dividing line. Figure 7.24 depicts a simplified drawing with three rectangular tread blocks and how the pitch dividing lines would delineate each pitch length. At the bottom of Figure 7.24, the two portions of each tread block are colored differently along the pitch dividing line. Finally, using the different colors for illustration, Figure 7.25 shows how those three pitch sizes could be combined in nine separate ways, resulting in nine separate tread block sizes. The first part of pitch block 1 combined with the second half of pitch block 1 produces the smallest tread block. The first half of pitch block 1 combined with the second half of 2 will produce a slightly larger tread block. By using the combinations 1-1, 1-2, 1-3, 2-1, 2-2, 2-3, 3-1, 3-

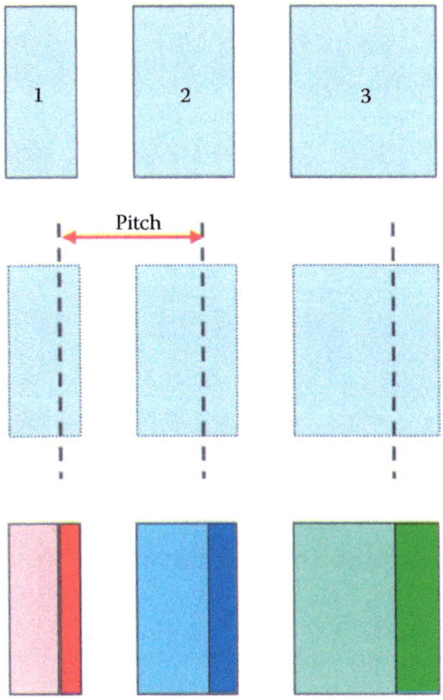

Figure 7.24. A simple illustration using three pitch lengths and how the pitch dividing lines divide each tread block. This enables nine combinations of each half with any other half, as shown in Figure 7.25.

2, and 3-3, there are a total of nine differently sized and proportioned tread block sizes that were created from only three pitch lengths. Note that a tread block could have the same overall size of another tread block but might be composed of different sections and thus have different proportions. Figure 7.26 depicts two of the nine choices depicted in Figure 7.25, which are approximately the same overall size but whose first and second halves are very different in proportion. This may not seem important when dealing with simple rectangular tread blocks as illustrated here, but in the case of more complex tread blocks, this will have an effect on the overall proportion, shape, and appearance of the tread blocks as was illustrated in Figure 7.5. Figure 7.27 depicts this with a more realistic drawing of a tread design, having four pitch lengths divided in a way that each pitch will be able to combine with

Figure 7.25. The nine possible combinations of three pitch lengths.

any of the others, resulting in various sized and proportioned tread blocks. Figure 7.28 illustrates the resulting tread appearance using these four pitch lengths.[8] With so many resulting tread block sizes and proportions, it becomes less likely to find any sizeable repetition of the same sequence along the length of the tire tread, thus providing the examiner a way of using this mixed arrangement of tread block sizes and proportions to reliably locate the exact position(s) around the tire's circumference that could have made the crime scene impression.

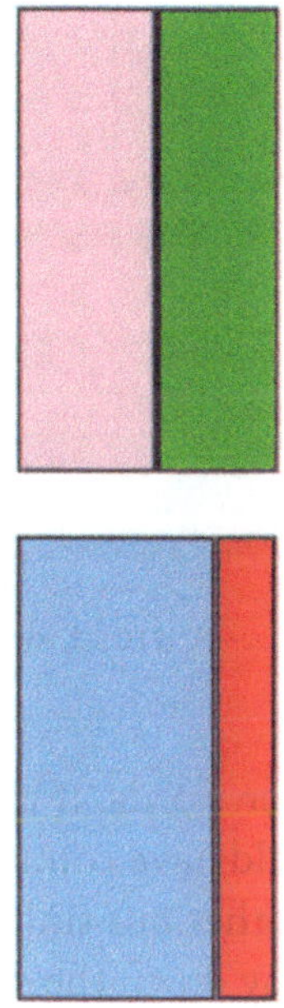

Figure 7.26. Two equally sized resulting tread blocks but with different proportions.

Modern Noise Treatment Differs on Each Tire Side

Noise treatment originally consisted of the same pitch sequence on one side of the tire as the other, as shown in the examples in Figures 7.21 and

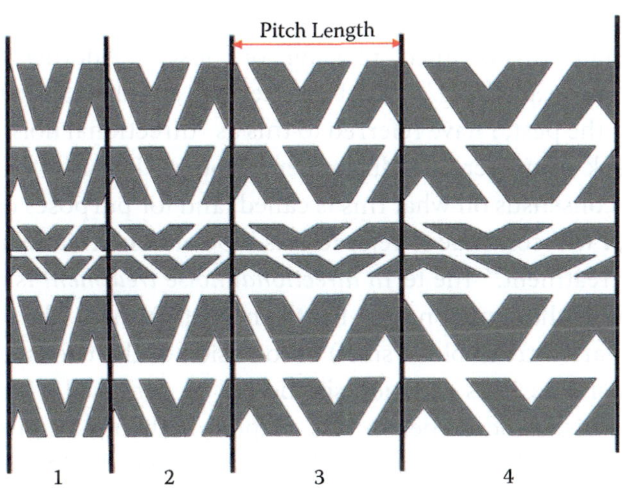

Figure 7.27. An example of four pitch lengths.

[8] This design example is similar to the Firestone Wilderness LE design depicted in the bottom photograph of Figure 7.2.

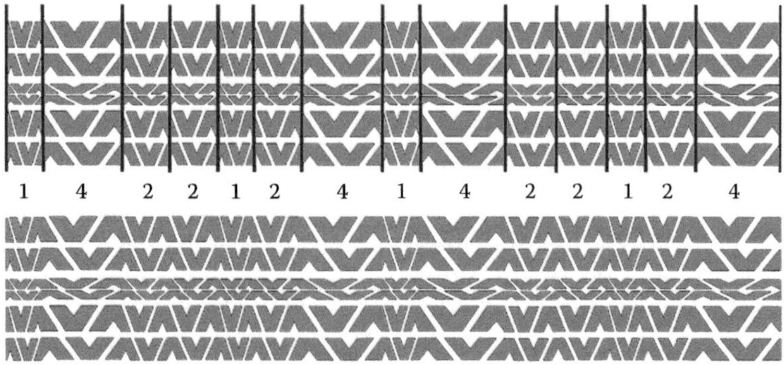

Figure 7.28. A tread design composed of the combined pitch lengths in Figure 7.27.

7.22. In other words, if a tire was divided down its centerline circumferentially, it would have contained the same sequence of pitch block sizes on one side as the other but simply running in opposite directions. This meant the tire would lay down the same sequence of tread block sizes regardless of the direction it was rotating. An impression made by a tire mounted with the whitewall side facing in could not be distinguished from an impression made by a tire mounted with the whitewall side facing out, simply because you could not determine directionality of the tire based on its pitch sequence.

Since the early 1990s, tire manufacturers have produced tires with a pitch sequence that is different on one side of the tire from the other. There does not seem to be any universal industry terminology that refers to this. One source states this is called "phasing" or "offset."[9] Another source states this is called "noise pitching."[10] Most say they still simply refer to this as noise treatment. In the past, I have referred to this as "directional noise treatment" simply for lack of universal industry terminology. Because there does not seem to be a consensus on what this is called, and for purposes of discussion in this book, I will continue to refer to this type of noise treatment as "directional noise treatment." The term *directional noise treatment* is clear in that the words define the situation, i.e., that the noise treatment (the specific pitch sequence of varied tread block sizes) on one side of the tire is not the same as on the other side. This situation should not be confused with directional tread designs discussed earlier in this chapter. It should also be noted that whereas a directional tread design is visibly detectable, the "directional noise treatment" of a tire cannot be seen on a tire, i.e., you cannot look at a tire and

[9] Gent, A. N. and Walter, J.D. The Pneumatic Tire (August 2005, p. 382).
[10] Larry Shelton (Goodyear Tire and Rubber Company), personal communication, April 17, 2007.

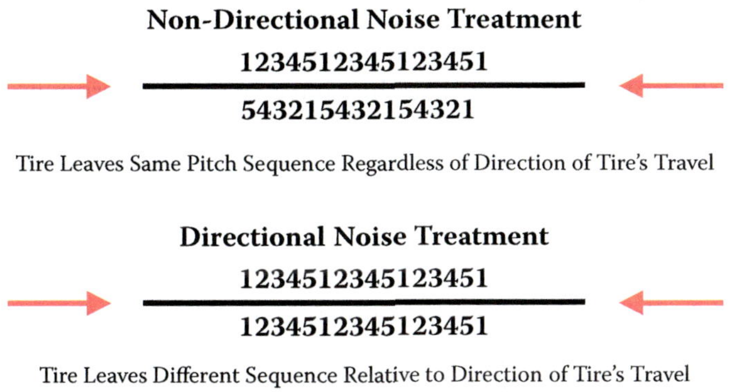

Figure 7.29. A simplified way to explain directional versus non-directional noise treatment. Look at each scenario from the position of the arrow. With the non-directional noise treatment, the sequences from the right and left sides are arranged the same. With the directional noise treatment they are different.

visually determine if it has directional noise treatment.[11] It should also be repeated here that virtually any tire developed today that has noise treatment will likely have directional noise treatment. Figure 7.29 depicts in a very simplified way the difference between a tire having non-directional noise treatment (or no noise treatment) and one having directional noise treatment.

When the pitch sequence is different on one side of the tread from the other (directional noise treatment), it becomes possible to do a number of different things as an examiner that have forensic significance. These include (1) determining directionality of the tire in relation to the impression and the way it was mounted on the vehicle (serial side in or out); (2) further reducing the areas of the tire that could have made an impression; and (3) being more specific when confirming agreement or disagreement of tire dimension. This also means that, with today's modern passenger and light-truck tires that have noise treatment, a crime scene impression will likely almost always correspond with only one position on the tire that made it and in one direction only. This added technology by the tire industry actually is a great assistance to the forensic examiner.

Tires without Noise Treatment

Most tires for medium trucks like 18-wheelers do not have noise treatment. Tires produced for agricultural vehicles and construction equipment that operate at very low speeds do not need noise treatment, nor does a noisy motorcycle require a noise treatment to produce a quieter

[11] Determining this will be covered in Chapter 10.

tire. Although most light-truck tires have some varied pitch sequence and mixed tread block sizes incorporated in their designs, some off-road mud tires are inherently noisy because they have such large grooves and tread blocks.

Tread Wear Indicators

Tread wear indicators (TWI), also known as tread wear bars, are required by the Department of Transportation (DOT). The DOT requires any tire 13 inches in diameter or larger sold in the United States to have at least six tread wear indicators placed around the circumference of the tire.[12] Often a tire will contain more than six tread wear indicators. Because the United States is the biggest consumer of both vehicles and tires, virtually all manufacturers in the world produce tires that conform to the DOT standards. A tread wear indicator is a raised bar of rubber that normally crosses the tread design and that is raised 2/32 inch above the bottom of the groove. The purpose of the TWI is to provide a visual indicator to the vehicle owner to indicate that only 2/32 inch of tread wears remains and the tire should be replaced.[13] Figure 7.30 depicts a tread wear indicator deep in a section of tread of a new tire. Figure 7.31 depicts a worn tire where the tread wear indicator is even with the worn tread and thus is more exposed. Tread wear indicators are technically part of the tread design in that they are mixed within the tire tread pattern and thus are part of the impression a tire leaves.

Given the proper conditions, tread wear indicators can appear in both two-dimensional and three-dimensional impressions. Tread wear indicators will not show up in a crime scene impression if (1) the impression is two dimensional and the tread has not been worn down to the last 2/32 inch of tread depth; (2) the impression is three dimensional and the depth

[12] National Highway Traffic Safety Administration, U.S. Department of Transportation, CFR Title 49, § 571.119 refers to Standard 119. Paragraph S6.4 reads: Tread wear indicators. Except as specified in this paragraph, each tire shall have at least six tread wear indicators spaced approximately equally around the circumference of the tire that enable a person inspecting the tire to determine visually whether the tire has worn to a tread depth of 1.6 mm [2/32 inch]. Tires with a rim diameter code of 12 or smaller shall have at least three such tread wear indicators. Motorcycle tires shall have at least three such indicators which permit visual determination that the tire has worn to a tread depth of 0.8 mm [1/32 inch].

[13] Tire Business, September 25, 2006, and October 9, 2006, reported research showing that wet traction drops off significantly as tread depth falls below 4/32 inch, twice the depth now allowed. Currently no states require greater than 2/32 inch minimum, with exception of a federal law that mandates 4/32 inch tread depth on the steer axle of medium- and heavy-duty trucks. Information reported from numerous sources support a change to a larger tread depth requirement in the future; however, that would reduce the life of a tire by about 20%.

Figure 7.30. Tread indicator in a new tire is raised 2/32 inch above the groove depth.

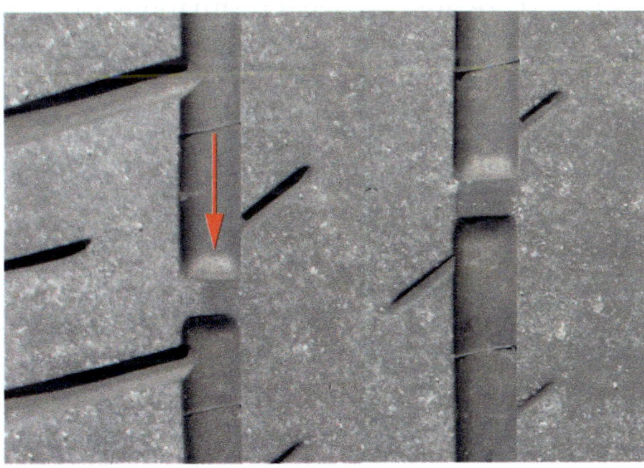

Figure 7.31. Tread wear indicator in a tire worn down to the remaining 2/32 inch depth and thus is flush with the rest of the tread design.

of the impression did not extend into the substrate to within 2/32 inch of the remaining tread depth; (3) the recovered crime scene impression is short and was not made by a portion of the tire having a tread wear indicator; and/or (4) the detail retained in the impression is poor or has been filled in with loose soil and debris that prevents visual recording and/or detection of the tread wear indicators.

Using Tread Wear Indicators and Noise Treatment Together

When present in an impression, tread wear indicators are part of the design. Because they are located in at least six positions around the tire, they can be used to assist in locating the area or areas of the tread surface that could have made the crime scene impression. When a tire has noise treatment, the tread wear indicator positions found at different locations among the tread combine with the varied pitch sizes to allow for even more distinguishable areas that occur only once around the tire's circumference. Figure 7.32 depicts a drawing of the pitch sequence around a tire. At the bottom of this drawing is the cast of a crime scene impression and the pitch sequence represented in that cast. If no tread wear indicators were present in that crime scene impression, then any of the four areas of the tire (underlined in orange) could have produced the same pitch sequence. However, if a tread wear indicator was present in the cast impression (dotted red line), then only one area of the tire (red arrow) could have made the impression.

Tread wear indicators have many appearances. Some are thin and some are wide. Some travel straight across the tread while others are either angled or staggered. Regarding the position of the tread wear indicator on any particular spot on a tire, there are two general situations that will be encountered. One is where all the tread wear indicators intersect tread blocks of different sizes and/or at different positions on each tread block. Figure 7.33 illustrates how this might appear, more typical of situations where the tread wear indicators were added in the finishing stages of mold making. A second

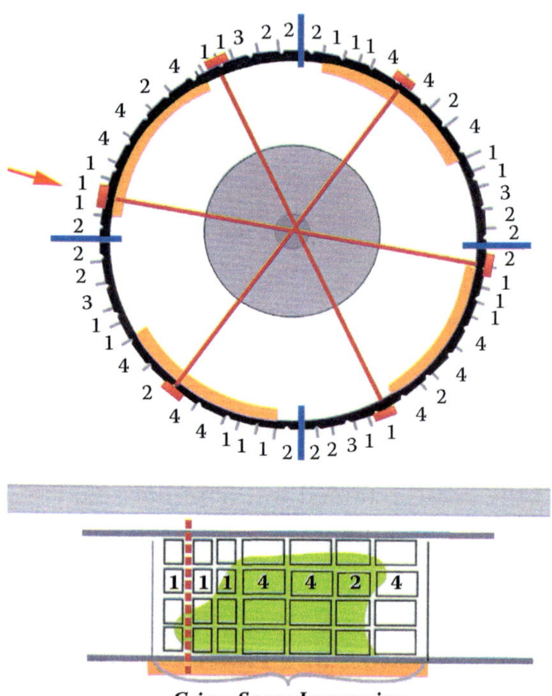

Figure 7.32. A pitch sequence around a tire, the position of the tread wear indicators, and their varied locations relative to the pitch lengths. A tread wear indicator in the crime scene impression will help locate the areas of the tire that could have produced that impression.

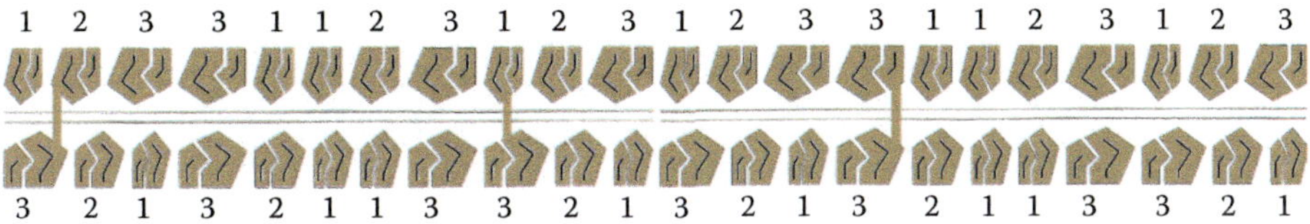

Figure 7.33. A tread design that has the tread wear indicators intersecting different size tread blocks will help reduce the number of areas on the tire that left an impression.

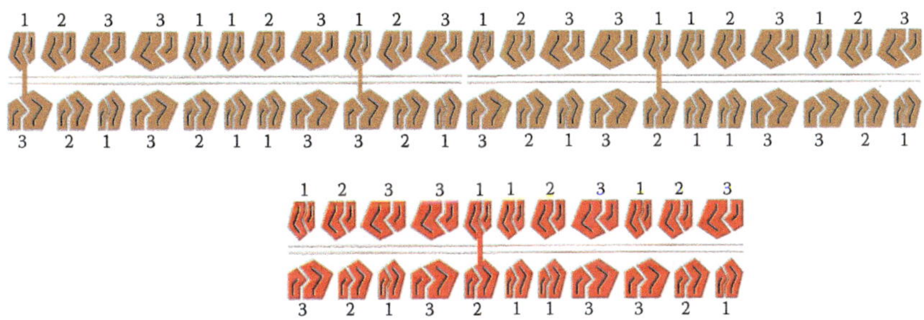

Figure 7.34. Some tread designs have the tread wear indicators adjacent to identically sized tread blocks around the tire. Regardless, the neighboring tread block sizes will still vary.

situation (Figure 7.34) is a tire with noise treatment that has the tread wear indicators all positioned on the same sized tread block, more typical of modern engraved mold making. Note in the case of the example in Figure 7.34 that although the tread wear indicators are present in the same location on the same tread block size, the adjacent tread block sizes will vary, thus still providing the same opportunity to use tread wear indicators to locate specific areas of the tire.

Noise Treatment and Tread Wear Indicator Combination Possibilities

The following examples represent some of the possible situations that may confront an examiner based on whether or not the tire has noise treatment, whether the tread wear indicators were retained in the impression, and how the tread wear indicators were placed during the mold-making process. Please note that the illustrations in this book only include three tread wear indicators (half the tire rotation) instead of the full circumference that would include all six, simply so the pictures could be made larger in the book for illustrative purposes.

Figure 7.35. A tire with no noise treatment and no tread wear indicator in the crime scene impression.

Example 1 Figure 7.35 illustrates a recovered impression made by a tire that does not have noise treatment and without the presence of any tread wear indicators in the crime scene impression. In this situation, there are many areas of the tire tread that fit the tread design and size of the crime scene impression at the bottom of that illustration. The examiners will therefore not be able to determine a specific point on the tire that may have made that impression based on pitch variation or tread wear indicators. Instead, they will have to examine the full tire circumference in both directions and rely on tread wear and/or individual characteristics to find the location(s) that could have made the impression.

Example 2 Figure 7.36 represents a recovered impression made by a tire that does not have noise treatment, but the impression displays one or more tread wear indicators. In this particular situation, the tire's six tread wear indicators all cross the tread, intersecting identical tread blocks of the same size and shape. Because the tread wear indicators are all in the exact same positions, because they all intersect the same portion of the identical tread blocks, and because there is no noise treatment, a crime scene impression from this tire could still potentially come from six locations on this tire in either direction for a total of 12 locations.

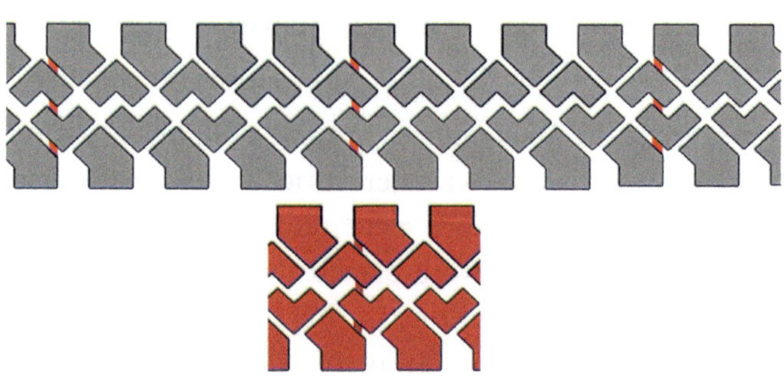

Figure 7.36. A tire with no noise treatment but a tread wear indicator present in the crime scene impression.

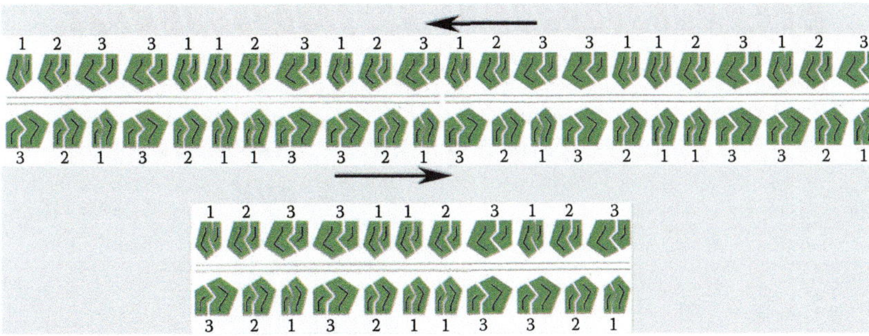

Figure 7.37. A tire with non-directional noise treatment and no tread wear indicator in the crime scene impression.

Example 3 Figure 7.37 illustrates a crime scene impression made by a tire that has non-directional noise treatment but no display of tread wear indicators. In this situation the examination must rely solely on the varied pitch sequence of the noise treatment to locate the area or areas of the tread that fit the crime scene impression and thus could have made the impression. Because the noise treatment is non-directional, the full circumference of the tire will have to be examined in both directions. As most tires made today that incorporate noise treatment employ directional noise treatment, this example may not be one that is encountered.

Example 4 Figure 7.34 illustrates a crime scene impression made by a tire that has non-directional noise treatment and the display of a tread wear indicator. In this situation the examination can focus on the area(s) of the tire with the same pitch sequence in combination with the presence of a tread wear indicator. In almost every case, this will result in only one position on the tire, because each tread wear indicator will be located among differently sized tread blocks, i.e., a different part of the pitch sequence of the tire. However, because the noise treatment is non-directional, the full circumference should be examined in both directions as well. As in Example 3, most tires made today that incorporate noise treatment have directional noise treatment, so this example also may not be one encountered.

Example 5 Figure 7.38 illustrates a crime scene impression made by an asymmetrical tire design having directional noise treatment but no display of a tread wear indicator. In this situation the examination must rely solely on the varied pitch sequence of the noise treatment to locate the area or areas of the tread that fit the crime scene impression and thus could have made the impression. Because the design is asymmetrical, the crime scene impression will only match the tire in one direction.

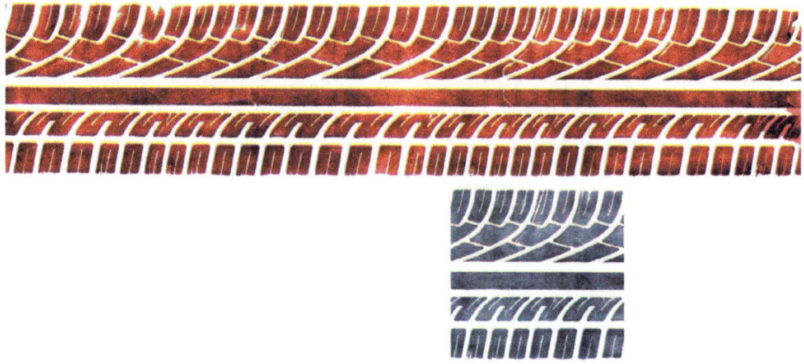

Figure 7.38. An asymmetrical tire with noise treatment but no tread wear indicator in the crime scene impression.

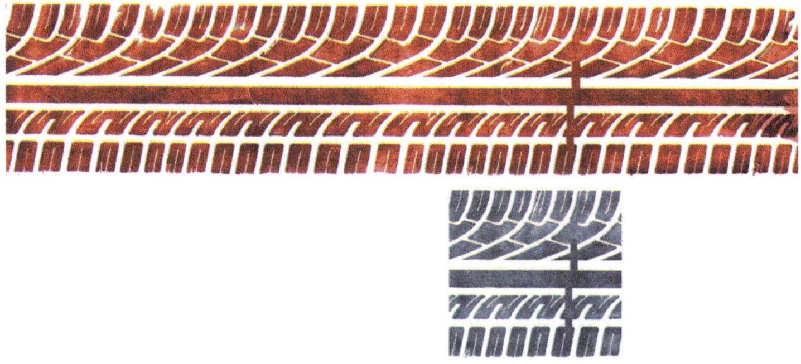

Figure 7.39. An asymmetrical tire with noise treatment and a tread wear indicator in the crime scene impression.

Example 6 Figure 7.39 illustrates a crime scene impression made by a tire that has an asymmetrical design and displays a tread wear indicator. In this situation the examination can focus on the area(s) of the tire with the same pitch size and sequence in combination with a tread wear indicator in the same position within that design. In almost every case this will result in only one position on the tire, because each tread wear indicator will be located among differently sized tread blocks, i.e., a different part of the pitch sequence of the tire, and also because the design on each side of the tire is not the same. (For symmetrical tires, the pitch sequence would be different on each side of the tire.)

Vehicles Tires of Multiple Tread Designs

Although new passenger cars and light trucks are equipped by their manufacturers with four tires of the same design, this may not always be the case throughout the life of that vehicle. Often more than one tire design is represented on a vehicle. When a vehicle has two, three, or four different tire designs, the occurrence of this form of evidence at a crime scene has added significance. The significance is greatest when more than one design has been found at a crime scene and, based on documentation of the treads, can be concluded to have come from the same vehicle, either because the tracks of that vehicle are isolated or because the tracking characteristics permit that conclusion.[14] An example of this is illustrated in Figure 7.40.

Common sense would dictate that vehicles having multiple designs are older, and this is the case most of the time. But it is certainly possible to find this occurrence on a newer vehicle as well where a damaged tire had to be replaced and the replacement tire was of a second design. In a study in Iowa,[15] tires were observed on 1,250 vehicles in parking lots of grocery and other stores as well as the state capitol parking complex. Ten percent of the vehicles observed were from law enforcement impound lots. That study found that 72.3% of the vehicles had all four tires of one design (AAAA); 5.9% had three tires of one design and one of a second design (AAAB); 14.3% had two tires of one design and two of a second design (AABB); 6.1% had two tires of one design, one of a second design, and one of a third design (AABC); and

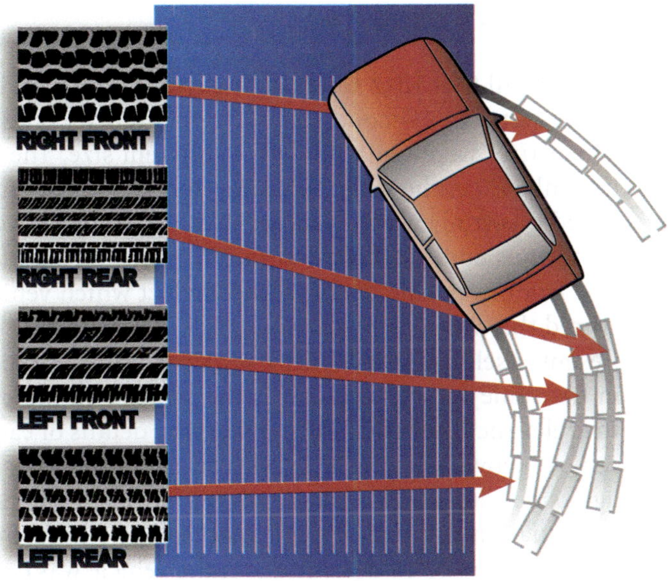

Figure 7.40. The combination of more than one tread design and/or sizes associated with the tracks of one vehicle can have added significance.

[14]Even in an area where neither of these is possible, the location of two designs at a scene that are later both found on a suspect vehicle may still carry some significance.

[15]Bessman, C. and Schmeiser, A., "Survey of Tire Tread Design and Tire Size as Mounted on Vehicles in Central Iowa" (2001).

only 1.4% of the vehicles had tires each of a different design (ABCD).[16] The study also reflected that the chances of having more than one tread design were even less when the vehicles from the impound lots were excluded. The results of this study were consistent with a prior study made in Jacksonville, Florida, where 66.6% of the vehicles had all four tires of one design (AAAA); 6% had three tires of one design and one of a second design (AAAB); 16.6% had two tires of one design and two of a second design (AABB); 8.4% had two tires of one design, one of a second design, and one of a third design (AABC); and only 2.4% of the vehicles had tires each of a different design (ABCD).[17] A more recent and ongoing study in Utah has shown very similar results based on the information they have collected to date. After collecting information from 318 vehicles, 77.04% of the vehicles had all four tires of one design (AAAA); 5.35% had three tires of one design and one of a second design (AAAB); 13.21% had two tires of one design and two of a second design (AABB); 3.46% had two tires of one design, one of a second design, and one of a third design (AABC); and only 0.94% of the vehicles had tires each of a different design (ABCD).[18]

Vehicle Tires of Varying Sizes

Some vehicles, where all four tires were originally one size, have been found to have one or more tires of a second size. One possibility would be a situation where the rear tires were replaced with a different size. The Iowa study determined that only 4% of the vehicles surveyed had any tires mismatched in size.[19] It is noted this study was conducted in 2001. Many new vehicles are now designed and thus come standard with different tire sizes for the rear tires than for the front tires. The study did not reflect which vehicles, if any, were manufactured that way.

If a case presents itself where a vehicle has a tire or tires of a different size than others on the same vehicle and this is the same as in the crime scene impressions, the relevance of this will depend on the details of each case and that specific vehicle. Obviously a vehicle with tires of different sizes on the left side and right side would be unusual and significant in any case. On the other hand, in a situation of a vehicle with rear tires of a different size than its front tires, it would have to be determined if the vehicle was designed that way or if this represented customized and unusual changes to that vehicle.

[16] A is the first design, B the second design, C the third design, and D the fourth design.
[17] Miller, T. A., "Tire Tread Design Combinations as Mounted on a Vehicle" (1994).
[18] Elliott, K. T. (Utah Bureau of Forensic Services, Salt Lake City, UT), personal communication, June 2007.
[19] Bessman, C. and Schmeiser, A., "Survey of Tire Tread Design and Tire Size as Mounted on Vehicles in Central Iowa" (2001, p. 591).

Tire Wear

8

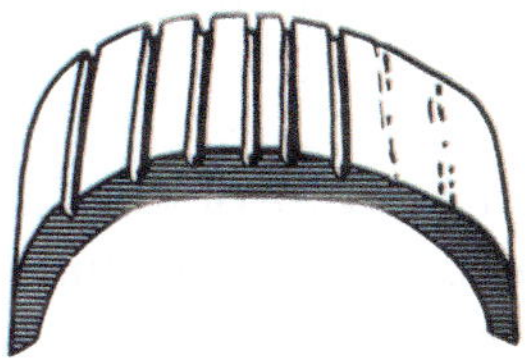

Use of Wear in Forensic Examinations

When new, tires exhibit their full and original tread design and depth. Most new passenger tires will have tread depths typically in the range of 9/32 to 13/32 inch. Light- and medium-size trucks will typically have greater tread depths. As a tire accumulates miles, the depth of its tread is reduced through friction, resulting in visible changes in the tread design. The impressions the tire leaves will reflect those changes. Although general wear is not sufficiently unique to make a tire's tread one-of-a-kind, the characteristics of tread wear are useful to distinguish one tire in a particular condition of wear from many other tires that were produced with the same tread design and dimension but that are now in different conditions of wear. Examination of the wear characteristics retained in a crime scene impression with those on a suspect tire is a significant part of the continuing examination process.

Wear Terminology

For the purposes of discussion in this book, some basic terminology that pertains to forensic comparisons is provided.

General Wear General wear refers to the gradual removal of rubber from the tread surface, creating gradual changes in the tread's depth and the resultant changes in its appearance. Those changes are noticeable not only on the tire but also in the impressions a tire makes. General wear correspondence is a term used to describe a situation where the overall wear of the tire closely approximates the wear reflected in the crime scene impression and thus could have produced the crime scene impression.

Excessive Wear Excessive wear is a term used to describe tread wear in an extreme state, such as the case when the majority of the tread is worn away and/or where tread is worn down to the tread wear indicators. It infers that the tire is worn past its intended usable life. A tire tread that is worn bald on its shoulder would be one example of a tire having excessive wear.

Irregular Wear Irregular wear is a term that refers to wear that is not symmetrical across the tread surface. For instance, a tire tread may exhibit more wear on one shoulder than the other, or the tread may exhibit uneven wear around the circumference of the tire, as in the case of cupping.

Specific Wear This is a term used to describe a specific feature of wear at a specific location of the tread or crime scene tire impression. It may include a worn sipe, an isolated bald area, exposed cordage, or other specific features attributed to wear.

Causes of Tire Wear

As the tire rotates in contact with the road surfaces, it goes through what is known as a flex cycle. At the contact patch, its round shape must change to match the flat surface of the road. The components of this process include compression of the rubber as it changes its shape; rolling forces as the tread accelerates through the contact patch area creating slippage; mechanical influences such as worn parts, load, and alignment; and the size of the contact patch. These all create or influence the abrasive frictional forces that result in the gradual removal of rubber from the tread. As rubber is worn away, changes in the appearance of the tread surface become increasingly evident.

In addition to there being many influences on the wearing of the tread, these influences may not remain the same during the life of the tire. Tires are often rotated from other positions; mechanical problems such as misalignment, poor shock absorbers, or suspension problems may develop and later may be repaired; and improper inflation of the tires may vary from time to time. No one can analyze a worn tire and accurately conclude that its total wear is due to precise percentages of the many factors that influence wear. Further, and most significantly, in almost every case the actual causes of the wear are not forensically relevant. What is relevant is whether the position and degree of wear evident in the crime scene impression does or does not correspond with the position and degree of wear on the respective portion of the tire's tread. This analysis is made in the context of whether the tire's tread could have produced the impression or whether its tread could be eliminated. In those cases where there is a very pronounced and specific wear feature that may be caused by extremely worn parts, a slipped belt, bad wheel bearings, and so forth, and the need arises to address the causes of that wear, a tire engineer or manufacturer should be contacted.[1] It should be clear that analyzing the cause of wear is not the role of the forensic tire impression examiner, nor is it his or her area of expertise.

Some causes of tread wear are discussed hereafter, not in any way to suggest an examiner can address possible causes of wear of a particular tire tread in a case but only to provide some general appreciation and understanding of the complexity of the wear process.

Some general types of wear are depicted in Figure 8.1. The most common cause of wear encountered is under-inflation of a tire, which causes both shoulders to wear more than the center of the tire. If tires are run in an over-inflated condition, they will wear in the center more than on the shoulders. Improper alignment such as damaged steering or suspension parts can cause a tire to wear more on one side than the other, producing what is known as irregular wear. Some other influences or causes of wear include:

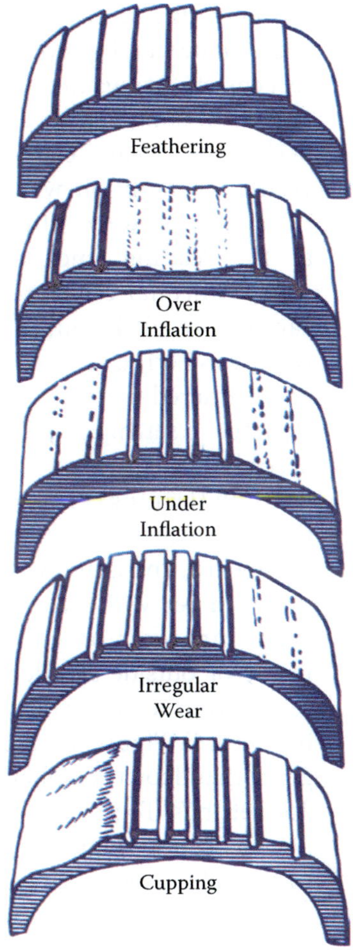

Figure 8.1. Some common types of wear.

- The degree of heat generated by the tire as it goes through its flex cycle.
- Wheel imbalance, which can cause uneven movements during tire rotation resulting in excessive wear to portions of the tread surface. This wear can include irregular wear and cupping.

[1] For instance, in one case where a vehicle had completely worn out wheel bearings, the tires wore excessively in certain shoulder areas. My examination concluded that the crime scene impressions and the suspect vehicle tire corresponded in wear, including specific wear on the shoulder. The mechanic from the repair shop where the suspect's vehicle was repaired and the engineer from B.F. Goodrich tire testified, respectively, to the vehicle maintenance, namely regarding the wheel bearings that needed replacing and that the shoulder wear was related to the wheel bearings.

- Caster settings. Caster is the angle of the steering axis. Incorrect caster settings can result in excessive shoulder wear and heel-to-toe wear. Heel-to-toe wear is a condition where the tread blocks wear differently at the leading and trailing edges. Unequal caster settings can also result in pulling that requires steering compensation and feathered wear.
- Camber settings. Camber describes the inward or outward tilt (leaning) of the tire. A tire with negative camber will tilt inward, and a tire with positive camber will tilt outward. Premature wear on either the inside or outside shoulder can result from an incorrect camber setting. Figure 8.2 is a diagram that depicts camber.

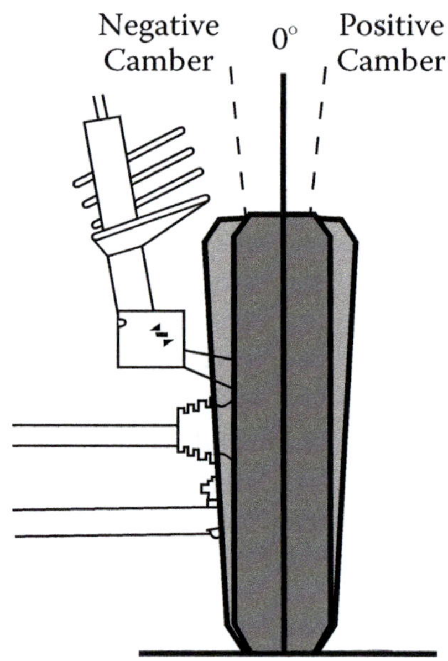

Figure 8.2. Camber is the inward and outward tilt of the tire. Incorrect camber settings can result in inside or outside shoulder wear.

- Toe settings. Toe, simply defined, is the direction the tires are pointing. Toe-in occurs when the fronts of the tires are closer than the rear of the tires, and toe-out occurs when the fronts of the tires are farther apart than the rear of the tires. Figure 8.3 is a diagram that depicts both toe-in and toe-out. Excessive toe-in or toe-out will result in a sawtooth wear pattern known as feathering and excessive shoulder wear on either the

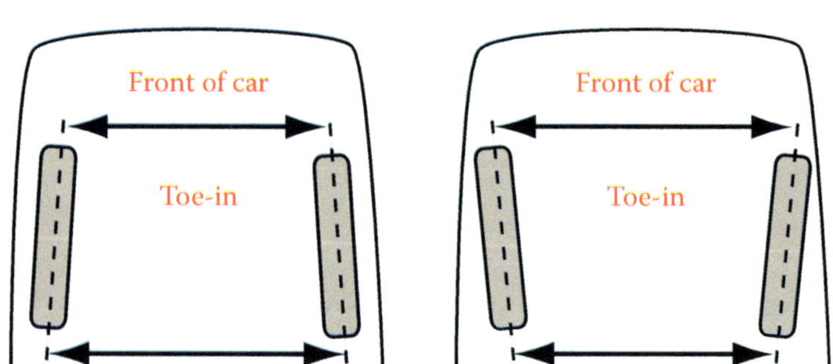

Figure 8.3. Toe-in and toe-out refers to the direction the tires are pointing. Excessive toe-in or toe-out will result in a wear pattern known as feathering.

inside or outside edges. Tires that are toed-in or toed-out are actually traveling slightly sideways instead of straight.

- Worn parts, suspension problems, bad shock absorbers, and other mechanical problems on the vehicle may result in the tire skipping or hopping, resulting in a wear pattern known as cupping.
- The type of road surface. A coarse or rough road surface will cause wear much quicker than a smooth road surface.
- Quick starts and stops, fast cornering, driving at excessive speeds, and other bad driving habits can cause heel-to-toe wear, a condition in which the leading edge of the tread block wears differently than the rear of the tread block
- The load the vehicle is carrying. The heavier the vehicle's load, the faster the tire will wear.

Characteristics of Tire Wear

Wear Characteristics Retained in Two-Dimensional Impressions

Wear features present on the surface of the tread are capable of being retained in two-dimensional tire impressions. These occur when the tread surface acquires various residues on or off the road and then deposits them onto a two-dimensional surface in the form of a tire impression. The surfaces could include the road itself, objects on the road the tire passes over, or victim's clothing or skin that may have been run over. Those residues could consist of the normal mixture of road dust, dust from crushed rock, soil residues, black tire residues, and blood. The resultant detail in a two-dimensional impression can range from poor to excellent, depending on the existing conditions. The impression may reflect the class characteristics of the tread design and dimension, wear characteristics including changes in the shapes and sizes of the grooves and sipes, and even the tread wear indicators, should the tread be worn down to that degree. Figures 8.4 and 8.5 depict two- and three-dimensional impressions of the same tire.

Wear Characteristics Retained in Three-Dimensional Impressions

When a tire makes a three-dimensional impression in a soft substrate, its tread surface is pressed into that substrate and recorded at the bottom of the three-dimensional impression. In addition, some detail of a three-dimensional nature is also transferred. Those additional features may include partial or full groove depth, the recording of additional tread width, and the three-dimensional features of the tread surface detail (such as a stone

Figure 8.4. A two-dimensional impression of a tire.

Figure 8.5. A three-dimensional impression of the same tire that produced the impression in Figure 8.4.

embedded within a groove or sipe). In deeper impressions, portions of the sidewall may even record. A photograph of a three-dimensional impression will usually not be capable of capturing all of the three-dimensional aspects of the impression. A cast, on the other hand, will almost always retain the greatest amount of three-dimensional information.

Sipe Characteristics Change with Wear

The comparison of sipe wear can be an integral and important aspect of the tire tread examination and often is a key factor in distinguishing one tire from another. Sipes are placed into the tread blocks on most tires to create additional edges for traction and to create more flexibility within the tread block. More often than not, they are not of uniform depth. Figure 8.6 depicts some sipe blades in a small section of a mold. The central portions of these sipe blades, identified by the arrows, are deeper than each end and will extend farther into the tread rubber. Each will result in a sipe that will have greater depth in the middle and less depth on the ends. In this example, when the tread wears down to a certain point the ends of the sipe will become solid rubber and disappear, yet the central area of the sipe, which is deeper, will remain. Eventually, the entire sipe, which is not as deep as the main circumferential grooves, will be worn from the tread design. These changes to the sipes as wear advances result in changes in the appearance of the tread and its impression over the life of the tire.

Figure 8.7 is a picture of a small section of tread when new. Figure 8.8 is a drawing of that portion of tread design including a circumferential groove, smaller transverse grooves (slots), and sipes. The color-coded drawing depicts the actual depths of each component. In the new tire, the white areas, which

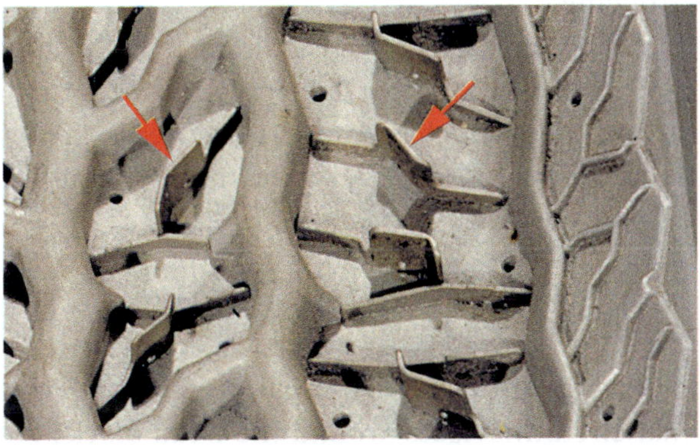

Figure 8.6. A close-up view of a small section of a mold. The sipe blades are not even in depth which creates sipes in a tire whose shallow portions wear away sooner than the deeper portions. The two red arrows point to two areas in the sipe blades that will correspond with the deepest part of that sipe.

Figure 8.7. A close-up view of a small section of new tread with tapered groove bottoms, slots, and sipes.

include the circumferential grooves and portions of the slots, are 10/16 inch deep. The red areas are only 3/16 inch deep and are the portions of the sipe, like in Figure 8.6, that are not as deep as the rest of the sipe. When the tread wears away 3/16 inch of rubber, those areas of the tire will appear solid as indicated in Figure 8.8. The blue areas are 5/16 inch deep. At 5/16 inch of wear, these areas will also be worn even with the tread surface. The green areas are 8/16 inch deep. When the tire wears away 8/16 inch of tread rubber, the green areas will disappear and the tread design will then appear as the last part of the drawing.

Figure 8.9 is a drawing of another tread design. On the left side is the full design of that tire when new. The portions of that design that are not at the full tread depth, and thus will change as the tire wears, are featured in red. On the right of that figure is the overall appearance of that tire design when it has become excessively worn.

Groove Depth and Taper

The main grooves that run circumferentially around tires and the larger open grooves that circumnavigate around the tread blocks on block design tires are normally equal in their depth. Sometimes these grooves are tapered, being wider at the top of the new tread surface and narrower at the bottom of the groove. When grooves are tapered, they become narrower as the tread wears down. In some tread designs, there may be very narrow circumferen-

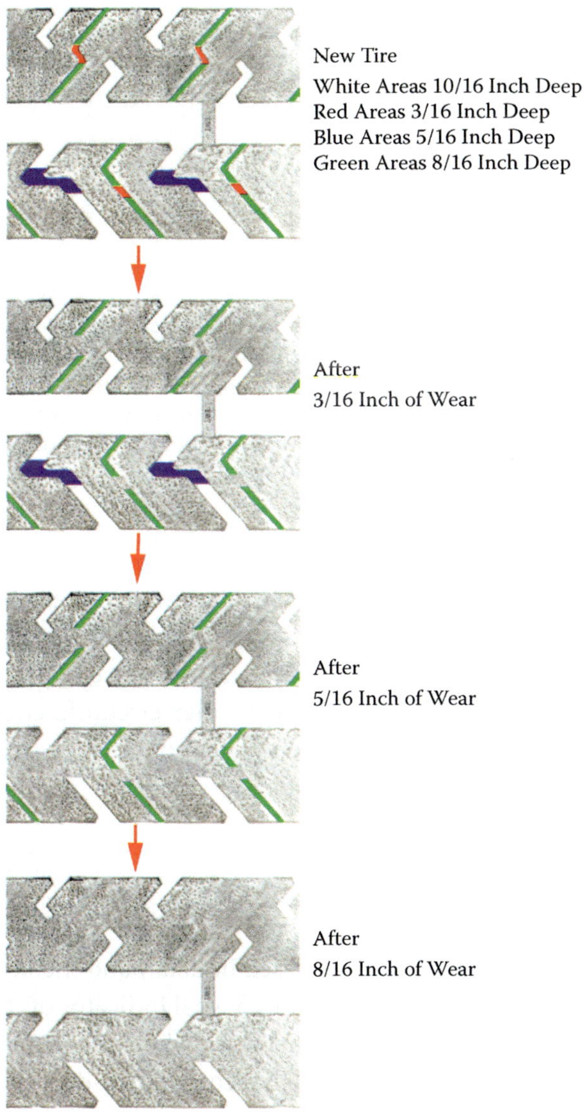

Figure 8.8. A drawing of the same section of tread as depicted in Figure 8.7 at different stages of wear. Notice through the color coding how the depth of the grooves, sipes, and slots changes as the tread depth wears down.

Figure 8.9. On the left side is a drawing of a new tire design. The portions of the sipes, smaller grooves, and other areas depicted in red are not as deep as the other portions and will eventually be removed through wear until the tire will appear as depicted in black on the right. Notice some of the lateral transverse grooves in the middle ribs have also worn away and the taper of the circumferential grooves has caused those grooves to narrow when worn.

tial grooves or channels that do not extend as deep as the larger circumferential grooves. When the tread surface wears down to a certain depth those grooves will disappear from the tread design. Figure 8.9 also depicts changes in the slots and groove widths as the tire wear advanced. The picture of the Michelin tires in Figure 8.10 shows the smaller circumferential groove on a newer tread has been worn away completely on a worn tire of the same design. Portions of the transverse slots and sipes have also partially worn away.

Tread Wear Indicators

Tread wear indicators have been discussed in detail and illustrated in Chapters 5 and 7. They are intended to provide a visual indicator of the tread depth to the consumer, with their visibility increased when only 2/32 inch or less of tread remains. Tread wear indicators will record in two-dimensional impressions only when the tread has worn down to that level (2/32 inch) and the actual tread wear indicator becomes even with the rest of the tread surface and thus makes contact with the substrate. But they may also record in three-dimensional impressions of all tires ranging from a new tread to an excessively worn tread, as long as the impression is of sufficient depth to record them. In either case, tread wear indicators are useful and reliable in visually documenting tread depth and general wear.

Figure 8.10. A tread that has a small groove running circumferentially around the shoulder area of the tire and a worn tread of the same design. The worn tread has resulted in the elimination of the smaller groove. Note also the changes in the small transverse grooves and sipes due to wear.

Figure 8.11. A tread depth gauge positioned on a tire. This is a plunger type of gauge with increments for each 32nd inch in depth.

Tread Depth Gauges

Tread depth gauges come in many different forms. Figure 8.11 depicts a basic tread depth gauge, incremented in 32nds of an inch. It is placed over the tire and depressed so that the bottom of the gauge rests on the bottom of the groove. The closest alignment of lines, incremented in 1/32 inch on the gauge, will provide the depth at that point.

Potential Unreliability of Tread Depth Measurements

Three-dimensional tire impressions at crime scenes are rarely perfect representations of the tires that made them. Tires will sink into the substrate partially in some instances and fully in other instances. Making a cast of those impressions and then using a tread depth gauge to determine the groove depths in the casts may provide different results in different impressions, even though the same tire in the same condition of wear produced both impressions. Below are a few situations relating to wear that could be encountered when comparing a crime scene photograph or cast with a tire.

- A tire impression in a three-dimensional surface such as snow, soil, and sand may or may not represent the full depth of the tread of that tire. Figure 8.12 depicts two impressions made by the same area of a tire that has a remaining tread depth of 6/32 inch. The left impression in Figure 8.12 was made in soft deep soil includes a recording of the tread wear indicators and is a slightly wider impression. In this case, because the tire was able to sink fully into the soil, the resulting impression is an accurate representa-

Figure 8.12. On the left is a photograph of a full-depth impression of a tire with 6/32-inch tread remaining and with a recording of tread wear indicators (arrows). On the right is a photograph of a partial-depth impression of the exact same section of the same tire that only sank 2/32 inch into packed sand, with no recording of the tread wear indicators.

tion of the actual tread depth of the tire that made it. The right impression, made from the same portion of the same tire, only sank 2/32 inch into the soil and did not record the full tread depth, thus there is no recording of the tread wear indicator in the impression. Using a tread depth indicator to measure the tread depth remaining on the tire and then comparing it with the depth of a cast of that impression could result in an erroneous conclusion, i.e., the tire that made the impression had only 2/32 inch of depth and therefore was not made by the tire having 6/32 inch of tread. This is a very common occurrence in impressions in fairly compact soil. It is also commonly encountered with vehicles traveling straight, because the front tires will compress the soft substrate first, followed by the rear tires, which are now tracking over compressed soil. The result is that the rear tires very often do not produce a very deep impression and will often not record the full depth of the tire tread that made it.

- A tire tread may extend fully into the substrate leaving a full-depth impression, but perhaps only a short segment of the impression, one that did not contain a tread wear indicator, is recovered. In this case there would

Figure 8.13. Dry soil will often fall back into the impression, partially filling the sipes and grooves of the impression, restricting detail and also misrepresenting tread depth.

be no way to reliably know if the tire did or did not produce a full-depth impression.

- A tire tread impression, as depicted in Figure 8.13, often contains debris and/or loose soil that have collapsed back into the grooves and sipes, preventing or covering the recording of the tread wear indicators and/or partially filling the grooves with loose soil. This interferes with the accurate determination of tread depth information.
- Tire treads often become temporarily filled with mud or snow, preventing the recording of tread depth accurately, as seen in Figure 8.14 and Figure 4.1 (Chapter 4).

Because of these aforementioned issues, the examiner should be aware of the limitations when comparing tread depth measurements between three-dimensional impressions and the depth of the tire tread. Although a tire that leaves its full-depth impression in soft and uncontaminated soil with its

Figure 8.14. A tread caked with mud or snow cannot produce an impression that accurately replicates its actual condition of wear.

tread wear indicators present could potentially produce a fairly clean impression that provides an accurate recording of tread depth, I have found that the opposite is equally likely.

Forensic Significance of Wear

After it has been determined that a crime scene tire impression corresponds in tread design and dimension with a specific area on a suspect tire, the examiner can then focus on that area and the correspondence or non-correspondence of the position and degree of wear. During this portion of the examination, the portion(s) of the tread that correspond in design and dimension should be compared, one tread block at a time, with the respective areas of the crime scene impression. Remember that this examination does not concern itself with how that wear was created on the tire but rather whether that tire could or could not have produced the wear features present in the crime scene impression. Depending on the wear characteristics in a particular case and depending on the degree of detail retained and recovered in the impression, a number of conclusions may be possible.

- It may be possible to eliminate a tire if wear features are sufficiently different to the extent it could be determined that tire was not capable of having produced the crime scene impression. This conclusion must take into consideration when the crime scene impression occurred as well as when the suspect tire(s) were obtained and any likely use in between. Tread compounds are very durable, and it is possible that thousands of additional miles on a tire tread may produce very little noticeable wear. Caution should be made to ensure that sipes filled with soil, soil compacted in the tread, or other factors have not misrepresented the tread depth of the crime scene impression.

- It may be possible to determine if the general wear of the tire of a vehicle corresponds with wear exhibited in the crime scene impression. This conclusion means the tire is capable of having made the impression but also recognizes many other tires of the design and dimension could be in that general condition of wear and thus could also have produced that impression.
- It may also be possible to conclude that irregular or specific wear features evident in the crime scene impression correspond with the suspect tire in the same respective areas. This conclusion means that the tire is not only capable of producing the crime scene impression, but only another tire with the same wear features could also have produced it.

Individual Characteristics

9

Individualization

Much has been written on the process of individualization and the principles of uniqueness. Tuthill and George, in their book *Individualization: Principles and Procedures in Criminalistics*, define and discuss uniqueness and individuality very capably and offer much discussion and background on that topic.[1] Man-made objects will always have manufactured variations, and things that occur in nature will always have natural variations. Whether man-made or a product of nature, these differences, although very minor and microscopic in some instances, will always be present.

The principle of individuality applies not only to forensic science but to everyday practical experiences. The concept that all things in the universe are unique, whether it be snowflakes, the annular rings of logs, the veins of a leaf, dermal ridge formation, the blood vessels in our eyes, the way a piece of paper tears, and so on, is a widely accepted principle. People recognize one another because of their individual appearances and the minor variations that exist between us all. Even monozygotic twins will have some distinguishable features. People also recognize their personal possessions for the same reason. A bicycle or pick-up truck may look very much like thousands of others when new, but after some wear and usage, its owner will recognize its acquired features that make it unique and separate it from the others.

The Individualization of a Tire

When new, the impression a tire leaves is essentially indistinguishable from impressions of other tires of the same tread design and dimension. Once

[1] Tuthill, H., and George, G., Individualization: Principle and Procedures in Criminalistics (1994).

mounted on a vehicle and subjected to thousands of miles of use over a variety of road surfaces, the general wear and individual characteristics tires acquire are often sufficiently distinctive to permit an impression to be identified as having originated from one specific tire.

Individualization through randomly acquired features has long been used to positively identify a tire with a crime scene impression. The FBI Laboratory began examinations of tire evidence with its inception in 1932, including the eventual creation of a tread design reference collection.[2] Forensically, tire impressions and tracks have been used and recognized worldwide as important physical evidence.[3,4,5,6] In fact, the identification of tracks, whether left by wagon wheels or tires, has undoubtedly been used by man for as long as the wheel has existed.[7] In recent years, the forensic use of both tire impressions and tire track dimensions to assist in proving a vehicle was at the crime scene has increased as modern-day criminals rely more on their vehicles to transport them to and from the crime scene.[8,9,10,11]

Examples of Individual Characteristics of Tires

Individual characteristics that are acquired by tires include those features that involve the removal of tread rubber in a random fashion resulting in cuts, scratches, tears, rips, abrasions, and the like. Individual characteristics also include added features such as stones that have become embedded in the tread design, known as stone holds, tire patches or plugs used in the repair of a tire, nails, metal objects, or other debris that have become embedded in the tread surface.

Cuts and Scratches

Cuts and scratches are inflicted on a tire's tread in countless ways from virtually anything sharp that a tire passes over; examples include the edge of a rock, a piece of broken glass, the sharp edge of a pothole, or a piece of metal in the road. Cuts can be small or large, long or short, shallow or deep, and

[2] Tire Tracks, FBI Reference Collection, FBI Bulletin, 6 (1936): 15.
[3] Walther, G., Les Empreintes d'Automobile, THÈSE présentée pour le doctorat en médicine, Strasbourg, 1923.
[4] Chavigny, M., "Tracks of Vehicles" (1930).
[5] Grogan, R. J., and Watson, T.R. "Tyres and Crime" (1971).
[6] Piette, H., "The Identification of a Tyre Track" (1961).
[7] Hamm, E. D. "Historical Overview of Footwear and Tire Tread Evidence" (1994)
[8] Hamm, E. D. "Tire Tracks and Footwear Identification" (1975).
[9] Bodziak, W. J., "Shoe and Tire Impression Evidence" (1984).
[10] Bodziak, W. J., Encyclopedia of Forensic Sciences (2000).
[11] Nause, L. A., Forensic Tire Impression Identification (2001).

straight, curved or multisided. The combined size and shape features that a cut ultimately possesses are the product of a set of random occurrences that, although theoretically, could repeat would be extremely unlikely to do so. The rubber used in the tread has tremendous resistance to cutting and abrasion. Despite the fact that a tire presses itself thousands of times over sharp objects and debris in the road, it is so durable that in most cases no damage is inflicted on it. Figure 9.1 depicts cuts on four different tires. In each of these examples, the cuts occurred because of a set of random circumstances that resulted in the removal of rubber in a precise way. Note in the top right example in the Figure 9.1 photograph that the object causing the long cut was a razor blade, a portion of which is still embedded in the tire above the tip of the arrow.

Tears and Rips

Tires can lose pieces of tread rubber through ripping and tearing actions that produce damage. This can occur on any road surface but occurs more when

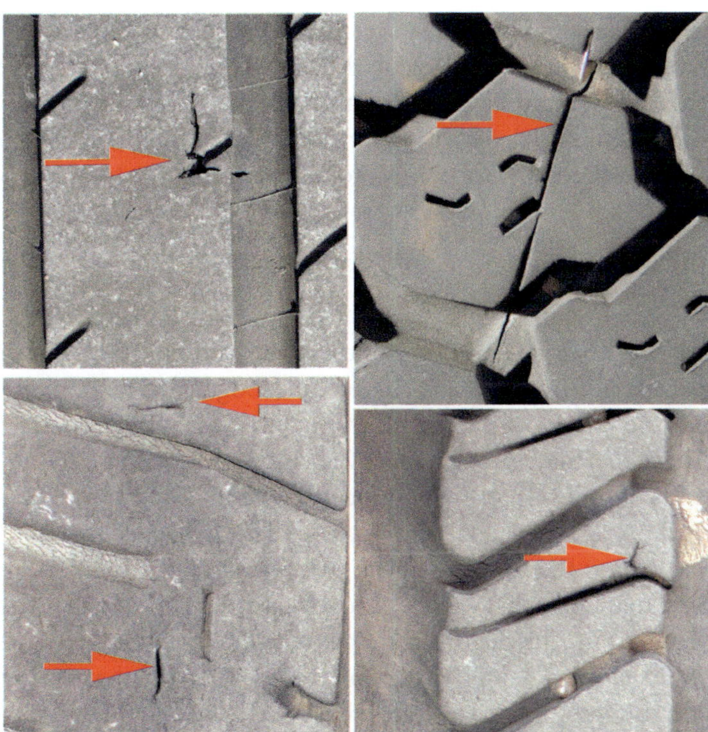

Figure 9.1. Examples of cuts found in the tread of several tires. The top left is a complex cut or possibly a combination of two cuts. The top right cut was made by a razor blade, part of which is still embedded in the tire.

Figure 9.2. The rubber tread can get torn or ripped due to a variety of causes. This is more common in heavier vehicles and vehicles driving over poor surfaces.

driving over off-road and rocky surfaces. This type of damage is more frequent on the tires of heavier vehicles, particularly those that must maneuver frequently as low speeds. These features are often larger, deeper, and often contain multi-sided features. Figure 9.2 depicts a section of tread of a truck tire with numerous chunks of rubber randomly torn away from the edges of the tread blocks.

Stone Holds

Stones come in all shapes and sizes and easily become lodged in the sipes and grooves of a tire. The size and shape of the stone caught in a sipe or groove as well as the exact position where it has become lodged are random. Stones are the most transient form of individual characteristics. Some stones are lodged very deeply and permanently in a groove or sipe and will remain in the tread for thousands of miles. In other instances they will only be in the tread for a very short time, either because they become dislodged or because they quickly break apart. Stones that do remain in grooves or sipes for a period of time will often permanently distort the groove or sipe. In these cases, even after the stone comes out, the distorted shape that remains will be an individual characteristic. Figure 9.3 depicts portions of two tires that have several stone holds. The arrows point to two stones that have begun to distort the grooves holding them. In more extreme cases, larger stones held in grooves or sipes will move or twist with each tire revolution, causing a drilling action that can erode and tear into the sides and bottoms of grooves or sipes and even drill into the carcass of the tire. This is referred to as stone drilling and is more

Figure 9.3. The two photographs on the right depict several stones that have embedded themselves in the grooves and sipes. On the left is a nail that has penetrated the tread.

predominant in heavier trucks. Some truck tires have narrow rubber strips at the bottom of the grooves to keep this from happening.

Nails

Anyone who has driven for a few years is likely to have had the unfortunate experience of having a nail puncture one of his or her tires. Figure 9.3 depicts a tire with an embedded nail. Nails not only come in many sizes but can puncture the tire at numerous angles, resulting in a variety of size and shape features.

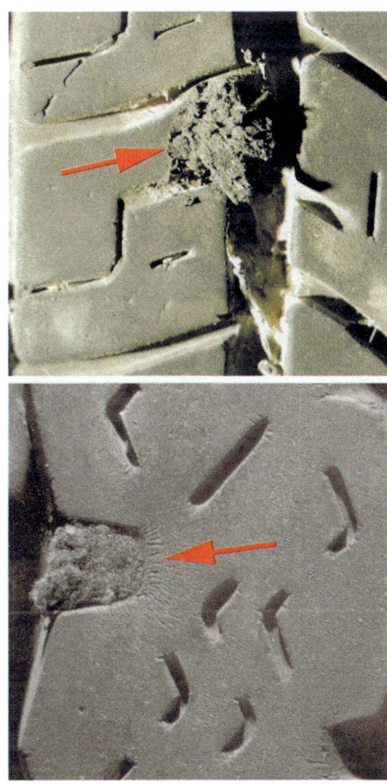

Figure 9.4. Tires often get punctured, and the plugs used to repair tires provide numerous random individual features.

Plugs and Patches

When a punctured tire is repaired, it will have a plug of rubber inserted into the punctured area of the tire. Although the materials and methods of doing this vary, plugs provide a wide variety of individual characteristics, not only from the location and size of the plug, but often from the fraying or tearing of the plug once driving is resumed. Stress lines in the rubber will also accompany plugged areas and add additional random features. Figure 9.4 depicts sections of two tires that contain plugs. Note the many stress lines in the bottom photo.

Excessive Erosion of Tread

When the tread surface of a tire wears excessively, either due to mechanical problems or a tire defect, the underlying belts and cordage can be exposed. This will result in a randomly shaped area of wear as well as many random features within this area. Figure 9.5 depicts a section of a tire that was on a vehicle that had serious mechanical problems, which eventually resulted in the random exposure of the steel tread belts and cordage.

Recording Individual Characteristics in a Substrate

The impression-making process is not a perfect process. When a tire rolls over a surface, whether it leaves a two- or three-dimensional impression, the detail retained by that surface is dependent on a number of factors, including the substrate type and condition, the type of substance on the tire, moisture, contaminates such as rocks, sticks, and debris that interfere with reproduction of detail, vehicle speed, and other factors. In some instances, remarkable

Figure 9.5. An exposed belt on a tire due to severe mechanical problems. The position and exact manner in which this belt becomes exposed and the resulting tearing of the exposed fabric and steel is random and contain numerous individual features.

detail is retained by the substrate, but in other instances only minimal general class characteristics of the tread design, or even less detail, are retained. Although this applies to all forms of impression evidence, it is undoubtedly more common with tire impressions because they leave their impressions over such a large variety of substrates in a variety of conditions. A typical soil substrate that is uneven in texture and compactness may also contain rocks, leaves, sticks, and other debris mixed in with it and consequently will not retain all of the detail of a tire passing over it. Further, because the quality of that substrate will vary over the length of the impression, the degree of detail retained may be better in some areas than others. In many cases, recovered impressions contain clear detail in one area while a few inches away in the same impression there is poor detail. This does not constitute a basis for elimination of that tire because some features were not reproduced in the impression. Rather, this is what normally occurs in this form of evidence. The fact that some details are retained and other details are not is normal and routine, even under controlled conditions. Certain detail in tire impressions, including individual characteristics, will be absent from the impressions simply because the conditions were not satisfactory to allow for replication of that detail. I observe this routinely in tire classes even though we make the impressions in soil that is capable of retaining fine detail and contains little or no debris.

Weight of Individual Characteristics

In the examination process, when individual characteristics are present, the examiner must determine the significance or weight of those characteristics toward establishing individualization. Experienced tire examiners know that virtually any random individual characteristic a tire acquires will not be found on another tire, much less on a tire of the same tread design and dimension, and at the same location along its 6- to 8-foot-long tread surface. An experienced tire examiner asked to make a study of random individual characteristics on tires, to visually examine hundreds of tires to establish the frequency of occurrence of each different characteristic, would know immediately, before even attempting such a study, that he or she would not find any two characteristics alike in the same precise area of the tire tread in another tire of the same design and dimension. To the best of my knowledge, no study of the frequency of random individual characteristics on tires would ever produce results of any value, other than confirming what is already known. A limited study of this type was recently performed with new footwear. That study concluded "the widely accepted proposition that the accidental damage found on footwear outsoles is randomly produced" inasmuch as no duplicate random accidental characteristics occurred on the various boots.[12] Whereas a limited study of this type can be done with footwear, the logistics of doing it with tires is much more involved.

Random characteristics differ considerably in their appearance and uniqueness. A small 1-mm cut or a tiny stone held in a sipe in the tire tread represent features that are about as minimal as you could find. Larger individual characteristics, in addition to their position on the tread, will have specific shape features and are capable of occurring in many different orientations on the tire. But the question is often asked: "How many individual characteristics are needed for the identification of a tire?" The answer depends on both the quality and quantity of those characteristics. One very small and featureless cut will not be enough. But a more dimensionally complicated cut such as depicted with an arrow in the top left picture of Figure 9.1 might, in itself, justify this conclusion.

When dealing with the evaluation of random individual characteristics shared by the tire and a crime scene impression, there are three quantitative components to consider: the position of the characteristic, its size and shape features, and its orientation. But their quality or degree of clarity will have the most influence on the weight that can be applied to characteristics of any type. An individual characteristic must be sufficiently clear to establish a reliable cause-and-effect type relationship between it and the respective feature on the tire. You cannot weigh heavily a blurred or indistinct feature in a photograph of a crime scene impression simply because something appears to be in the same position on the tire and therefore presume they are related to each other. There must be sufficient clarity to see a relationship between the two, i.e., the crime scene impression must contain a reasonably good replication of the characteristic to the extent you can conclude one is related to the other. Only then should the quantitative aspects of the feature be considered. As characteristics become more complex in their size and shape features, they grow in their importance and the weight they carry toward individualization. A clear but short cut could carry more weight than a more complex and multidirectional cut in the tire that was not clearly evident in the impression.

One excellent statistical accounting of the tremendous weight a clear and confirmable individual characteristic carries was offered by Rocky S. Stone in a recent forensic journal article.[13] Stone, in his abstract stated:

[12] Adair, T., Lemay, J., McDonald, A., Shaw, R., and Tewes, R., "The Mount Bierstadt study. An experiment in unique damage formation in footwear" Journal of Forensic Identification, 57(2) 2007 199–205.

[13] Stone, R. "Footwear Examinations–Mathmatical probabilities of theoretical individual characteristics" JFI 56(4), 2006 pp. 577–599.

> Objectivity, in most cases, is reinforced by quantification. The individual characteristics that appear on a shoe print or shoe impression can be quantified using two primary variables. Their location on the print and their configuration and orientation yield measurable, discriminating data values.... With marks or combinations of marks of reasonable complexity, the magnitudes of the resultant numbers, though entirely abstract and based upon conservative assumptions, are remarkable."

Stone used a metric grid with divisions of 1 mm^2. By placing that grid over a size 8½ flat-bottomed shoe sole, he determined that the sole contained a surface area of 16,000 mm^2.[14] He used a very small cut on that sole as an example of a minimal area of random damage that could occur on the sole, but which he could easily and accurately differentiate its position within 1 mm. For simplicity, in this example, he treated that cut as if it were a two-dimensional feature. Using the formula for simple probability, $P = m/n$, where P is the probability, m is the number of ways of success (the proper position), and n is the total number of possible locations (16,000), he calculated the probability of another shoe sole containing that cut in the same position as being 1 out of 16,000.[15]

The same formula can be used for calculating the chances of a tire having a similar small cut in the same exact position. Virtually all passenger and light-truck tire designs have noise treatment, which means the size and arrangement of its tread blocks changes around the circumference of a tire. Thus a tire's design is different over the entire length of the 6- to 8-foot-long rolling circumference of the tire tread. Any characteristic acquired on such a tire would not be the same as one on another tire of the same design and size unless it appeared in the same exact position along its long tread surface. Using 6.5 feet (1,981.2 mm) as an average length of the tread around the tire and a tread width of 7 inches (177.8 mm) as an average width, the surface area of the full tire's tread surface would be approximately 352,257 mm^2. Figure 9.6 represents a portion of the 6.5-foot-long tire impression in the example, with an arrow pointing to the small cut whose position on the tire tread could accurately be differentiated within 1 mm. Figure 9.7 is an enlarged view of that space. Using the above formula for simple probability, the chances of another tire having a small cut at that same position on that tread, would be 1 out of 352,257. This example does not take into account the design of the tire tread or any general tire wear.

[14] For purposes of Stone's study, the design of the shoe was not considered. In a real case, the design and size of the shoe would be factored in since there are thousands of shoe designs, each coming in many sizes

[15] This simple probability formula is the same for calculating the toss of a coin being heads or tails, which is 1 out of 2 chances.

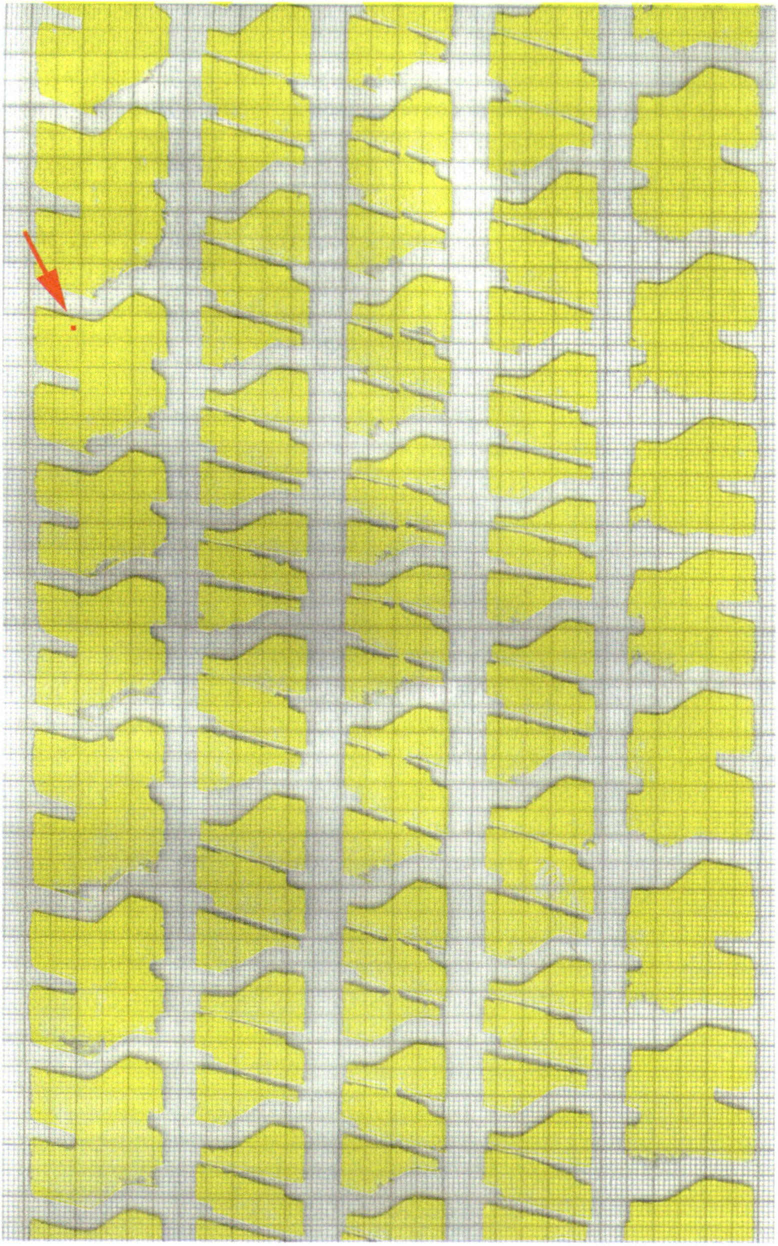

Figure 9.6. A 1 mm^2 metric grid superimposed over a portion of a 6.5-foot-long (1,981.2 mm) by 7-inch-wide (177.8 mm) tire tread. For a tire tread of that size, there are approximately 352,257 mm^2. The arrow points to a red dot representing a very small random individual characteristic whose position can be accurately be differentiated within 1-mm of the tread.

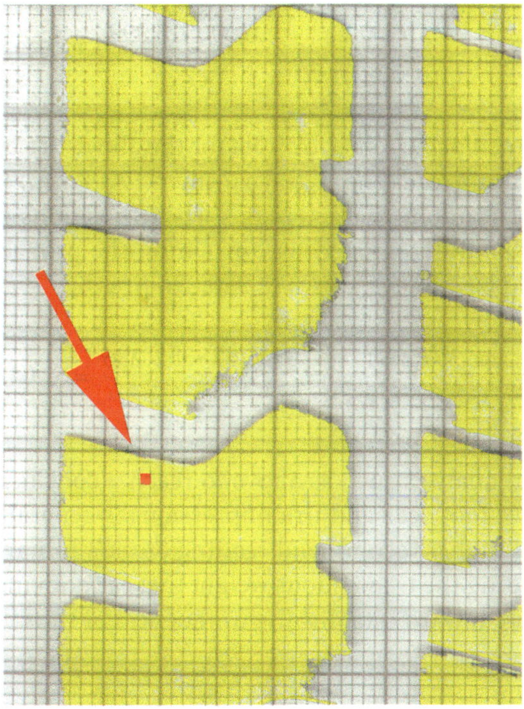

Figure 9.7. An enlargement of the portion of Figure 9.6.

Stone also demonstrated what the probability would be for a shoe sole with two or more very small cuts to be present on another shoe sole in the same two positions. For this combination, he uses the formula:

$$nC_r = \frac{n!}{(n-r)!r!}$$

Where ${}_nC_r$ = the combination of n things taken r at a time
n = the number of possible positions
r = the number of characteristics
! = factorial after a number like n, it means

$$n \bullet (n-1) \bullet (n-2) \bullet (n-3) \text{ and so on}$$

For the position of the two cuts on a shoe to be the same, the probability of a random duplication would be 127,992,000, calculated as follows:

$$ {}_{16,000}C_2 = \frac{16,000!}{(16,000-2)! \bullet 2!} = \frac{16,000 \bullet 15,999}{2} = 127,992,000 $$

Using this combined occurrence formula for the above tire example having a 6.5 foot (1981.2 mm) tread length and a 7-inch (177.8 mm) tread width, and two small cuts or random characteristics whose positions on the tire tread could accurately be differentiated within 1 mm, the probability of random duplication would be 1 in every 62,042,320,896 tires:

$$ {}_{352,257}C_2 = \frac{352,257!}{(352,257-2)! \bullet 2!} = \frac{352,257 \bullet 352,256}{2} = 62,042,320,896 $$

Using a statistical analysis such as above to reach a conclusion in the forensic examination of footwear and tire impressions is generally not practiced; however, I would highly recommend reading Stone's full article as a way of better understanding the tremendous weight that random individual characteristics contribute toward establishing uniqueness of tires.

Changes in Individual Characteristics with Additional Wear

The examiner should always know the date the impressions were recovered (date of crime) and the date the tires were seized.[16] As a tire continues to be used, additional tread rubber is worn away and cuts, scratches, and other individual characteristics will eventually be lost. Additional individual characteristics will likely be acquired. If the perpetrator's vehicle is not recovered for a period of time after the crime, it may have traveled considerable distances, and that additional mileage may have worn away the shallow individual features. The absence of individual features that might have been present on the tread surface when the crime scene impression was made, but are no longer present, is not a basis for elimination. Deeper cuts or scratches in tires would likely remain for more miles than a shallow cut or scratch, but eventually all will change or wear away. A stone held in a groove or sipe might last for a mile or several thousand miles, depending on how tight and deep it is within the tread.

To illustrate the durability of the tread rubber on modern tires, five very shallow superficial cuts were intentionally placed within a small tread area.

[16]In a 2-year-old serial homicide case, I was asked to examine tires on a suspected vehicle. The first thing I did was to record the DOT numbers on each tire. The DOT numbers revealed the tires had been produced after the date of the crime. The examination ended.

These cuts were so shallow that their depth would be far less than 1/32 inch. A lift reflecting those characteristics was made on the day the damage was inflicted on the tire, at 118,798 miles. Three-thousand miles and almost 2 months later, at 121,798 miles, a second lift of the area was made. Figure 9.8 depicts both lifts and the arrows point to the five damaged areas. There are no significant changes to those areas, and all five cuts are still present 3,000 miles later.

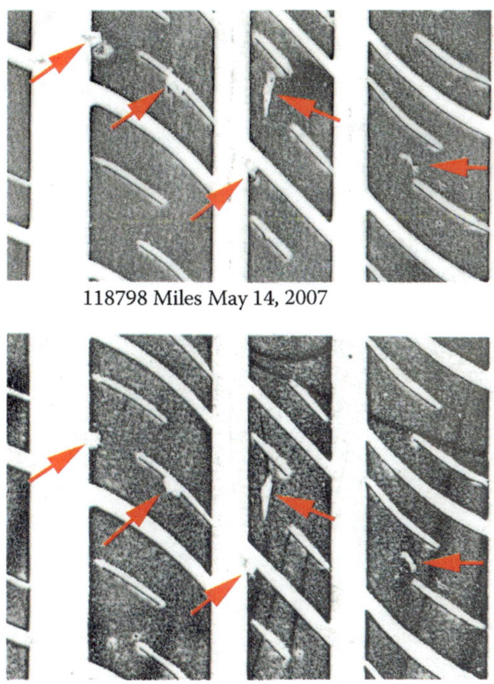

Figure 9.8

Examination Methodology and Procedure for Comparison of Tire Impressions

10

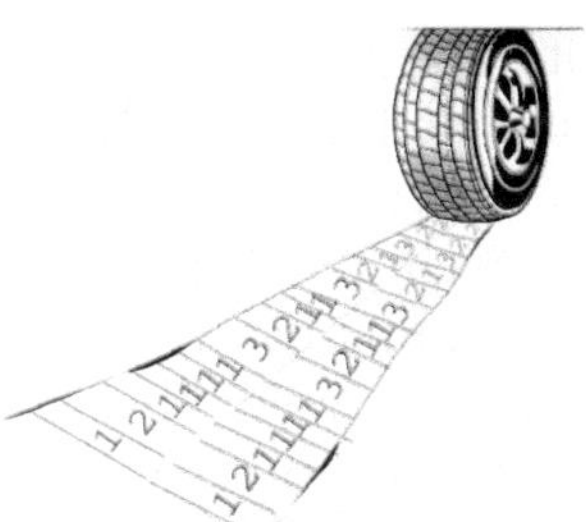

Structured Examination Procedure

Prior chapters have described and provided discussions on tread design, tread dimension, tread wear, and individual characteristics. This chapter uses this information while providing a method of comparing the crime scene tire impression with a known tire.

Many new or inexperienced examiners erroneously shortcut certain steps and hastily attempt to visually connect a tire to a crime scene impression. I cannot emphasize enough the importance for the examiner to follow a full and structured methodical procedure when making these comparisons. It should be emphasized that although the process described herein will provide assistance in the comparison and examination, the evidence in each case is different, and likewise, the conclusions and opinions rendered from the evidence in any particular case is not something you can obtain from a book or checklist, but rather from your training, experience, and a thorough examination. Examination results will sometimes be severely limited by the lack of detail or other factors, while other results will range in their conclusions from one of correspondence of tread design and dimension to those providing the necessary detail to enable a positive identification.

Note Taking

Along with conducting a thorough examination, taking good notes and keeping adequate photographs to document the examination is essential. For some, digital cameras and computers now provide an easier means for better documentation than may previously have been the normal practice. Good note-taking habits should not be regarded as more work for the examiner but a way to organize and clarify the entire work process. Good documentation is also a good way to self-check your work product.

Most laboratories have evidence receiving units that receive incoming casework and evidence, enter data into a computer, and track evidence within the laboratory. Regardless, the examiner should keep his or her own notes regarding what was examined, when it was received, the disposition of that evidence, and observations made during the examination. A list of evidence with a good description of each item should be created. This list not only serves as an organizational tool for the examiners by causing them to check and describe each item in detail, but provides an opportunity to make a good initial assessment of the evidence, the examinations that are requested, and any preparation that will be required before the examination can begin. Some examiners prefer to include this listing of evidence on a worksheet that will contain other relevant information about the case, including the case number, case title, the crime committed, the suspect's or victim's names, when the evidence was received, and the like. When this worksheet is composed on a computer, the same information may be used to create the basic format for the final examination report.

Figure 10.1 is an example of a worksheet in a tire impression case in which two cast impressions and two tires have been submitted for examination. Notice the description of the casts includes where each was poured. In the description of the tires, the brand name and line of tire, size, and DOT number are included, as well as an explanation of the location and date when those tires were manufactured. More detailed descriptions of evidence not only clarify information about the evidence, but reflect a more thorough manner of describing that evidence. Pages following that worksheet will accumulate as the examiner proceeds through the examination process. Examiners who take few notes are risking possible loss of information they might need at a later date. If they examine evidence and offer testimony or conduct additional examinations months or years later, they and their casework will benefit immensely from good note-taking habits. A worksheet and notes should be sufficiently clear and thorough to allow another examiner to review and completely understand all that has been done and the basis for any conclusion. The Scientific Working Group on Shoeprint and Tire Tread

Laboratory Worksheet

Case No. 07-1201-078
Arlee Bailey – victim
M. Whitford Hall – suspect
Homicide
Date of Crime: November 24, 2007

The following items were received on 12/1/07:

Crime Scene Items

Item #1 Cast of tire impression marked #5, recovered from edge of road adjacent to victim's body

Item #2 Cast of tire impression marked #6, recovered from turn-around area on opposite side of road from body

Two rear tires obtained from 2006 Honda Accord, bearing license number HIL 098 on November 28, 2007, further described as follows:

Item #3 B. F. Goodrich G-Force T/A, P215 50/R15 91H bearing DOT number BDXM FRL9 2307, and mold number 01-318933-03. The DOT number indicates this tire was manufactured in Miami, Oklahoma during the 23rd week of 2007.

Item #4 B. F. Goodrich G-Force T/A, P215 50/R15 91H bearing DOT number BDXM FRL9 2107, and mold number 01-318933-05. The DOT number indicates this tire was manufactured in Miami, Oklahoma during the 21st week of 2007

Notes:

Items #1-4 recd from evidence unit 12/1/07 10:25 am

Items #1 & 2 photographed and natural size prints made on 12/17/07

12-18-07 – in evidence bay - 2 known exemplars each made of #3 and #4 tires using wet media film and speedball oil based ink.

Figure 10.1. The first page of a simple worksheet providing basic information about the case, date of the crime, date the evidence was recovered and received, and a good description of that evidence is important. To this subsequent pages of the examiner's notes can be added.

Evidence (SWGTREAD) has published guidelines for casework documentation, which can be accessed online.[1]

Preparation for Examination

Tire examiners often face the obstacles of poor evidence recovery and documentation and, even worse, the submission of only part of the evidence. Although in some cases, the examiners themselves might be the ones who recovered the evidence, more often than not this evidence is collected, documented, and recovered by an investigator or crime scene technician who later transmits the evidence request to the laboratory. An unfortunate consequence of this is that the full amount of information and physical evidence that might otherwise contribute to the examination result may not be provided. The standard request of "Here's the evidence. What can you do with it" is often accompanied by only a portion of the evidence. This may be combined with an unfortunate case policy of "I only compare what they send me" and/or "I only make the comparisons they request." The forensic tire examiner should always ensure he or she has the totality of the evidence in its best form and consider all questions that may surround the items recovered and the examination of that evidence. As with other evidence, tire cases vary in the quantity of evidence and their complexity. One case may only involve a few photographs and/or a cast of a single impression. Another case may involve multiple tire impressions, several tires, and many photographic images and casts. On average, a tire case typically takes longer to work; takes more preparation, including the production of known exemplars of the tires, and involves direct contact between the examiner and the contributor to ensure all aspects of the case are understood and that all evidence has been submitted.

Below are some examples of different forms of tire evidence and general considerations that should be given those forms of evidence.

Original Impressions Original tire impressions, such as those on clothing or other objects the tire ran across, should be photographed for documentation and considered for possible enhancement methods.

Negatives of Tire Impressions All film negatives of both general crime scene and examination-quality photographs of tire impressions should be reviewed and evaluated to determine what enlargements need to be made. Any exposures of impressions that depict similar or same tread design as the suspect tire, and that have been properly taken with a scale, should be enlarged to natural (1:1) size.

[1] SWGTREAD Guidelines for Casework Documentation are published on the IAI Web site (www.theiai.org).

Digital Images of Tire Impressions The full digital files of each exposure are needed to ensure the greatest detail is available. Examiners should be aware that those contributing digital evidence often have an innocent misunderstanding of the existence and/or need for the full digital file. For instance, some departments routinely use film at the crime scene and then, when having that film commercially developed, opt to have a disc prepared with those images on it. They are later unaware of the fact those images on the disc may be considerably smaller digital files. The same may also occur when larger digital image files have been copied by someone else at a reduced file size. Be sure you have the full digital files. As with film, any exposures of impressions that depict the similar or same tread design as the suspect tire, and that have been properly taken with a scale, should be enlarged to natural (1:1) size.

Photographs or Computer Prints of Tire Evidence In the event photographs or prints of tire evidence are submitted, the examiner should request the original negatives or full digital files as mentioned above to ensure he or she has the greatest amount of detail for examination as well as the full content of the original exposure.

Notes and Scene Diagrams Any crime scene diagrams, photo logs, or other information should accompany photographic images of tire evidence to assist the examiner in interpretation and evaluation.

Casts All casts should be thoroughly air-dried if not already done. Air drying a freshly poured tire cast takes 48 hours. Only then should the cast be cleaned. Casts should be photographed with a scale and oblique light for documentation.

Lifts Any lifts of tire impressions should be photographed to both record and enhance the impression.

Tires Tires should be described fully, including the DOT number, noting the week and year the tires were manufactured, and the mold number. In those cases where a full examination is required, two full-circumference exemplars of each tire, as outlined in Chapter 4, should be made. When presented with the tires of a vehicle suspected of leaving the crime scene impressions, the examiner should be as thorough as possible and account for all tires that were on that vehicle, including the spare tire. Often a well-meaning investigator may believe he or she has been able to determine which tire made the impression as a result of an eye-witness account or his or her own theory of what might have happened. But it is always best for the forensic examiner to have and examine all of the tires similar in design. For example, two dead-end tracks at the scene might be presumed to be the two front tires of a vehicle pulling in straight and then backing out before leaving the scene. The suggestion here might be to only examine the front tires. However, there is the distinct possibility that the vehicle backed in with the rear tires leaving the impressions. Likewise, if sufficient time has passed between the date of the crime and the seizure of the tire, there is also the possibility that the tires have been rotated or that one tire may have been replaced by a full-size spare. Examination of only one or two tires might result in a false elimination of that vehicle and/or the failure to identify the actual tire that made the impression.

Elimination Tires Elimination impressions or photographic images of elimination tires should be accounted for and examined to confirm the crime scene impressions in question are not those of police vehicles, the victim's vehicle, or other vehicles not related to the crime.

Database or Tread Design Searches In cases where no suspect vehicle has been seized, searches for tread design information or track data may be called for. The process of searching tread design reference materials is discussed later in Chapter 12.

The Process of Examining Tire Impressions

A physical comparison of a crime scene impression with a tire should be performed as objectively as possible. In reality, there are only two possibilities, i.e., either the tire made the impression or it did not. Yet not all crime scene impressions will have retained sufficient detail to permit one of those definitive conclusions. The process of the examination is to go through a structured and unbiased method of comparison that will support or dispute those possibilities. During this examination process, the tread design and tread dimension, including any pitch sequence; the general condition of wear as well as specific wear features; and the presence of any individual characteristics in common, will be examined in that order. The examination of any of these areas will always be directly related to and limited by the detail that has been retained and recovered in the impression.

Tread Design and Dimension

Design is the most obvious feature of the tread and is the area examined first. The examination of design will allow for either inclusion or exclusion of the tire. If the questioned impression and tire are clearly two different designs, the tire can be excluded and there is no need for further examination. A tire of one design can simply not produce an impression of another design. An example of this is provided in Figure 10.2, where the tire is clearly a different tread design than depicted in the scene impression on the right. If this is the result, these differences should be documented and the examination between

Figure 10.2. The tire on the left is clearly a different design from the design in the crime scene tire impression on the right and therefore could not have produced that impression.

those two items is over. On the other hand, if the initial design comparison reveals the design is similar or the same, further examination will be necessary. Presuming the impression has sufficient detail for further examination, full-circumference inked impressions of the tire or tires of that design will be required. Examination of the design after this point will simultaneously include the examination of the tread dimensional features which are incorporated in that design.

The conclusion that the tread design in a crime scene impression is the same precise design and dimension as the tire being examined requires more than simply a visual inspection. Although in a general descriptive way, all tires in all sizes sold for a particular brand and line of tire could be said to be of the same design, the forensic examination will be more specific, taking into consideration any variables between tire molds, the position of tread wear indicators, and the specific size and arrangement of the tread blocks which will vary from tire size to tire size within the manufacturer's same line of tires.

If you are comparing several tires of the same design from one vehicle, the mold numbers found on the sidewalls will inform you whether all of the tires came from the same mold or different molds. Molds are frequently damaged during their use. Either the damage itself or subsequent repairs may distinguish one mold from others. A good case example of this involved the examination of four truck tires in a homicide case. During the examination, it became apparent to the examiner that a portion of a tread block on one tire was shorter than the corresponding tread blocks of the truck's three other tires. Contact with the manufacturer determined that the plaster cast model used to manufacture the molds for three of the four tires were damaged at that location and repaired, resulting in a slightly greater dimension of a tread block in three molds but not in the fourth tire mold (Figure 10.3).[2] Another case example involved the four rear tires on a rental truck used to dispose of the victim of a homicide. During mold production, four sipe blades were mistakenly positioned backwards near the parting line of a shell mold that produced one of the four tires. These characteristics were present in one of the four tire tracks that were cast at the scene. Examination of the mold at the tire manufacturing facility confirmed this. A photograph of this area of the shell mold is featured in Figure 10.4, showing two sipe blades pointing in opposite directions.

Using the Inked Impressions to Learn about Tire Design and Dimensions

Chapter 4 outlined the procedure for preparing two full-circumference inked impressions on clear wet media film. These impressions were obtained with an approximate 180-degree or half-rotation offset. Before proceeding with the comparison of tread design and dimension, an examiner should use the

Figure 10.3. The tire on the bottom has an elongated tread block as a result of repairs made to the plaster cast model during mold production. The tire at the top was from a mold that was not repaired and contained the original shorter tread block. (Case example courtesy of Teresa A. Stubbs, Sr. Crime Laboratory Analyst, Florida Department of Law Enforcement, Tampa, FL.)

[2] Case example and photographs contributed by Teresa A. Stubbs (Sr. Crime Laboratory Analyst, Florida Department of Law Enforcement, Tampa, FL), June 14, 2007.

known inked impressions to become familiar with the tread design as well as possible slight variations between tires of the same design, examples of which were provided in Figures 10.3 and 10.4. To do this, place both of the clear inked impressions of the tire being examined side by side on a table or workbench and in the same direction, as shown in Figure 10.5. It helps to place a piece of chart board behind the impressions to allow for better contrast. At this point, you may already be able to visually determine that the tread blocks of the tire design vary in size, i.e., that the tire being examined has noise treatment. Next, take the end of one impression and place it over top of the other inked impression so that its end is over the first few inches of the opposite end of the inked impression on the bottom. Figure 10.6A represents a segment of one of the known tire impressions in Figure 10.5 and has been colorized blue, and Figure 10.6B represents a segment of the second

Figure 10.4. Case example where one mold had some sipe blades inserted backwards. The red arrows point to one sipe blade inserted correctly and one of four blades that were positioned incorrectly. This produced an impression that was visibly different on one tire but not on the others, which came from different molds. Also notice the bent sipe indicated by the blue arrow.

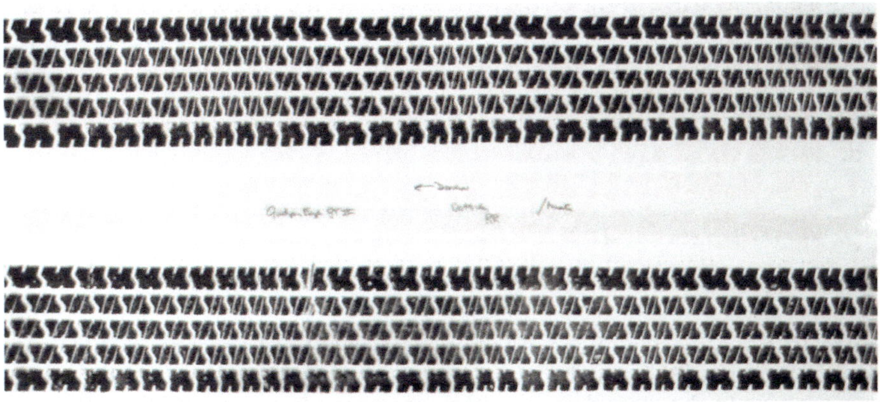

Figure 10.5. A portion of two full-circumference inked impressions laid side by side. An initial study of these and the tread block sizes and pitch sequence will assist in the examination of the crime scene impression.

known impression of the same tire and has been colorized red. In real case work, as in Figure 10.5, these would both be full-circumference impressions offset about 180 degrees from one another, but for illustration purposes in this book, shorter sections are illustrated. In casework, to see how often the tread block sizes and pitch arrangement correspond, move the top impression over the bottom impression one tread block at a time until you reach the point where the tread blocks all superimpose exactly. This result is shown in Figure 10.6C, which is a composite of Figure 10.6A, which is superimposed over Figure 10.6B and fits perfectly, producing the purple combination. Getting the tread block sizes to superimpose exactly confirms there was no slippage or distortion when the impressions were produced. Moving one

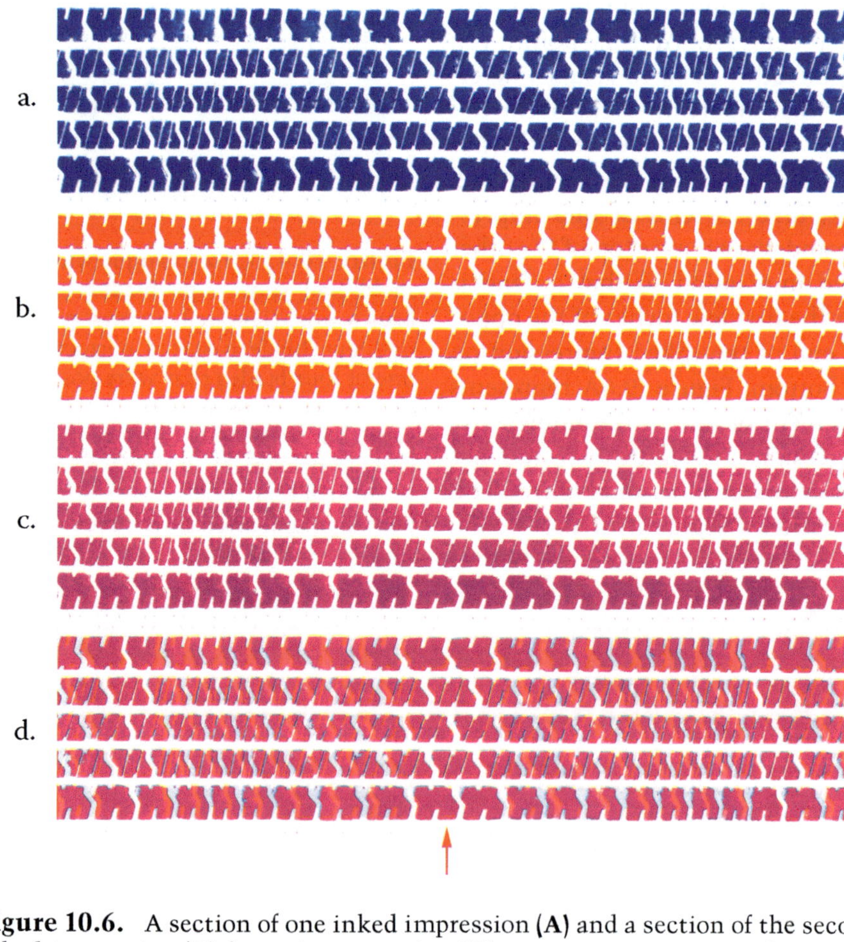

Figure 10.6. A section of one inked impression **(A)** and a section of the second inked impression **(B)** from the same tire. When one is superimposed over the other running in the same direction, they correspond perfectly **(C)**, but when one is placed over the other in the opposite direction, they do not superimpose **(D)**. This means this tire has directional noise treatment, i.e., the pitch sequence on one side of the tire is different than on the other side.

inked impression over the other also provides some familiarity regarding the features of the overall design and tread blocks and how the pitch sizes of the tread blocks vary in size and shape around the tire's circumference. Next, take the top inked impression, turn it around 180 degrees in the opposite direction, and repeat the process, running it over the bottom impression one tread block at a time from one end to the other. This process will likely reveal that one side of the tire has a different pitch sequence or noise treatment than the other.[3] Figure 10.6D is a composite of a portion of Figure 10.6A running in the opposite direction over Figure 10.6B. Nowhere along the full length of each impression does one impression superimpose over the other, meaning the majority of the tire will have a different pitch sequence on one side than the other. Because they do not match in the opposite direction, they have directional noise treatment. This is the reason why the coloration in Figure 10.6D is scattered. A very small area in Figure 10.6D, indicated by the red arrow, illustrates how occasionally a small isolated area of tread blocks will superimpose, but clearly not a larger area. Tires having directional noise treatment might contain very short segments (2 to 6 inches) of the same pitch sequence in the opposite direction. This feature is not one that is visually detectable when simply placing the two impressions side by side, as in Figure 10.5, or by just looking at the tread design of the actual tire. Directional noise treatment will only become detectable when trying to superimpose one impression over the other running in opposite directions. If you can match the full design in the opposite direction, then the tire does not have directional noise treatment. It should be re-stated here that virtually all passenger and light truck tires now have directional noise treatment. Tires that have directional tread designs or asymmetrical tread designs are visually obvious. Figure 10.7 depicts a section of a directional tread design, and the same section running in the opposite direction. It is easy to see that the tread design is directional.

Going through the above described procedure confirms the quality and accuracy of the exemplars and provides insight into the features of the tire design you are examining and will prove useful later when comparing the tire with the crime scene impressions.

Next, take one of the clear inked impressions and wrap it around the tire it came from to synchronize it with the tread design of the tire (Figure 10.8). The inked impression should be matched with the precise parts of the tire it came from. There are a couple ways of doing this. If the tire has obvious cuts or scratches or other damage on the tread, the inked impression can be used to synchronize those areas of damage that have recorded on the inked impression with the location of the corresponding damage on the tire. Note

[3] In the case of directional tread designs and asymmetrical tread designs, it is already known that one side of the tire will be different from the other side.

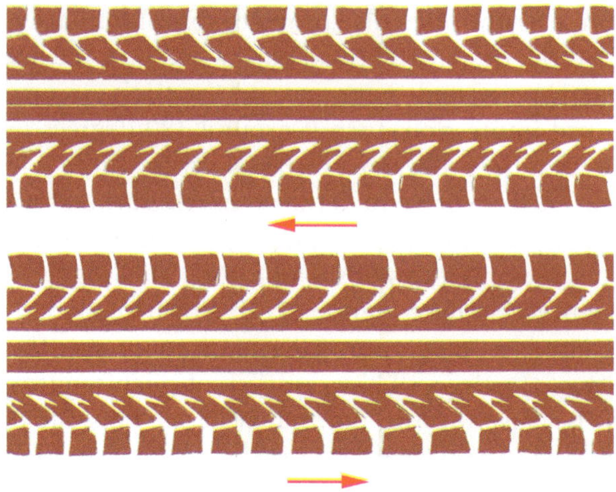

Figure 10.7. A directional tread design is visually obvious when placed in opposing directions.

Figure 10.8. Synchronizing the inked impressions with the tire they came from, including marking the positions of each of the tread wear indicators, is part of the preparation prior to examination.

that the impression was made under load and the tire you are examining is not under load, so the inked impression will not perfectly superimpose around the entire circumference. Also, be sure you are positioning the inked impression in the right orientation against the tire, i.e., ink side against the tread and the portion of the inked impression you labeled outside on the same side as the outside of the tire as it was mounted. Another way to synchronize the tire with the inked impressions is to simply use any segments you may have marked on the inked impression as it was being made and line them up with the respective part of the tire, as illustrated in Figure 4.22. If you still are having a hard time matching the inked impression to the tire, and the tire has noise treatment, then you could use the varied pitch lengths and pitch sequence to help with this. Find a distinct area on the tire where the pitch varies dramatically, such as an area where perhaps there is a small tread block followed by a large tread block and then three small tread blocks. Then look for the same sequence on areas on the inked impression and see if the other tread portions also match.

Once the clear known impression is synchronized with the tire, mark both the tire and the inked impression in a way that will allow you to easily find these same locations again. Then, with the inked impression still held in place around the tire, locate each tread wear indicator and, using a colored marker, mark each precise tread wear indicator position. The tread wear indicators should be marked across the full tread design (Figure 10.8). Figure 10.9 depicts three of the tread wear indicators marked in red. Note the uneven spacing of the tread wear indicator positions on this particular tire, which had tread wear indicators in eight positions instead of the minimum six positions. When the tread wear indicator positions have been marked on the first inked impression, the second inked impression can be superimposed on top of the first inked impression and the respective tread wear indicator positions transferred to the second impression.

You now have two full-circumference inked impressions on clear film that can quickly be associated with the respective corresponding areas of the actual tire and that also have the tread wear indicators marked on them. You can now superimpose the known exemplars over similar known exemplars made of other tires of this design being examined in the same case. This will provide a way to become aware of any mold variations due to bent or missing sipes, mold repairs, different locations of tread wear indicators and any other relevant variations between tires of the same design from one vehicle.

After this preparation and procedure, the examination of the tread design and dimension can continue. More often than not, the full crime scene impression has not retained good detail over the entire impression. Whether examining a photograph or cast, selecting an area that contains the clearest representation of the tread blocks is always a good place to begin the comparison. Also, areas where the tread block sizes change dramatically, such as an area with a large tread block adjacent to two smaller tread

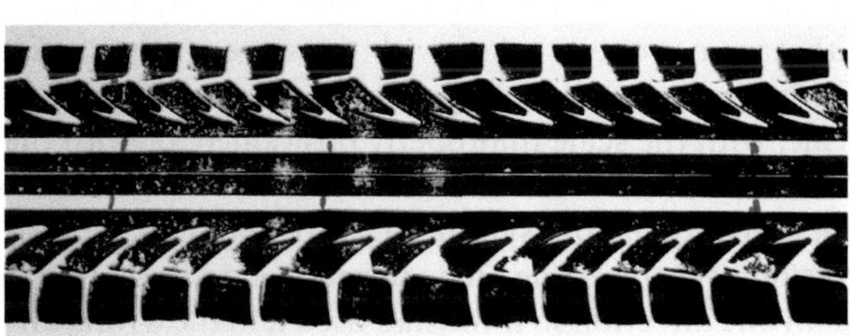

Figure 10.9. The tread wear indicators marked on this known impression will assist during examination.

blocks, are easier to work with. Superimpose the end of the inked impression over the selected area of the questioned impression. Then move the known impression, one tread block at a time, in an attempt to locate corresponding areas where the tread blocks and their specific sizes and pitch arrangement correspond. It is important to emphasize that this should be done initially with a short section of the crime scene impression, perhaps only including 4 to 6 tread blocks. If you find an area matches, then look and see if other tread blocks on either side of this area also match, eventaully expanding the comparison over the full impression. The object is to find a location where the inked impression will superimpose over the entire crime scene impression. During this examination process, always be aware of the relationship between an inked impression and the crime scene impression. For instance, when examining an original impression or photograph of an impression, the clear inked known impression is simply superimposed over top of those items, ink side up. However, when examining cast impressions, because the casts were turned over when lifted from the ground, the known impression will also have to be turned over (ink side against the cast) before superimposing it over the cast during the examination.

This above described process of examining the tread design and dimension by moving the known impression over the crime scene impression needs to be done patiently. As stated above, you are attempting to locate an area or areas of the tire and impression where there is agreement of both the physical size and pitch sequence of the tread blocks. In cases where there is directional noise treatment, as is the case of almost all passenger and light-truck tires, it is likely that only one area of the inked impression will correspond with the precise size and arrangement of tread blocks recovered in the crime scene impression. If one or more areas agree, then further examination of those areas will be made. For tires not having any noise treatment, the tire will contain tread blocks of one size only and there will be many areas that will fit.

Because this dimensional analysis portion of the examination is extremely sensitive to slight inaccuracies of size, only the best and most original evidence should be used. This would include, first and foremost, any casts or original impressions recovered. If examining photographs, only photographs of the impression that were properly taken with the scale on the same level as the bottom of the impression will likely produce any success. Photographs taken without a scale, with the scale improperly positioned, or with the camera at an angle will normally be of limited use for any dimensional evaluation. If the tire is not a directional or asymmetrical tread design, be sure to run the inked impression over the crime scene impression in both directions. It will likely only fit in one direction so if you had tried it in the wrong direction first, you would not have been able to find any agreement. If an area containing the same sequence of tread block sizes cannot be found, be sure to re-attempt this with the second inked impression as the crime scene impression may coincidentally intersect the end of the first inked impression which would make finding the corresponding pitch sequence using that inked impression impossible. This was illustrated in Figure 4.5 in Chapter 4.

At this point, there are a couple possibilities. You might find the tire's inked impression corresponds in tread design and dimension with the crime scene impression. An example of this is provided in Figure 10.10. If so, you would then locate the corresponding areas on the tire itself and continue the examination directly between the impression and the tire, looking for wear and individual characteristics in those areas. It is also possible that you might have difficulty locating an area of the inked impression that corresponds precisely with the crime scene impression. This means that either the tire did not make the impression or there is some legitimate reason why the precise pitch size arrangement is not lining up. It is important to understand that there are many reasons why the tread pitch arrangement of the tire that made the impression may not correspond exactly, even though the tire made the impression. Some of these reasons are discussed below.

Figure 10.10. The tread design and dimension of the tire's ink exemplars correspond with the cast.

Confirming Correspondence in Tread Design and Dimension

Examiner Experience

There is a certain degree of knowledge, experience, methodology, and patience involved in this type of examination. It is entirely possible that the tire does correspond in design and dimension with the crime scene impression, but the examiner has simply not been able to establish this. Physical comparisons of crime scene impressions with several tires is often time consuming and tedious. If the impression is the same design, but the dimensions and pitch sequence of the inked impression do not appear to correspond, a number of reasons might account for this. If you have carefully followed the above procedure and are frustrated, it may be wise to simply put the case aside for a day and later, with fresh eyes, start over and repeat the examination procedure. Always be sure you have used both of the known impressions, running them in both directions over the crime scene impression. If your experience is limited, you may wish to get assistance from a more experienced examiner. Some of these examinations turn out to be very straightforward, but others are more challenging.

Using Tread Wear Indicators

Tread wear indicators are invaluable to help locate and confirm the precise area of a tire that potentially made the crime scene impression. This is why in the above described procedures it was suggested to transfer the locations of the tread wear indicators to the inked impressions. Tread wear indicators will not always be retained in the crime scene impression, but when they are, the location of a tread wear indicator in relation to the size and arrangement of the adjacent tread blocks is an excellent way to confirm you have the proper location on the tire. It is also useful to eliminate other portions of the tire in the same way. The varied possibilities that you might encounter with regard to tread wear indicators are discussed in Chapter 7. Figure 10.11 shows two areas of an inked impression over top of a crime scene cast. The tread wear indictors are lined up in both situations, but the pitch sequence of the various tread block sizes only corresponds with one.

Deflection Variables

The differences in the deflection of a tire on a hard surface versus its deflection in a softer surface such as soil, sand, or snow are known and demonstrable and were discussed in Chapter 7. A tire leaving its impression in a soft substrate will leave a slightly longer impression than its inked impression on a hard substrate. Receiving a cast of a deep impression will be a clue that differences may be encountered during the examination. This size variation will be along the circumference of the tire and could interfere with an examiner's attempts to find agreement of the arrangement of tread block sizes over the

Figure 10.11. The bottom portion of this photograph depicts the correspondence of the inked impression, including tread wear indicators (blue arrow). The top portion of this photograph depicts the non-correspondence of the tread blocks when the tread wear indicators are aligned, meaning this is not the proper position of the tire.

full impression. Some key points should be remembered. The deeper and longer the recovered portion of the crime scene impression is, the greater the differences that will likely exist. Shallow impressions and very short impressions may not reflect sufficient differences for this to be noticeable. In those instances where greater differences exist between the known and questioned impressions, the question to be addressed is whether those differences are due to deflection or whether they could be due to the impression being made by another tire of that design but of a different size.

When attempting to superimpose the known impression over the crime scene impression, deflection differences will not be noticeable within a short length of the impression. Thus the first thing to do is to try to align the tread blocks and pitch sequence between the known and questioned impression over a short section of four to six tread blocks. If you locate an area that corresponds in a short section but then gradually changes as you continue to move along the length of the impression, this is due to differences in deflection and simply requires you to make minor adjustments in the position of the known overlay. An example of this would be to find agreement between four tread blocks at one point with the superimposed impression and then find that after 10 inches there may be a 1/8-inch discrepancy between the position of the tread blocks at that point, then after 20 inches a 2/8-inch discrepancy in the same direction, and after 30 inches a 3/8-inch discrepancy in the same direction, etc. Figure 10.12 depicts an example depicting a section of a cast with the proper portion of known impression superimposed. This cast, taken in deep soil, is slightly larger than the known inked impression taken on a hard surface, due to differences in deflection. The enlarged areas show the inked impression lined up properly over the cast at location 1, a very slight shift at location 2, and slightly more at location 3. On the other hand, if during an examination you were to find that a short area corresponded and then, all of a sudden, there was a significant disagreement in the size or position of the next tread block, as in the top picture of Figure 10.11, then this indicates that either you do not have the proper section of the tire that made this impression or the impression was made by another tire.

Inflation Differences

Inflation differences will present minor changes in the length of the impression, but the degree of difference is not a significant one. If you inflated the tire to its approximate recommended pressure when taking the known inked impressions, there would only be a measurable difference if the crime scene impression were made by a tire with substantially lower pressure and that difference would be very small. It would also be gradual.

Soil Movement and Condition

In cases of supersaturated soils, very loose soils, or other soils that are dimensionally unstable (e.g., peat), the dimensional features of a tire may not record accurately as the soil may actually move during and/or after the impression-making process, causing the dimensional features to actually change after they are impressed into the soil. This is not common, but I have seen this occur in both footwear and tire impressions. If you did not have first-hand knowledge of the crime scene conditions, you may want to talk to the crime scene technician who recovered this impression regarding information about the soil conditions.

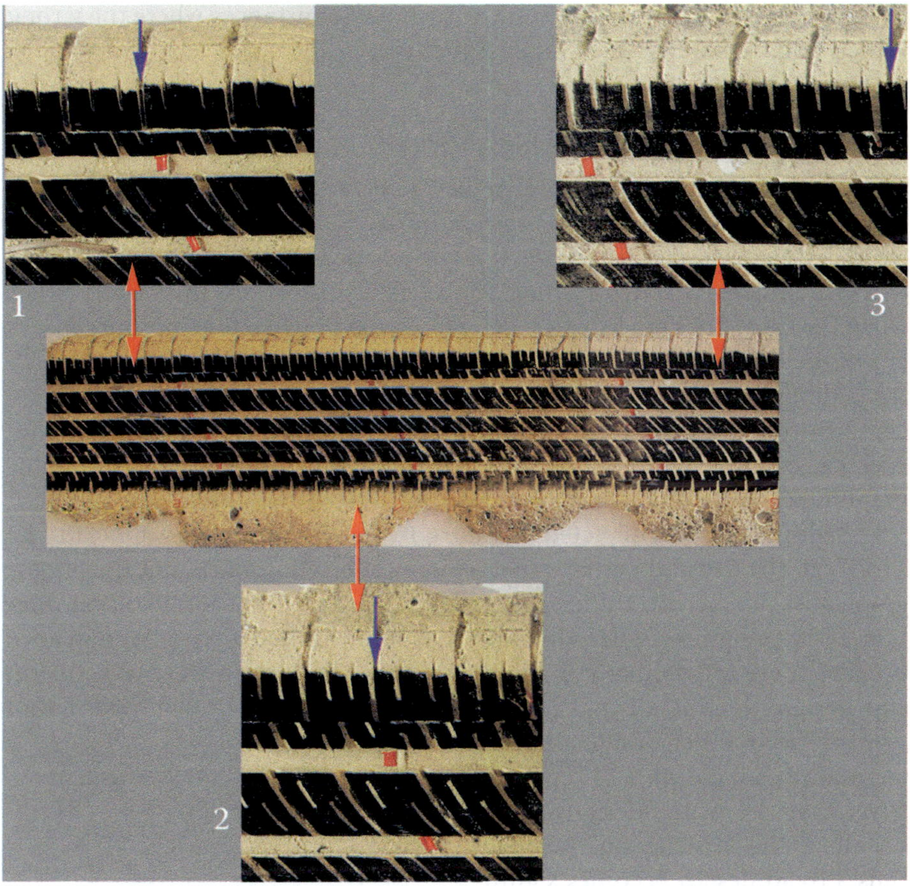

Figure 10.12. Deflection difference between impressions made in soft substrate and on a hard surface creates slight variances in the dimensions between the two. In the center is a 3-foot long cast with the inked impression of the tire superimposed over it. At area *1* the alignment is perfect; at area *2*, the alignment is slightly off and at area *3* the alignment is further off. This very slight but gradual shift along the length of the cast is characteristic of deflection differences.

Possible Results Regarding Tread Design and Dimension

Different Tread Design

When the tread design recovered from the crime scene is determined to be different from that from the suspect vehicle, it can be said that the suspect vehicle, with the tires currently on it, could not have made that impression. An example of this is depicted in Figure 10.2. This limited examination and conclusion is extremely useful in the elimination of impressions at the scene, such as those made by emergency vehicles or other vehicles that may have passed through that area, but would also apply to instances where the wrong vehicle and tires were seized for examination.

Similar or Same General Tread Design

In some examinations it may only be possible to conclude that the tread design in a crime scene impression is similar to or the same as the general tread design of the suspected tire. It is entirely possible that impression failed to retain sufficient detail for a more thorough examination. This occurs either when the tread does not leave a clear impression or when the improper recovery of the evidence limits the examination. In those cases where a detailed tread design is not available, the examination may not allow a full design comparison, and it may only be possible to conclude the design is similar. A classic example of this is the situation where the only evidence is a photograph taken at an angle and a good distance from the impression and with poor lighting, such as depicted in Figure 10.13. The design may appear to be similar to the tire and perhaps the tire cannot be eliminated, but the photograph does not provide sufficient detail for an accurate or thorough examination. If the design is similar, this alone has some limited forensic significance because there are so many different tire tread designs in the marketplace, and design alone is all that is needed to discriminate tires of one design from those of other designs. Even a common tread design will represent fewer than 1% of the designs found on all of the vehicles on the road, thus a tread design becomes significant when the suspect vehicle's tread design turns out to be the same or similar as found at the crime scene. In these instances, of all the designs that the suspect vehicle could have potentially possessed, it contained a design either the same or similar enough to the extent that it could not be eliminated as having made the impression recovered from the crime scene. This conclusion does not prove that suspect vehicle's tires were the source of the impression but simply allows for that possibility. It should be recognized that the possibility also exists that another vehicle, having a tire(s) of the same

Figure 10.13. A poorly taken photograph will limit the examination of tread design and possibly prevent any meaningful examination.

or similar design, could also have left the impression. In conclusions of this sort, varied reactions are often expressed by prosecutors and defense attorneys. Defense attorneys are quick to accept eliminations of their client's tires when the design is different but often object to the admissibility of conclusions in cases where the design is determined to be similar or the same but identification cannot be made. These objections would include attacks on the relevance, because so many tires of that design have been produced and the argument that a jury can make this decision themselves and do not need an expert to do this. This of course is not true, as jurors are ill prepared to make any physical comparisons and certainly are not aware of many aspects of the comparison, such as subtle changes in wear, pitch variation, and other technological aspects of tires and the impressions they leave. On the other side, the prosecutor will often choose not to put this conclusion into evidence for the simple reason that they are not aware of the significance of a design-only conclusion, that being that any particular design represents fewer than 1% of the tire designs on vehicles.

Note there are also cases where the tire either did not record clearly or there was a problem in the recovery, and the detail recovered warranted the conclusion that the impression was insufficient to permit any meaningful examination.

Tread Design and Dimension Correspond

When the crime scene impression and a tire correspond with regard to both tread design and tread dimension, as depicted in Figure 10.10, this is a significant examination conclusion. It means the suspect tire contains the specific tread design and dimensional features that are capable of having produced the tire impression recovered from the crime scene. This conclusion must recognize the possibility that other tires possessing the same tread design and dimensional features could also have produced that impression. This would include other tires of the same design and size from the suspect vehicle as well as other tires of the same design and size from other vehicle sources.

Continuing the Examination Process

Once it can be concluded that the specific tread design and dimension of a crime scene impression corresponds with a portion or portions of a suspect tire, the examination thereafter should be made directly between that impression and the precise portion(s) of the actual tire. Up to this point in the examination, the inked impressions have been used as a tool, a sort of blueprint of the tire in its current condition, to assist in locating the area or areas of the tire that contained the same pitch sequence and tread block sizes that could have made the impression. Although the known impressions may continue to assist in the examination of wear and individual characteristics, the greatest amount of detail is contained on the tire itself. Thus the examination should now focus, one tread block at a time, between the crime scene impression and the dimensionally corresponding area(s) of the tire itself. High-intensity oblique lighting should be used as needed to help see and enhance the fine detail in casts and tires. Because the tread blocks are similar and easy to loose track of, it helps to stick a piece of tape or other temporary mark on a specific location of the crime scene impression as well as one on the corresponding tread block of the tire as a beginning reference point. In this way, it is always easy to keep track of each tread block you are comparing in the crime scene impression with the corresponding tread block of the tire. Figure 10.14 depicts two known inked impressions positioned over a cast representing two overlapping tire impressions. The several temporary pieces of colored tape are being used to help maintain the proper relationship between the tires being examined and each cast impression. The tires will be similarly marked. When characteristic in common are confirmed and deemed significant, a more permanent form of marking and documentation can be used.

Figure 10.14. Two cast impressions with inked impressions positioned. The colored pieces of tape have been placed on the cast and inked impressions as well as the tire to help organize a systematic examination with the respective portions of the tires.

Wear Characteristics

The next area to examine is the tire wear. The tread rubber used in tires is exceptionally durable; nevertheless, its constant contact and movement over the road surfaces gradually wears that rubber away. The forensic tire examination concerns itself with the degree and position of wear that is present on the tire at the time it is examined and whether or not this wear corresponds with the wear reflected in the crime scene impression. The agreement of general wear characteristics can provide significant and detailed features that contribute toward the individualization of the tire. Wear is a changing and variable class characteristic, and for that reason the examination of the wear on a tire should always take into consideration the date of the crime and the date on which the tires were seized to account for any additional wear that might have occurred between those dates. A vehicle seized within a short period of time after the crime will have tires in essentially the same condition of wear. A vehicle seized several months later may or may not show a similar condition of wear, depending on the mileage added since the crime. To this extent, it should be noted that many tires on passenger vehicles and even light trucks have high tread wear expectancies. Thus the wear features on tires of a vehicle driven an additional few thousand miles since the date of the crime will not likely change significantly. An example of this was shown in Figure 9.8.

During the examination, the general condition of wear and the condition of the sipe wear on each tread block should be compared between the tire and impression, one tread block at a time. When conducting this type of comparison, the detail present in the crime scene impression is the only limiting factor. It is normal for one particular portion of the impression to be clearer than others. Figure 10.15 depicts a photograph of a portion of a cast depicting several commonly encountered features, including a small cut and a stone hold (green arrows), tread wear indicators (blue arrows), an area of less detail which will limit some aspects of the comparison with the tire at that location (yellow arrow), and sticks, stones, and debris (top red arrows) that were near or on the surface of the ground when the tire left its impression, which will often interfere or prevent examination of those areas. Flow marks sometimes encountered in casting (bottom red arrow) can also interfere with detail. The interpretations of these items are fairly straightforward. A stone trapped between a sipe or groove (stone hold) is easily distinguished from a loose stone on the ground that was trapped in the cast as it was poured. The same is true for sticks, grass, or other debris.

As the examination proceeds, significant similarities or dissimilarities should be noted and documented. A car with four tires of the same size and design, suspected of leaving an impression at the scene of a crime may have the same class characteristics of tread design and dimension, but one tire

Figure 10.15. Casts reflect not only the detail of the tire but also unwanted detail of the surface and debris.

may vary in its wear features that might distinguish that tire from the rest. This could be due to lack of tire rotation or due to one of many issues on that particular vehicle that is causing one tire to wear differently than the others. It could also be due to the prior use of a full-size spare tire to replace one of the original four tires. If sufficient detail is retained in the crime scene impression, a close examination of these four tires will often enable elimination of three tires and inclusion of the fourth.

The correspondence of wear is significant in that it further narrows down the tires of a particular design and dimension that could have left the impression.

In a case where the driver's rear tire was in relatively unworn condition and the passenger rear tire had worn shoulders that corresponded respectively with two scene impressions, the conclusion would have added significance. When specific wear such as a portion of a sipe that is worn away corresponds, the number of other tires of that design and size that would have a sipe worn in that same way at the same position in the pitch arrangement would be extensively less, thus making a conclusion of this type an even more significant one.

Tread Depth

Impressions may not accurately represent the true condition of wear of the tire. As previously discussed, tires will not leave an accurate representation of their condition of wear and tread depth if the full depth of their tread does not sink into the substrate, if their tread is packed with snow or mud, and/or if loose soil falls back into the impression.

As illustrated in Chapter 8, sipes and smaller grooves usually have different depths, meaning the more shallow portions of a groove or sipe will wear away before other portions of the same sipe. These changed features are on the surface of the tread and are thus visible, in even two-dimensional and shallow three-dimensional impressions. When sipes in the impression are clear and present, they are better visual indicators of the condition of wear than measuring the tread depth. Figure 10.16 depicts a tire whose worn condition reflects portions of sipes. Once continuous, the remaining portions of the sipes are now interrupted. Both the tire and cast possess similar sipe conditions.

Forensic Significance of Wear

Correspondence of wear, even specific wear features, is never a basis for the identification of a tire. Thousands of tires are produced in each design and size and their wear characteristics gradually change as they are used. The observation of a specific degree of wear on a tire or even a specific sipe wear characteristic could never be said to be unique to only one tire. But wear, in many cases, will contribute significant weight to the overall examination. Wear is useful in both elimination and inclusion. Confirmable and clear wear characteristics can serve to further narrow down the number of tires that could have made the impression.

Because wear changes over time and can be misrepresented in impressions, the only safe, accurate, and reliable way to use wear in examinations is to rely only on those features that reproduce clearly in the crime scene impression. Using tread depth measurement of crime scene impressions, particularly in cases where there is poor retention of detail, could erroneously result in elimination of the actual tire that made the impression. Elimination of a tire due to wear can only be made when clear impressions offering clear detail can be confirmed to be different from the tire, enabling a conclusion that, at the time the tire impression was made, the tire could not have had the same wear characteristics.

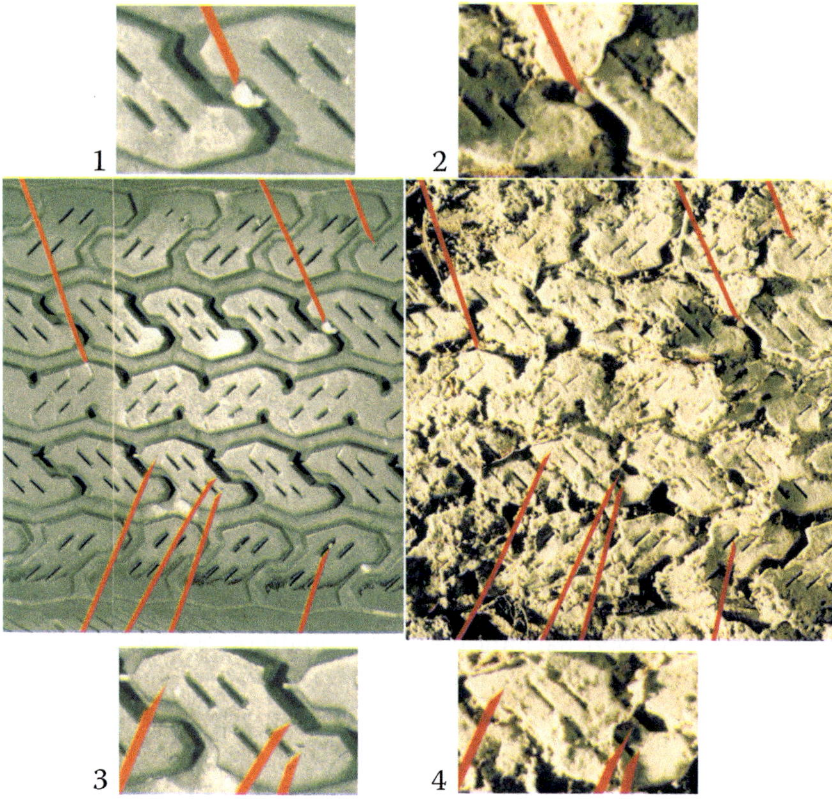

Figure 10.16. A small portion of a 3-foot-long cast that was identified with a tire. **(1)** and **(2)** depict a stone hold and **(3)** and **(4)** depict three small cuts.

Individual Characteristics

Individual characteristics, discussed in Chapter 9, are those features randomly acquired during a tire's use that contribute to or make a particular tire different from others. They include characteristics where rubber has been removed from that tire, including scratches, cuts, tears, abrasions, and other physical damage. They also include the acquisition of stones that have become wedged in grooves and sipes, other debris that might have become embedded in the tire's surface, and patches from tire repairs. An identification of a tire, i.e., the conclusion that a tire, to the exclusion of all others, made a particular impression, can only be based on the presence of these randomly acquired individual characteristics. The incorrect evaluation of these characteristics could result in the failure to identify the tire that made the impression, the erroneous identification of an impression with a tire that did not make it, or the identification of an impression when it was simply not warranted based on the evidence at hand. As with the other components of the tire examination, it is necessary to be as objective as possible. During the assessment of these features both the quality and quantity of the individual characteristics will relate to the weight and relevance they will provide to the conclusion. Figure 10.16 depicts a short portion of a 3-foot dental stone cast from a homicide scene. Two areas have been enlarged to show individual features. The first area shows a stone hold in the cast impression (2) and the corresponding stone still present in the tire (1) and the second area shows three small but clear cuts that correspond with individual features on one tread block. These characteristics were accompanied by numerous additional individual and wear characteristics allowing for a positive identification of that tire. The cast was taken from the impression shown in Figure 3.42. Figure 10.17 depicts a small area of a tire and a cast where portions contained excellent detail enabling identification.

Clarity of Characteristics

Clarity is the qualitative portion of the examination and an extremely important part of the individualization process. An individual characteristic must appear with sufficient clarity in order to reliably associate its features with those respective features on the tire. For the individual characteristic to

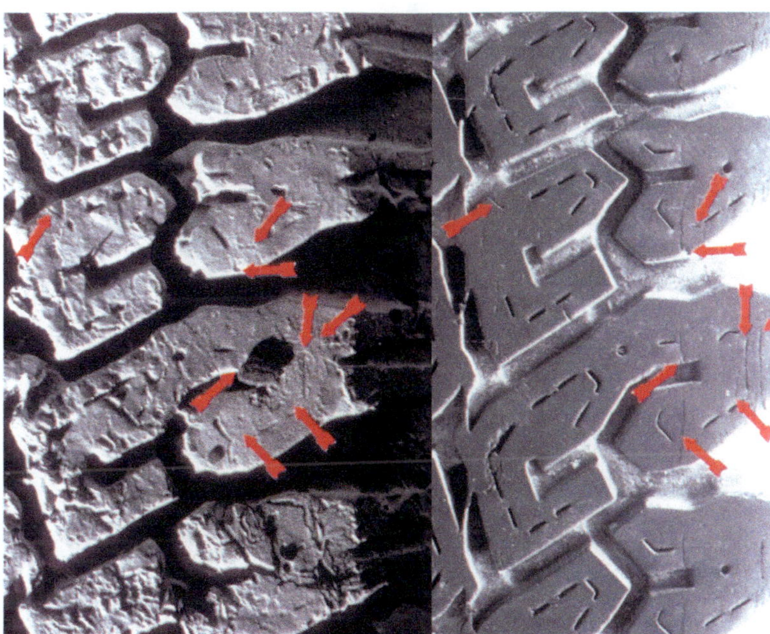

Figure 10.17. This cast contained excellent detail in some but not all areas. In those areas that did retain detail, there were sufficient individual characteristics to identify the tire.

carry much weight, the clarity must allow for a cause (the feature on the tire) and effect (the feature in the impression) relationship to be confirmed. From my training days, I will share with you some excellent advice I was given with one simple phrase—"If it's there, it's there, and if it's not, it's not." This old expression simply means sometimes you will find some features present with sufficient clarity, while other times there may be some indication the feature is present, but the level of clarity is insufficient to be sure. Figure 10.18 depicts a photograph of an area on a cast that attention was brought to because of the presence of a small cut on the tire and the resulting cut-like shape produced on the inked impression of the tire. The area of the cast that corresponds with that spot on the tire is circled in red. Notice that the detail in the cast in that area shows some possible disturbance, but it is not clear and it is not the same shape as the cut on the tire and inked impression. There is insufficient clarity to relate one to another. It is entirely possible that the disturbance reflected in the cast is simply due to the topography of the soil and had nothing to do with the cut on the tire. On the other hand, Figure 10.19 depicts a small cut on a tire that does correspond well with a characteristic in the cast.

It is important to understand that individual characteristics in crime scene impressions never are exact reproductions of the respective individual

Figure 10.18. The circled area on top reflects a disturbance of some type but does not reflect the shape of the cut that was on the tire, as represented in the inked impression. Without some relationship, it is not possible to simply presume one has caused the other.

Figure 10.19. A cut on a tire and the resulting clear cut in the impression recovered by the cast.

characteristics that caused them. In fact, even in repetitive inked impressions the same characteristic will vary slightly. This is normal and demonstrable. But sufficient transfer of detail to establish some relationship, i.e., that the characteristic in the tire can be linked to that respective feature in the impression, is essential. The clearer the relationship is, the greater weight that feature carries because of its increased reliability and detail.

I have found that some examiners tend to have a lower expectation of what is required in terms of clarity. I have witnessed on many occasions, in both casework and classes, instances where examiners point to a feature in a tire and then point to the corresponding area of the crime scene impression, yet no clear or confirmable features are present. It is a serious mistake in impression analysis for an examiner to find an individual feature on the tire and then try to convince themselves that they can see it in the crime scene impression when there is simply insufficient clarity to do so. As a result of this type of improper evaluation, I have seen trial charts with arrows pointing to areas where little or nothing can be seen. Some of these examiners actually believe that they can actually see things that others cannot see. This is simply not being objective nor reasonable and will likely lead to erroneous conclusions. As a rule of thumb, any characteristic that is used as part of the basis of your opinion should be sufficiently clear that an average observer can see it when it is brought to his or her attention. If this is not the case, then the value of that characteristic must be reduced or perhaps should not be used at all.

Weight or Value of Characteristics

On the issue of how much weight is put on a particular characteristic, it might seem that studies could be made to tabulate the frequency of various individual features, i.e., that a simple count of individual characteristics such as cuts of different shapes and sizes could be tabulated by looking at a large number of tires, to the extent that the frequency of any cut of a particular size and shape cut could be predicted. But the issue of individual characteristics is not that simple. If a person were to collect used tires of the same design and try to count the frequency of similarly sized and shaped individual characteristics, he or she would find all of the individual characteristics were different from one another based on their combined position, size, shape, and orientation. Thus there would be a continually growing category of individual characteristics, all being one-of-a-kind. An attempt at making a study of this type would simply confirm what is already known, i.e., that individual characteristics are extremely random and unique in their size, shape, and orientation and can be acquired on any position of the tread surface. The only way to realize the weight or value of these features would be through a mathematical computation such as was provided by Stone and referenced in Chapter 9 and/or based on a complete understanding of this process along with the experience of the examiner.

Absence of Individual Characteristics

Failure to find a corresponding individual characteristic in a crime scene impression for each and every one that appears on the tire is in no way a basis for elimination of that tire. This is because these features, many of which are very small and/or shallow, do not reproduce in most cases, as the conditions need to be just right for them to do so. It is also because the tire is constantly acquiring individual characteristics, so additional individual characteristics may now be present on the tire that were not on that tire on the date the crime scene impression was made.

Partial Width Impressions

Some impressions at crime scenes do not represent a full recording of the width of the tread surface but only a portion. Regardless, the same analysis can still be performed with regard to tread design and dimension, including the pitch sequence of a suspected tire, followed by the examination of wear and individual characteristics. Although fragmented or partial width tread impressions, by volume, contain less information for the examiner to compare, the potential of a good result is still there.

Reporting Results

The purpose of a written report is to effectively transfer the results of your forensic examination to the person who requested it. Although the report may be addressed and directed to an investigator or other individual who submitted the evidence to you, the report may also be read by the prosecutor, defense counsel, and others and may even be introduced to the jury as a court exhibit. Those who read the report are going to have distinctly different reasons for reading it. Most will not have access to or any familiarity with the evidence. Reports that only offer brief or inadequate descriptions of the items that were examined and/or that offer brief opinions may not provide adequate information for the reader to fully comprehend and understand what was examined, what the results were, or what those results mean. Adding pictures to the report provides all who read the report with an understanding and some familiarity, albeit small, of the exact cast(s) or photograph(s) that were examined as well as the tread design of the tire(s) examined.

In the results portion of the report, it is important to recognize that each case and each examination result is based on different evidence. Thus the wording for each observation or opinion should simply report what was observed and what can be concluded from those observations. In cases where the final opinion is that of an identification or elimination, the core wording of the results is rather uncomplicated and could simply be expressed and understood as follows:

> "It was determined that the K4 passenger rear tire made the impression represented by the Q21 cast."

> "It was determined that the K3 driver's side rear tire did not make the impression represented by the Q21 cast."

In many examinations, identifications or eliminations are not possible, and the conclusions that have been reached vary immensely. Attempting to provide a final opinion of those examination results with a choice of only a few predetermined phrases will often be inadequate and will often result in a misunderstanding of the results. Instead, the results in these instances should be filled with details about what was observed and what could be concluded, such as correspondence or dissimilarities in tread design, tread dimension, general wear, and so forth. To bring some continuity to this process, SWGTREAD has published "Standard Terminology for Expressing Conclusions of Forensic Footwear and Tire Impression Examinations."[4] This resource specifies certain core terminology and discourages other terminology for use in connection with footwear and tire examination results. These are guidelines only and are not meant to be the only choice or the actual recommended

[4] SWGTREAD Standard Terminology for Expressing Conclusions of Forensic Footwear and Tire Impression Examination guidelines are published on the IAI Web site (www.theiai.org).

wording for any particular examination. Examination results should ideally provide additional information and, as needed, be supplemented with photographs either inserted directly in the report or provided as an attachment.

Scientific Method

Physical comparisons, such as a tire impression examination, are straightforward and best conducted by using a simple application of the scientific method. This includes identifying the problem (did the tire make a certain impression?); developing basic hypotheses (the tire made the impression/the tire did not make the impression); making tests or comparisons to test the hypotheses (making known exemplars and physical comparisons between the impression and the tire); and projecting a conclusion (your opinion).

In this chapter I have outlined considerable information that can be used to proceed through a tire examination in a very structured and organized way, provided the crime scene impressions reflect sufficient detail. During these procedures, it is important to reach out and assure you have all of the best evidence and to keep as objective as possible, reaching an opinion based only on observations that are clear and confirmable and expressed in a fair and plainspoken way.

Additional Comments

There are those who maintain the only way to prove there are not two tires, shoes, or fingerprints exactly alike would be to actually check all the shoes, tires and fingerprints in the world. If this could be done, there would be no need for forensic tire examiners, but instead, we would simply have ordinary individuals check all the tires in the world. Of course this would not be practical or possible, regardless of the case importance. Further, this argument does not really disagree with the concept of uniqueness and natural variation, but addresses the burden of proof some believe is necessary before anything could be determined to be unique.

Others argue that physical comparisons are highly subjective and not very objective. Objective observations are those that are outwardly factual and uncontested. A general example would be the statement, "It is pouring down rain outside." The fact that it is raining is not an opinion but an objective statement of fact. On the other hand, the term *subjective* is a statement based, in part, on someone's opinion. An example would be, "The sandwich tastes good." Another person tasting the same sandwich might have a different opinion. With regard to a physical tire examination, an objective observation would be clearly demonstrable tread design, tread dimension, general wear, and individual characteristics. Although any forensic examination will have some subjectivity, the forensic tire examiner, with proper training and experience, who makes a structured, methodical analysis of tire evidence can provide the basis for his opinion in a demonstrable and objective way.

Presenting Tire Evidence in Court

11

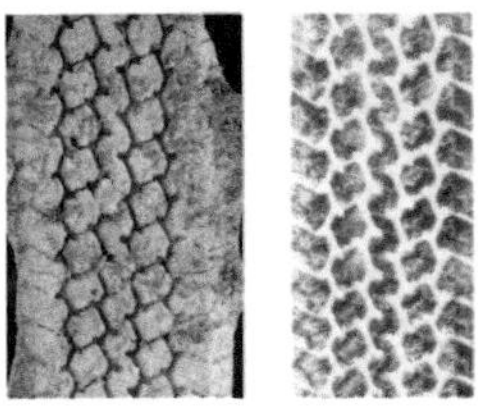

Preparation

The role of the expert witness in court is to educate the jury regarding his or her knowledge about the evidence in a way the jury can then understand and apply the appropriate weight to that evidence. Thus, an important role and responsibility of forensic tire examiners is to use the best available presentation methods to graphically display their examination observations and the basis of their opinion to the jury so they will be able to easily understand the examination process and results. Presenting a case in court begins when you are working it. If you do not keep sufficient records of your examination via photographs, test impressions, and the like, you will not have the materials necessary to adequately present your results.

When I first began testifying in court in the mid-1970s, the utilization of large photographic charts and occasional transparent photographic overlays was the leading-edge technology. Some also used 35-mm color slides for the same purpose. These were and still are effective ways of sharing demonstrative physical evidence. Today, there are many additional choices available, and these continue to evolve as technology advances. Some courts are equipped with LCD or DLP projectors while others have TV screens and monitors. Unfortunately, some courts still have no technical aids or equipment.

Demonstration Aids

During testimony involving physical examination of tires, graphic demonstration in court is often required and recommended. Prior to giving testimony, it is a good idea to check ahead to determine what technology and equipment will be there. Some of the equipment or programs used to assist demonstrations in court are described below.

Photographs

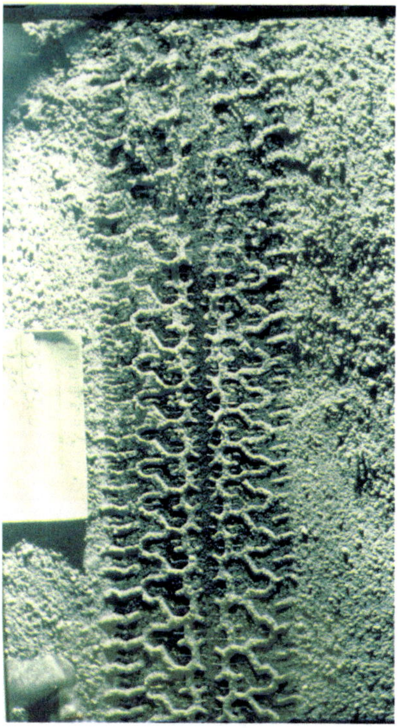

Figure 11.1. An enlargement of a hardcopy photograph mounted on hard board, to which an actual transparent known impression has been taped.

Photographs enlarged to natural size like those used in the actual examination can be used to effectively present the results of a tire examination. Figure 11.1 depicts an enlarged photograph of a tire impression with an attached transparency of the inked impression. By manually lifting and lowering the transparency, the correspondence of features can be demonstrated. In some cases, adding lines with numbers or arrows to draw attention to important points will be appropriate. The use of transparent overlays attached to the photographs or an actual re-enactment of the examination process on a table in front of the jury is also a commonly used technique. If necessary, the jury can be asked to stand or might even be allowed to parade around the table and see the photographs and full-circumference impressions superimposed over the impression or cast. The main disadvantage of the hardcopy demonstration is the fact that regardless of whether the photographs used are large, it is often difficult for the entire jury to have the appropriate time and position to see all details either because of the distance from which they are viewing the photographs or because of glare or some other interference. However, one distinct advantage of the hardcopy photographs is that they can be admitted as an exhibit that can, if necessary, be viewed further by the jury during deliberation. If smaller photographs are used, they could also be projected via a visual presenter and/or used very effectively in conjunction with the other computer graphic presentations.

PowerPoint Presentations

Microsoft's PowerPoint has been around for several years and continues to be a popular choice to present evidence in court. Scanned or photographed digital images can be imported to create individual slides that can then be projected onto a screen. Figure 11.2 depicts nine slides used in part of a court

Figure 11.2. PowerPoint is a relatively easy-to-use and effective way of presenting the entire range of illustrations, from general scenes and pictures to enlarged detailed comparative pictures. When projected onto a screen, it allows for better viewing of fine detail than seen on a monitor. This is part of a slide presentation using PowerPoint.

presentation. The content of each slide can be labeled with numbers, arrows, or other appropriate information as needed. This program works best for presenting the evidence in a side-by-side manner. It is possible to use overlays in the PowerPoint program but is not nearly as versatile as other programs in this regard. Each slide prepared can be printed in hardcopy form if an exhibit is necessary to be admitted into evidence or is necessary to send to the jury. PowerPoint presentations are quick, easy, and inexpensive to prepare and often form the core portion of a court presentation.

Adobe Photoshop

Adobe System's Photoshop is one of the most popular graphic arts programs used, although it is expensive and so court computers may not have the software. This may only mean that you would have to bring your own laptop computer into court to use it. Like PowerPoint, it is best used with a projector and a screen. It is the best program for showing detail, as it has the capability of zooming in on specific areas to ensure that everyone in the court will be able to see everything. Adobe Photoshop also has the ability to portray an impression such as a crime scene tire impression with an overlay of the known inked impression showing important comparison features. This allows the same versatility as you would have had with an actual overlay over a hardcopy photograph with the added advantage of knowing everyone can easily see everything you are projecting. The overlay can actually be moved during the demonstration just as if you were moving an actual inked transparency over a photograph. Further, this program has numerous additional tools, including the ability to adjust the opacity of the overlay or zoom in on certain key areas, as well as projecting greater resolution.

Visual Presenters

Visual presenters are made by a number of companies. Perhaps the most well-known brand name is the Elmo Legal Presenter (Elmo Company Ltd.), but numerous brands exist. Unlike conventional overhead projectors where only transparencies can be used, the visual presenter can project either opaque photographs or transparencies onto a large screen. The video camera on the unit can zoom in on specific areas of the photograph and project highly detailed and enlarged images of those areas on the screen. The advantage of a visual presenter is that it can be used to project almost any document or photograph brought into the courtroom. Disadvantages are occasional glare when projecting glossy photographs and the limitation of the size of the area being projected, normally an 8 × 10 area.

Screens versus TV Monitors

A projector screen is preferred to the use of a TV monitor for a number of reasons. First and foremost, monitors do not have nearly as high as resolution as a projector. Showing a highly detailed Adobe Photoshop or PowerPoint presentation through a TV monitor would be counterproductive and would result in much less detail as compared with what could be projected onto a screen. In addition, a projection screen is normally much larger than a monitor. Other problems also encountered with monitors include glare, monitor size, and the limited ability to see a monitor from an angle. Even when several monitors are located throughout the courtroom, a single projection screen will allow for better detail. If the courtroom is not equipped with a screen, consider the possibility of projecting the presentation against a wall.

Planning Ahead

The size and layouts of courtrooms vary considerably. Some courtrooms are equipped with screens, visual presenters, and projectors necessary to project images. Others have monitors in various locations and others have no equipment at all. Further, some presentations may be before a judge only, while others may take place in a larger room and will need to be viewed by a jury. Whenever asked to provide testimony in court, you should discuss the presentation options with the attorney and determine the equipment that is available. A presentation in a small hearing before a judge may be best served with a few 8 × 10-inch pre-labeled hardcopy exhibits to facilitate a quick presentation with no setup time required. On the other hand, testifying to significant results in a trial before a jury may only be best served with a detailed PowerPoint and/or Adobe Photoshop presentation projected on a large screen. In some cases, provisions may have to be made to acquire or bring a projector and screen to the courtroom.

Pre-Trial Meeting with Attorney

As an examiner, when you are testifying in a strange courtroom and for an attorney you have never met, the pretrial meeting is normally something that is mutually desired. On the other hand, some examiners have testified numerous times in the same courtroom and for the same attorney, and with many witnesses to tender, the attorney may wish to do without the pre-trial meeting. I would always encourage the pre-trial meeting, even if it needs to be brief and on the phone. This minimally ensures there is a clear understanding of why you are being called as a witness, allows you to arrange for the evidence that you will be testifying about to be in court as well as to discuss the best method of presentation that you believe will be beneficial.

Testifying to Your Conclusions

The ability to present your observations and conclusions to a jury in a clear and concise way is not a trait shared by all. Many examiners are new and others have had little occasion to testify in a tire case. The graphic presentation is an important component in most tire evidence cases, should be used whenever possible, and is often the core of your testimony.

When you take the stand and qualify as an expert in the area of tire impression evidence, keep in mind that most jurors will not have much of an idea what this examination involves. In addition to the normal qualification questions, it is a good idea to explain what a forensic tire expert does, how tire impressions may be left at the scene, that tires come in different designs and sizes, that tires wear which causes visible changes in the design, and that tires also acquire random damage which can make them unique. The jurors should understand you are making a comparison of tires from a particular vehicle that is suspected of having caused impressions at the crime scene, and you should explain the process you go through in making such a comparison. Although all of this may seem elementary, it will ensure that the jurors know who you are, why you are there, and what examination you have performed. Your testimony, like in many other physical comparisons, may involve a positive identification, eliminations of tires, or other relative conclusions. The best way to present this evidence is to stand in front of the jury and, with the evidence and your form of graphic presentation at hand, walk them through the process of your examination, share with them your observations, and finally state your conclusions.

Resources and Databases 12

Resources

A number of resources are available that provide assistance with regard to the search for tread designs and track measurements, as well as information and assistance in the investigation and examination of tire evidence. These are set forth below in this chapter with a brief explanation. As usual, any information published in these guides that becomes significant in casework or the examination should be verified with the tire manufacturers.

Tire Guides, Inc.[1]

Tire Guides, Inc. was founded by Bennett Garfield in 1950 to provide a source for more detailed information about the various tire designs and brands that are sold. By 1966 the company published the *Tread Design Guide* and the *Who Makes It and Where Tire Directory.* Today, the company produces numerous reference guides and, in conjunction with Pearl Communications, also produces an electronic version of tread designs available on a CD-ROM known as the Tread Assistant. Those Tire Guides publications most used by forensic examiners and investigators are described below.

Tread Design Guide

The Tread Design Guide, featured in Figure 12.1, is published annually and consists of a compilation of thousands of photographs of tread designs subdivided into passenger, light truck, medium and large truck, off-road, agricultural, ATV and motorcycle, and retread sections. Within each respective

[1] Tire Guides, Inc., 1101 South Rogers Circle Ste 6, Boca Raton, FL 33487-2748; 561-997-9229; www.tireguides.com.

Figure 12.1. The *Tread Design Guide* contains thousands of photographs of tire designs. (Courtesy of Tire Guides, Inc.)

section the tire designs are arranged alphabetically by manufacturer name. Although the primary use of this guide is to serve the tire industry, forensic examiners and investigators routinely use this guide, for it provides invaluable assistance when attempting to identify a tire brand and line of tire that left an impression at a crime scene through its tread design. Figure 12.2A depicts a page from the passenger tire section inside this guide. The photographs of the tires are provided to the publisher by the various manufacturers each year and represent about 95% to 98% of the tires available. Approximately 400 to 500 new tire designs are placed into this guide each year. At the bottom of each page is information that indicates whether the sidewall lettering comes in white letters (WL), outlined white letters (OWL), or outlined black letters (OBL). Figure 12.2B depicts some of these lettering choices. Crimes where a tire impression is left at a scene in rural areas and smaller towns, which is determined to have been made by a high profile tire that has raised white or outlined white lettering, can provide significant

Figure 12.2A. A page from the passenger tire section of the *Tread Design Guide*. The code at the very bottom indicates the lettering type, such as outlined white letters (OWL), white letters (WL), and outlined black letters (OBL). (Courtesy of Tire Guides, Inc.)

Figure 12.2B. White letters (WL) and outlined white letters (OWL) on a tire will make that tire a high-profile tire and may be of value in locating suspect vehicles in smaller cities.

investigative leads. For instance, if an impression from a crime scene in a small town were determined to correspond with the Republic Invader Radial GT tire in Figure 12.2A, available in raised white letters, an all-points bulletin might quickly locate the vehicle because these tires are high profile. The same lead would likely not work in a larger city. Photographs of tread designs featured in prior years that are no longer being manufactured are removed from the Tread Design Guide in subsequent years. Using this guide to search for a tire recovered from a crime scene involves looking photograph by photograph and page by page of each annual edition. Some simple tips for conducting this type of search are:

- A cast from of a crime scene impression will show its tire design the same as the tire pictured in the *Tread Design Guide*. On the other hand, a photograph of a tire impression will represent a reversed image of the tire design as compared with that pictured in the guide. When viewing a photographed impression, you should reverse the photograph so it will then appear in the same way as the tire photographs in the guide. Reversing a photograph simply means that you flip the negative over and then make a print. Digitally, horizontally flipping the image will accomplish the same thing.[2] Figure 12.3A depicts a picture of an

[2] For instance, in Adobe Photoshop, click on Image>Rotate>Flip Canvas Horizontal.

Figure 12.3A. A regular photograph of a tire impression in soil.

Figure 12.3B. The same photograph as Figure 12.3A but reversed.

Figure 12.3C. A cast of the tire impression in Figure 12.3A.

Figure 12.3D. The tire that made the impression in Figure 12.3A.

impression in soil. Figure 12.3B is a reverse print (or horizontal flip) of that same picture. Figure 12.3C depicts a cast of that impression, and Figure 12.3D is a picture of the tire similar to what you would find in the guide. Note that the transverse grooving and element shapes run at different angles in the Figure 12.3A photograph, seeming to be different when compared with the photograph of the tire (Figure 12.3D). When using this photograph to search for that tire design, the tire design could easily be missed. However, a reversal of that picture (Figure 12.3B) eliminates that problem, as it now presents the crime scene impression in the same way as the tire appears in the reference material. Also note that the cast impression (Figure 12.3C) is the same likeness as the tire photograph (Figure 12.3D), thus a direct comparison between the cast and that photograph can be made and no reversal will be necessary.

- Since the *Tread Design Guide* is published yearly, when searching for a tread design you must decide which year's guide you will begin your search with. If the crime occurred in 2007, then you could search the 2007 guide or earlier years. If you were searching a cold case that occurred several years prior, you would only search for tires made in that year and before. Based on the crime scene impression alone, you would not likely know if the car that made those impressions was new or old and thus you would not know if the car was equipped with original equipment tires or replacement tires. It is noted that some tire designs are made for many years and thus appear over and over again in each year's edition, while other tires are only made for one year and only appear in that single year's edition. The choice of what year to begin the search with should be well reasoned. Searching for a tire design through the *Tread Design Guide* is a procedure that often requires searching several years' editions before finally locating the tire.
- As mentioned above, the *Tread Design Guide* includes more than one category of vehicle, such as passenger, light truck, medium truck, etc. Even though you normally would not know what type or size vehicle made the crime scene impression, you must decide which category in the guide to search first. Most vehicles involved in a crime are made by either a passenger vehicle or a light truck. If the impression was made by a light truck and you only search passenger tires, you may not have any success and will not find the tire until you search the light-truck category, unless that particular design appears in both. The size of the impression, any available track measurements, and even possibly witness information may provide clues as to which category should be searched first.
- From the crime scene impression, select a primary feature, such as the number of circumferential grooves as well as a couple secondary features that appear to be the most appropriate and reliable for the search. A secondary feature might be something as obvious and simple as an angled transverse groove or the features of the center rib. As you search the section, you can skim over most tires that do not contain the primary feature, and when one does, quickly look at the other features you wish to focus on.

- As tires wear down, their design features change. Be aware of the possibility that the tire that made the impressions was well worn, and take this into consideration when you select the primary and secondary design features for your search. Select features that are less likely to change as the tire wears.
- If you happen to find a tire that is almost an exact match but contains only minor differences, you may want to contact that company and to see if the design is theirs. If it is not, they will probably be aware of whose design it is.
- The advantage of searching the *Tread Design Guide* is that you do not need a computer or computer program. However, the disadvantage lies in the fact that you may not be searching the correct year and thus may have to search through editions of several years.

Tread Assistant CD-ROM (*Computerized Tread Design Guide*)

In 1998, Tire Guides, Inc. along with Pearl Communications began placing the images of its tires from the *Tread Design Guide*s onto a CD-ROM. It contains many thousands of pictures of tire designs covering numerous years. Today, if someone in the tire industry wants to look up a certain 2005 Goodyear tire design, he or she could enter the manufacturer name, style, and other information and the computerized program would locate that tire along with an image of its design. Likewise, if while examining a well-worn tire, a forensic examiner wanted to see what the tire tread looked like when new, he or she could also use the CD in this manner. One strength of the CD is that it provides ways to search for specific tire designs based on the category of the tire (passenger, light truck, etc), the number of circumferential grooves (0 to 8), and other criteria. Since it contains several years of designs, all of these years are being searched at the same time. Thus, in cases where a crime scene impression was recovered, but no suspect vehicle was located, the Tread Assistant could also be used to assist in determining the manufacturer and brand of the tire that left the impression. Designs are added yearly, and Tire Guides, Inc. is considering improving the search capability of this program. Figure 12.4 depicts the screen shot displaying some of the 257 hits for a passenger directional design having four circumferential grooves.

Who Makes It and Where Tire Directory

Published by Tire Guides, Inc. (Figure 12.5), the *Who Makes It and Where Tire Directory* contains pages of brand names of domestic and foreign tires with the corresponding manufacturers/importers of those tires, as well as addresses and phone numbers for contacting them in the first part of the guide. That is followed by pages of the Department of Transportation (DOT)

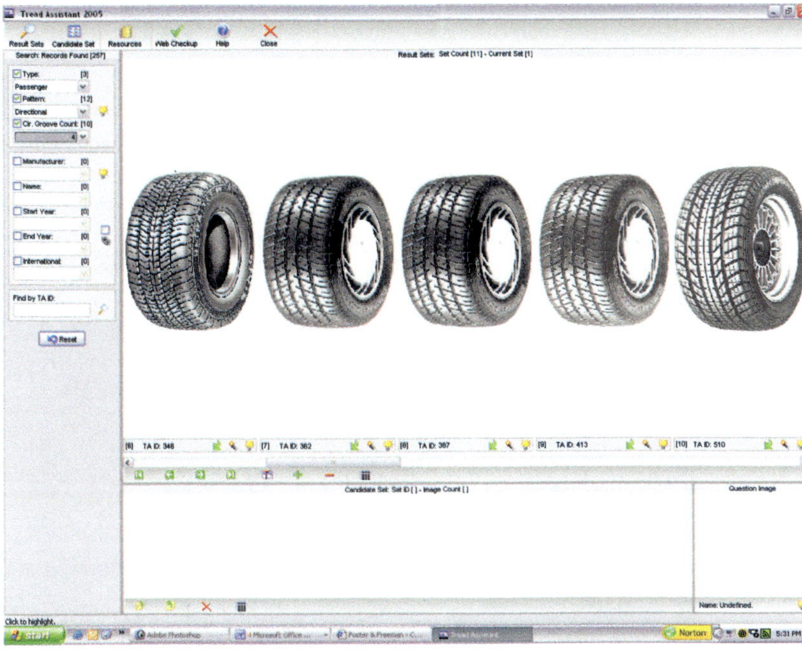

Figure 12.4. Computer screen shot showing the Tread Assistant program. The selections of the possible tires will scroll across the screen. (Courtesy of Tire Guides, Inc.)

code numbers. Code numbers appear as the first two letters or numbers of the DOT number and designate the manufacturer and actual address of the manufacturing facility that produced the new tire. So, if the DOT number on a tire were DOT MDXY ABCD 1806, then the "MD" (Figure 12.6) shows the tire was manufactured at The Goodyear Tire & Rubber Company, 922 East Meighan Blvd., Gadsden, AL 35903. The additional knowledge of where that tire was actually produced provides valuable contact information if the examiner should need to consult with that tire manufacturer on some aspect of that tire.

OEM Tire Size Guide

The *OEM Tire Size Guide*, published by Tire Guides, Inc. (Figure 12.7A), was first published in 1996 and provides information regarding tire brands and sizes used as original equipment on new vehicles. Each year's edition covers vehicles for the present year and approximately 10 years prior as well. This resource also provides an index of tire sizes and what vehicles used those sizes. For instance, on page 57 of the 2007 guide, a portion of which is depicted in Figure 12.7B, under the tire size P205/45R16 you would see that only one

Figure 12.5. *The Who Makes It and Where Guide.* (Courtesy of Tire Guides, Inc.)

vehicle, the Hyundai Accent SE, used this size as OEM equipment. This has potential forensic and investigative value. If a tire impression recovered at a crime scene, with assistance from the manufacturer, were determined to be a Kumho Solus 716 tire of size P205/45R16, a search through the OEM guide would indicate that only the Hyundai Accent SE used this tire. Elsewhere in the OEM guide, the Hyundai Accent SE is listed as using the Kumho Solus 716 tire as original equipment. Although in some instances this tire may also be sold in the aftermarket, it may be possible this tire is only found as OEM equipment on the Hyundai Accent SE vehicle. This could be of great assistance investigatively and could also affect the evidence in the case. This information could also be cross-checked with other recovered information such as track widths or with eye witness accounts. Other examples shown in Figure 12.7B, such as tire size P195/75R15, include 11 vehicles between 1998

CODE No.	NEW TIRE MANUFACTURER
LK	Productors Niacional de LLantas S.A. Cali, Colombia
LL	SICUP S.N.C. Usine Uniroyal de Clairoix Cedex 60 Compiegne, France
LM	Continental AG Werk Aachen Huttenstrasse 7 D-52068 Aachen 1, Germany
LN	Uniroyal S.A. de C.V. Lago Aullagas 60 11280 Mexico, D.F. Mexico
LP	Uniroyal Englebert Tyres Ltd Midlothian EH 28 8 LG/Scotland Newbridge, Midlothian, Scotland
LR	TVS Srichakra Limited Perumal Patti Road Vellaripatti Melur Taluk Madurai Tamil Nadu 625122, India
LT	Uniroyal Endustri Turk Anonim Sirketi Fabrika Posta Kutusu 27 Adapazari, Turkey
LU	Uniroyal, C.A. Apartado 98 Valencia, Venezuela
LV	General Tire Canada Ltd. John Street Barrie, Ontario, Canada
LW	Trelleborg Ummifariks Aktiebolag S-23101 Trelleborg, Sweden
LX	Mitsuboshi Belting Ltd. 4 Chome, Hamazoedori, Nagataku Kobe, Japan
LY	Mitsuboshi Belting Ltd. Hara Tsuda-Cho Okawag-gun, Shikoku, Japan
L1	Goodyear Taiwan Ltd. Nanking East Rd., Sec. 2 Taipei, Taiwan
L2	Woosung Tire Corp. - Yangsan Plant 30, Yusan-ri, Yangsan-eup, Yansan-kun, Kyungsangnam-do South Korea 626-800
L3	Tong Shin Chemical Products Co., Ltd. CPO 4104, Seoul, Korea
L4	S.C. Danubiana S.A. Judetul Ilfov, Comuna Popesti Leordeni Sos. Olteni ei Nr. 181 Romania
L5	Brisa Bridgestone Sabanci Izmit Tire Plant Alikahya, 41220 Izmit, Turkey
L6	Modi Rubber Limited Medipuram Plant, Meerut UP 250110, India
L7	SC Silvania SA 83 Mihai Viteazul St. Zalau, Salaj County, Romania
L8	Dunlop Zimbabwe Ltd. Domington, Bulawaye, Zimbabwe
L9	Panther Tyres, Ltd. 45 Ormskirk Rd. Aintree, Liverpool, United Kingdom
L0	Manufacture Francaise Des Pneumatiques Michelin, Zone Industrielle Des Gravanches 63040 Clermont Ferrand Cedex, France
M	
MB	The Goodyear Tire & Rubber Co. Martha Ave., Plant No. 2 Akron, OH 44316
MC	The Goodyear Tire & Rubber Co. P.O. Box 920 Danville, VA 24541
MD	The Goodyear Tire & Rubber Co. 922 East Meighan Blvd. Gadsden, AL 35903
MJ	The Goodyear Tire & Rubber Co. P.O. Box 1069 Topeka, KS 66601
MK	The Goodyear Tire & Rubber Co. P.O. Box 57 Union City, TN 38261

Figure 12.6. A page of tire codes from the inside of the *Who Makes It and Where Guide*. (Courtesy of Tire Guides, Inc.)

Figure 12.7A. The *OEM Tire Size Guide*. (Courtesy of Tire Guides, Inc.)

and 2004 that used that particular tire size. Other tires sizes are used by even a larger numbers of vehicles.

Another section of the OEM guide lists vehicles by model year and then lists the brands and lines of tires as well as the sizes that were used on each new car or truck. For example, information for the 2001 Mercury Sable LS in the OEM guide (Figure 12.7C) indicates that model came equipped with Continental Touring Contact AS P215/60R16 tires. In the case of this Mercury Sable, both the front tires and rear tires are the same size. However, in other instances, vehicles will have one tire size in the front and another tire size on the rear positions, as seen on the Mercedes SLK models, also depicted in Figure 12.7C. The OEM guide should always be considered as a guide only, thus any information should be confirmed with the respective vehicle's manufacturer or tire company.

	P205/45R16		
HYUNDAI	Accent SE	83V	2007
	P195/75R15		
CHEVY Tracker	4x2	94S	01-04
CHEVY Tracker	4x2 Convertible	94S	99-00
CHEVY Tracker	4x2 Convertible	94S	1998
CHEVY Tracker	4x2 Hardtop	94S	98-00
SUZUKI	Sidekick 2 Dr. 4x2	94S	1998
SUZUKI	Sidekick 4 Dr. 4x2	94S	1998
SUZUKI	Vitara 1.6L 4x2	94S	2000
SUZUKI	Vitara 4x2 2 Dr.	94S	1999
SUZUKI	Vitara JS 1.6L 4x2 2 Dr.	94S	2002
SUZUKI	Vitara JS 1.6L 4x2 2 Dr.	94S	2001
MAZDA	MPV LX 4x2	94S	98-99
	P195/75R14		
NISSAN	Frontier Pickup 4x2 Reg. Cab	92S	1998
NISSAN	Frontier Pickup XE 4x2 King Cab	92S	1999
NISSAN	Frontier Pickup XE 4x2 Reg. Cab	92S	1999
TOYOTA	Tacoma 4x2 Reg. Cab	92S	98-00
	P195/70R14		
BUICK	Skylark Custom	90S	1998
CHEVROLET	Cavalier	90S	98-05
CHRYSLER	Sebring LX	90H	98-99
DODGE	Avenger	90H	98-00
DODGE	Stratus	90S	98-99
DODGE	Stratus SE	90S	2000
EAGLE	Talon	90H	1998
EAGLE	Talon ESi	90H	1998
OLDSMOBILE	Achieva	90S	1998
PLYMOUTH	Breeze	90S	98-00
PLYMOUTH	Breeze Expresso	90S	98-99
PONTIAC	Grand Am	90S	1998
PONTIAC	Sunfire SE	90S	98-02
PONTIAC	Sunfire SE Convertible	90S	1999
HONDA	Accord DX	90S	98-02
HYUNDAI	Sonata		98-00
HYUNDAI	Sonata V6		1998
KIA	Optima	90H	2001
MITSUBISHI	Eclipse GS Spyder	90H	98-99
MITSUBISHI	Eclipse RS	90H	98-99
TOYOTA	Camry LE	90S	98-99
TOYOTA	Camry SE	90S	98-00

Figure 12.7B. A page from the OEM guide listing vehicles by tire size. (Courtesy of Tire Guides, Inc.)

2001 OEM Data

Model/Option	Weight	Base	Tire Size	Ply	Brand	Line
MERCEDES (Cont.)						
SLK 230 (Rear)			225/50R16 92V		CONTINENTAL	CONTI SPORT CONTACT
					MICHELIN	PILOT SX MXX3
					MICHELIN	PILOT SPORT
SLK 230 Sport (Front)			225/45ZR17		CONTINENTAL	CONTI SPORT CONTACT
					MICHELIN	PILOT SX MXX3
					MICHELIN	PILOT SPORT
SLK 230 Sport (Rear)			245/40ZR17		CONTINENTAL	CONTI SPORT CONTACT
					MICHELIN	PILOT SX MXX3
					MICHELIN	PILOT SPORT
SLK 320 (Front)			205/55R16 91V		CONTINENTAL	CONTI SPORT CONTACT
					MICHELIN	PILOT SX MXX3
					MICHELIN	PILOT SPORT
SLK 320 (Rear)			225/50R16 92V		CONTINENTAL	CONTI SPORT CONTACT
					MICHELIN	PILOT SX MXX3
					MICHELIN	PILOT SPORT
SLK 320 Sport (Front)			225/45ZR17 91W		CONTINENTAL	CONTI SPORT CONTACT
					MICHELIN	PILOT SX MXX3
					MICHELIN	PILOT SPORT
SLK 320 Sport (Rear)			245/40ZR17 91W		CONTINENTAL	CONTI SPORT CONTACT
					MICHELIN	PILOT SX MXX3
					MICHELIN	PILOT SPORT
MERCURY						
Villager		112.2	P215/65R16 96S		CONTINENTAL	TOURING CONTACT AS
			P215/70R15 97S		GENERAL TIRE	AMERI*GS60
Villager Estate		112.2	P225/60R16 97T		GOODYEAR	EAGLE LS
Villager Sport		112.2	P225/60R16 97T		GOODYEAR	EAGLE LS
Cougar			P205/60R15 90T		FIRESTONE	FIREHAWK GTA
Grand Marquis w/Handling Pkg.			P225/60R16 97T		GOODYEAR	EAGLE LS
Grand Marquis w/Police Pkg.			P225/60R16 97V		GOODYEAR	EAGLE GA
Grand Marquis			P225/60R16 97S		MICHELIN	SYMMETRY
Sable GS			P215/60R16 94T		CONTINENTAL	TOURING CONTACT AS
Sable LS			P215/60R16 94T		CONTINENTAL	TOURING CONTACT AS
Mountaineer 4x2 V6	5380	111.6	P235/75R15 105S		FIRESTONE	WILDERNESS AT
Mountaineer 4x2 V8	5380	111.6	P235/75R15 105S		FIRESTONE	WILDERNESS AT
Mountaineer 4x4 V6	5380	111.6	P235/75R15 105S		FIRESTONE	WILDERNESS AT
Mountaineer 4x4 V8	5380	111.6	P235/75R15 105S		FIRESTONE	WILDERNESS AT

Figure 12.7C. A page from the OEM guide listing tires by vehicle.

Who Retreads Tires

Who Retreads Tires is in a retread tire guide (Figure 12.8) published annually by Tire Guides, Inc. It lists over 5,000 retread codes along with the name and address of the respective retreading facilities attached to those codes. Each retread facility is assigned a three-letter code, such as "LWM," that, according the Department of Transportation, must be placed on the sidewall of the retread tire. An explanation of retread codes was previously discussed and illustrated in Chapter 6, in Figure 6.14 and Figure 6.15.

Tire Guide

The *Tire Guide* (Figure 12.9A) is published annually by Tire Guides, Inc., and provides tire and wheel fitment information for cars and trucks listed by their year, make, and model. It covers approximately 10 years. Although the information contained therein is not used as frequently by forensic examiners, it does provide a resource when certain tire size information might be

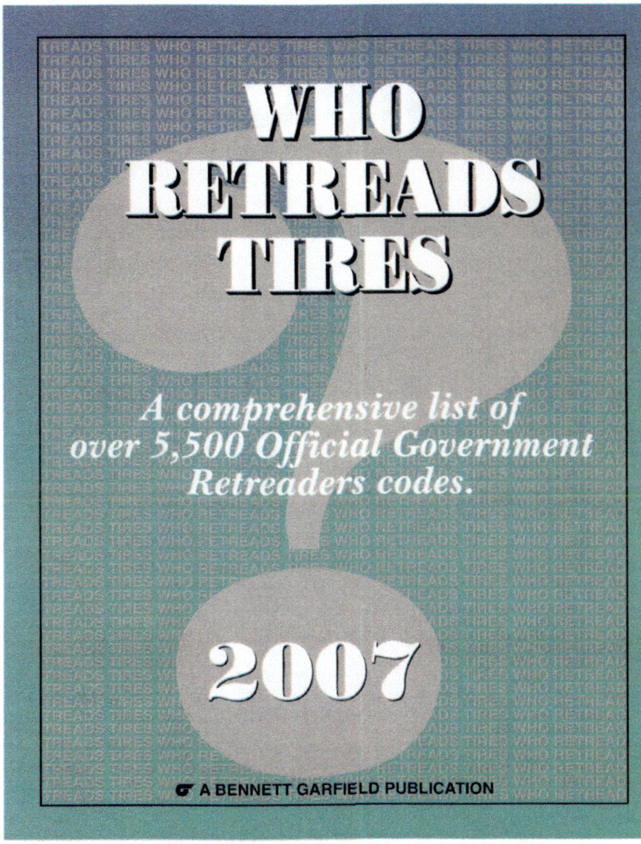

Figure 12.8. The *Who Retreads Tires* guide. (Courtesy of Tire Guides, Inc.)

needed. For instance, the guide lists a 2005 Corvette came standard with P245/40ZR18 tires on the front positions and with P285/35ZR19 tires on the rear positions. This page in the guide is depicted in Figure 12.9B. As another example, it lists a 2005 Ford Taurus as coming standard with P215/60R16 tires on all four positions. Should an older suspect vehicle being examined be thought to have replacement tires of an incorrect size, this guide would provide initial assistance in determining this. The guide also provides some rim size and bolt circle information that might be useful if trying to find a comparable car for the purposes of making known exemplars.

Figure 12.9A. The *Tire Guide.* (Courtesy of Tire Guides, Inc.)

AMERICAN CAR MODEL	YEAR	STANDARD TIRE SIZE & INFLATIONS FR. RR.	OPTIONAL TIRE SIZE & INFLATIONS FR. RR.	RIM SIZE NO. HOLES | BOLT CIRCLE	LUG NUT TORQUE (FT. LBS.)
CHEVROLET (Cont.)			When Using Torque Information See Note on Page 30.		
Cobalt SS	2005	215/45ZR18 89Y 32 32		7J 5-100mm	100
Corvette		P245/40ZR18 88Y 30 (Front)	P285/35ZR19*90Y (Rear) 30	8.5J/10J* 5-120.7mm	100
Corvette w/Z51 Sport Pkg.		P245/40ZR18 88Y 30 (Front)	P285/35ZR19*90Y (Rear) 30	8.5J/10J* 5-120.7mm	100
Impala w/Police Pkg.		P225/60R16 97H 30 30		6.5J 5-115mm	100
Impala		P225/60R16 97S 30 30	P225/60R16 97H 30 30	6.5J 5-115mm	100
Impala LS		P225/60R16 97H 30 30		6.5J 5-115mm	100
Impala SS		P235/55R17 98W 30 30		7.5J 5-115mm	100
Malibu		P205/65R15 92S		6.5J	100

Figure 12.9B. Part of a page from the *Tire Guide.* (Courtesy of Tire Guides, Inc.)

Tire Business[3]

This bi-weekly newspaper (Figure 12.10) is the trade newspaper of the tire industry. It includes a variety of articles on topics such as tire sales data, tire technology, industry trends, tire designs, and so forth. For a forensic examiner, the primary purpose of subscribing to this paper would be for continuing education as there is often information relating to manufacturing, designs, retreads, new technology, and the like.

a crain publication

TIRE BUSINESS

September, 25, 2006 | THE TIRE DEALER'S NEWSPAPER SINCE 1983 | $79 per year, $4 per copy

INSIDE

White Tire defends N.C. retreading contract ... 3
$3 million blaze guts Express Tire's San Diego store ... 3
Contl realigns replacement passenger/LT marketing team ... 4

Getting the Ride Right
Replacement tire speed ratings create concerns ... 10
Shops missing opportunities to boost parts sales ... 12
Stability control to become standard under NHTSA proposal ... 15

DEPARTMENTS
Associations ... 30
Automotive Service ... 6-7
Calendar ... 30
Classifieds ... 25-28
Commercial Tire Service ... 23
Editorials ... 8
Marketplace ... 30

LATE NEWS

CMA names Weller to post

MONROVIA, Calif.—Walter Weller, a former Goodyear and Bridgestone/Firestone (BFS) executive, has joined China Manufacturers Alliance L.L.C. as vice president of strategic accounts.

Mr. Weller will be responsible for CMA's Double Coin brand strategic growth, the firm said.

"CMA L.L.C. is excited to employ the knowledge and strengths of a person like Walt," the company said in a statement. "His past experience and abilities will assist Double Coin medium truck tires in achieving our strategic objectives."

Mr. Weller held several posts with BFS during a 20-year career, including president and managing director for its Mexican subsidiary as well as vice president, commercial truck tires. He joined Goodyear in 2002 as marketing director, commercial tire systems.

Get up-to-date information at the Tire Business Web site
http://www.tirebusiness.com

'Soft restructuring'

Cooper Tire interim CEO outlines plan to cut costs, enhance profits

By Bruce Davis
Tire Business staff

NEW YORK—Cooper Tire & Rubber Co. will embark on a "soft restructuring" in the coming months, hoping to cut costs by $70 million a year, enhance profits by $100 million and reduce inventories by $100 million, interim CEO Byron Pond told analysts in New York recently.

"In the past we focused too much on growth and not enough on profitability," Mr. Pond said to analysts attending Credit Suisse's Automotive Industry Briefing.

"Our results have been disappointing," Mr. Pond said. "To continue on this course is unacceptable."

To get the company on the right track, Cooper will institute a more flexible manufacturing schedule, opting to operate three of its four U.S. plants—Findlay, Ohio, Tupelo, Miss., and Albany, Ga.—on round-the-clock schedules and put its unionized Texarkana, Ark., plant on a variable schedule, Mr. Pond said.

See Cooper, page 29

"In the past we focused too much on growth and not enough on profitability."
Byron Pond, Interim CEO
Cooper Tire & Rubber Co.

Pond

COOPER TIRES

Shoring up the bottom line

Among initiatives outlined by interim Cooper Tire & Rubber Co. CEO Byron Pond to help shore up the bottom line, the tire maker will:

- Reduce SKUs in North America by 10 percent;
- Consolidate its ultra-high-performance tire offerings into one brand;
- Rationalize associate brand offerings;
- Limit "loader" incentive programs by capping participation based on the market, inventory levels and flex capacity; and
- Reduce its low-end product offerings.

Tread depth

Is 2/32nds inch too shallow?

By Bruce Davis
Tire Business staff

AKRON—Has the widely accepted minimum tread depth of 2/32nds inch—a relic of the bias-ply tire era—outlived its usefulness and should it be increased to improve safety on the nation's highways?

That's the contention of a vehicle dynamics engineer from Palo Alto, Calif., who has studied the situation for years, and the subject of two studies published recently in Europe.

William Blythe, a retired mechanical engineer who taught applied mechanics at San Jose State University for 42 years, has published a paper showing wet traction falls off "significantly" as tread depth falls below 4/32nds inch—or twice as deep as most states allow.

In his study, presented Sept. 12 at the International Tire Exhibition and Conference (ITEC) in Akron, Mr. Blythe notes there is no national standard for minimum tread depths. Instead, each state sets its own and is responsible for policing it.

See Time, page 29

A-maze-ing

Tire distributor and retailer Terry's Tire Town partnered with local farmer Bill Bakan for the annual Maize Valley Fall Experience in Hartville, Ohio, to support local charities. Every year, Mr. Bakan mows his cornfield into a maze of stunning aerial images as part of the festivities. This year, Alliance, Ohio-based Terry's brought in a BigFoot monster truck, immortalized in Mr. Bakan's eight-acre corn maze along with the logos of Terry's, Ford and Firestone. "Creating an image like this is not rocket science but it's not falling off a log either," Mr. Bakan said. "We hire a graphic designer and use global positioning satellite technology to help us figure out where to mow. It's a pretty high-tech process."

USW, Goodyear at crossroads?

Goodyear is resisting being labeled as the next "target" in the United Steelworkers (USW) union's tire maker negotiations, and the USW appears to be losing patience in talks with the Akron-based company that haven't progressed much since they began earlier this year. The two sides appear to be heading toward a bargaining crossroad.

— See story on page 29

Figure 12.10. *Tire Business*, a bi-weekly trade newspaper.

[3] Tire Business, published bi-weekly by Crain Communications, Inc., 1725 Merriman Road, Suite 300, Akron, OH, 44313; www.tirebusiness.com.

Tire Retread Information Bureau[4]

The Tire Retread Information Bureau (TRIB) is a nonprofit, member-supported industry association with hundreds of members in North America and many other countries. TRIB provides the public with information about the economic and environmental benefits of tire retreading and tire repairing. They host a Web site at www.retread.org and disseminate much information relating to the retread process.

JATO DYNAMICS[5]

JATO Dynamics developed and maintains a vehicle identification system search program called TirePrint™ (www.tireprint.com) in response to increased demand by law enforcement agencies for vehicle data to aid criminal investigations. It is a Web-based tool that helps to identify vehicles used during a crime, based on track dimensional information such as track width, wheelbase, vehicle type, and so forth. This type of database includes information such as body type, number of doors, front versus rear drive wheels, and front and rear track dimensions. Each time additional criteria are entered, the number of vehicles on the hit list is reduced. To use this resource, a subscribing agency can plug in the vehicle's dimensional and other information relating to a crime scene and a list of possible vehicles will be produced.

An example of this type of search is provided in Figure 12.11A, where a rear track width measurement of 54.5 inches, plus/minus 0.5 inch, combined with a tire tread width of 6 inches was made. The search was for the years between 1990 through 2007. The results produced a short hit list of 14 vehicles. In a second example, I searched for a vehicle with a rear track width of 59.5 inches plus/minus 0.5 inches for the years 2000 to 2007. This resulted in a much longer hit list of 400 hits.[6] Obviously a track width of 59.5 inches is a common rear track width and without additional information for the search would not be very useful for identifying the type of vehicle. I then searched the same rear track measurement of 59.5 inches and the years 2000 to 2007 but added eyewitness information about the crime scene vehicle, which described the vehicle as being a three-door (hatchback). This reduced the search hits to 59. Using a different rear track measurement, 53.5 inches, and 2000 to 2007, I tried again. That produced only two vehicles.

[4] Tire Retread Information Bureau, 900 Weldon Grove, Pacific Grove, CA 93950; www.retread.org.

[5] JATO Dynamics, Inc., 2851 High Meadow Circle, Auburn Hill, MI 48326; www.tireprint.com.

[6] The program will only publish the first 400 hits, so there could have been many more.

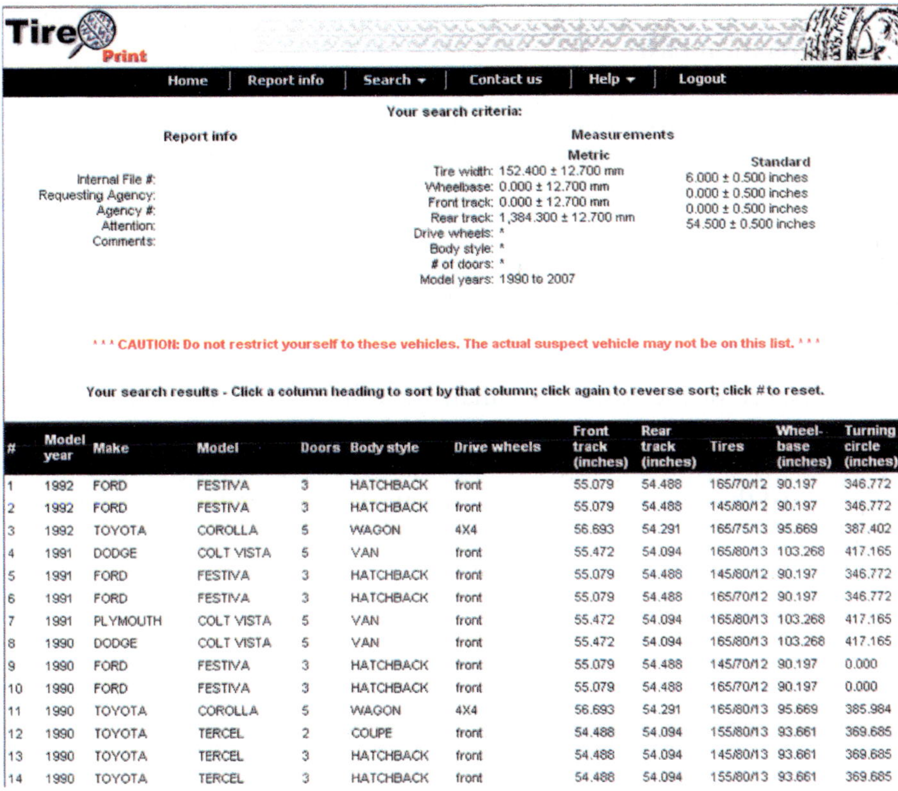
Tire Print

Home | Report info | Search | Contact us | Help | Logout

Your search criteria:

Report info

Internal File #:
Requesting Agency:
Agency #:
Attention:
Comments:

Measurements

	Metric	Standard
Tire width:	152.400 ± 12.700 mm	6.000 ± 0.500 inches
Wheelbase:	0.000 ± 12.700 mm	0.000 ± 0.500 inches
Front track:	0.000 ± 12.700 mm	0.000 ± 0.500 inches
Rear track:	1,384.300 ± 12.700 mm	54.500 ± 0.500 inches
Drive wheels:	*	
Body style:	*	
# of doors:	*	
Model years:	1990 to 2007	

*** CAUTION: Do not restrict yourself to these vehicles. The actual suspect vehicle may not be on this list. ***

Your search results - Click a column heading to sort by that column; click again to reverse sort; click # to reset.

#	Model year	Make	Model	Doors	Body style	Drive wheels	Front track (inches)	Rear track (inches)	Tires	Wheel-base (inches)	Turning circle (inches)
1	1992	FORD	FESTIVA	3	HATCHBACK	front	55.079	54.488	165/70/12	90.197	346.772
2	1992	FORD	FESTIVA	3	HATCHBACK	front	55.079	54.488	145/80/12	90.197	346.772
3	1992	TOYOTA	COROLLA	5	WAGON	4X4	56.693	54.291	165/75/13	95.669	387.402
4	1991	DODGE	COLT VISTA	5	VAN	front	55.472	54.094	165/80/13	103.268	417.165
5	1991	FORD	FESTIVA	3	HATCHBACK	front	55.079	54.488	145/80/12	90.197	346.772
6	1991	FORD	FESTIVA	3	HATCHBACK	front	55.079	54.488	165/70/12	90.197	346.772
7	1991	PLYMOUTH	COLT VISTA	5	VAN	front	55.472	54.094	165/80/13	103.268	417.165
8	1990	DODGE	COLT VISTA	5	VAN	front	55.472	54.094	165/80/13	103.268	417.165
9	1990	FORD	FESTIVA	3	HATCHBACK	front	55.079	54.488	145/70/12	90.197	0.000
10	1990	FORD	FESTIVA	3	HATCHBACK	front	55.079	54.488	165/70/12	90.197	0.000
11	1990	TOYOTA	COROLLA	5	WAGON	4X4	56.693	54.291	165/80/13	95.669	385.984
12	1990	TOYOTA	TERCEL	2	COUPE	front	54.488	54.094	155/80/13	93.661	369.685
13	1990	TOYOTA	TERCEL	3	HATCHBACK	front	54.488	54.094	145/80/13	93.661	369.685
14	1990	TOYOTA	TERCEL	3	HATCHBACK	front	54.488	54.094	155/80/13	93.661	369.685

Figure 12.11A. Computer screen shot showing results of a JATO tireprint.com tread width search. (Courtesy of JATO Dynamics, Inc.)

These quick examples illustrate the fact that when searching a tire track database the resulting hit list is not only dependent on the number of items you enter but also that some track widths are less common than others. It is also pointed out that in these examples, the minimum of plus/minus 0.5 inch was used, but very often tracks at a crime scene are not sufficiently distinct to permit that accurate of a measurement. In those cases a larger variance, such as plus/minus 1 inch or more, may have to be used and will result in a larger hit list. Also, you must be cognizant of the fact that if any search was made with a significantly inaccurate measurement, the hit list might not include the actual vehicle that left the tracks. Also, should the vehicle that left the impressions be equipped with aftermarket wheels or an optional axle other than the original equipment on that vehicle, it might have a substantially different track width than maintained in the database. In this program, there does not seem to currently be any way of including a turning diameter as part of the search process, although the turning diameter for the vehicles is provided on the hit list.

In another type of search possible using this program, the make and vehicle type, such as Nissan sedan, can be entered and, as depicted in Figure 12.11B, a list of vehicles and their track dimensions will be produced.

Michigan and RCMP Track Databases

In the early 1980s, Roger Bolhouse of the Michigan State Police (MSP) and Lawren Nause of the Royal Canadian Mounted Police (RCMP) created a computerized forensic database for vehicle track measurements and other data for forensic and investigative reasons. This original program was used and updated through the year 2002 and can still be operated today for older cases prior to 2002. The program provides a "hit list" of possible vehicles based on track width, turning diameter, wheelbase measurements and other data collected from the crime scene. For those agencies that are considering

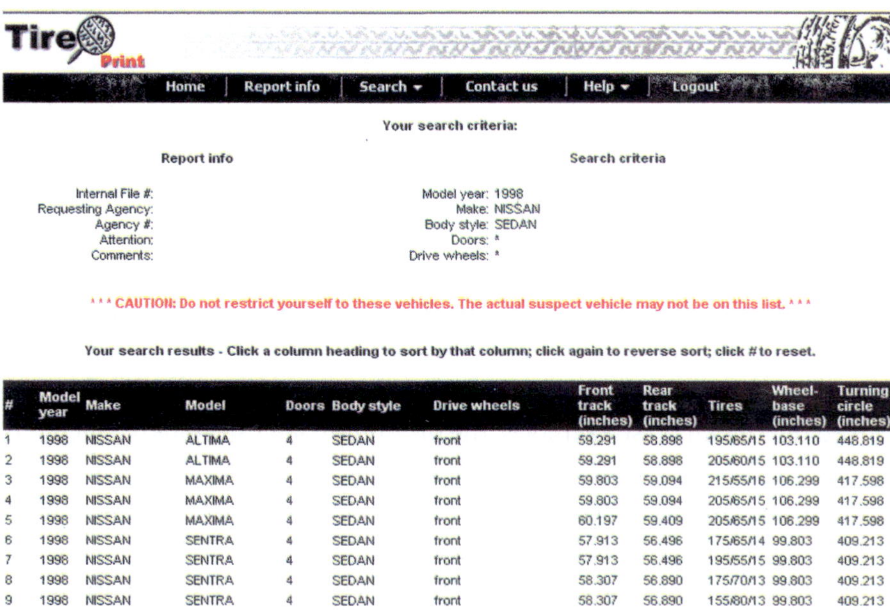

#	Model year	Make	Model	Doors	Body style	Drive wheels	Front track (inches)	Rear track (inches)	Tires	Wheel-base (inches)	Turning circle (inches)
1	1998	NISSAN	ALTIMA	4	SEDAN	front	59.291	58.898	195/65/15	103.110	448.819
2	1998	NISSAN	ALTIMA	4	SEDAN	front	59.291	58.898	205/60/15	103.110	448.819
3	1998	NISSAN	MAXIMA	4	SEDAN	front	59.803	59.094	215/55/16	106.299	417.598
4	1998	NISSAN	MAXIMA	4	SEDAN	front	59.803	59.094	205/65/15	106.299	417.598
5	1998	NISSAN	MAXIMA	4	SEDAN	front	60.197	59.409	205/65/15	106.299	417.598
6	1998	NISSAN	SENTRA	4	SEDAN	front	57.913	56.496	175/65/14	99.803	409.213
7	1998	NISSAN	SENTRA	4	SEDAN	front	57.913	56.496	195/55/15	99.803	409.213
8	1998	NISSAN	SENTRA	4	SEDAN	front	58.307	56.890	175/70/13	99.803	409.213
9	1998	NISSAN	SENTRA	4	SEDAN	front	58.307	56.890	155/80/13	99.803	409.213
10	1998	NISSAN	SENTRA	4	SEDAN	front	58.307	56.890	175/65/14	99.803	409.213

Figure 12.11B. Computer screen shot showing another page of the JATO tire-print.com program. (Courtesy of JATO Dynamics, Inc.)

using a track database, the MSP would be a good source to contact for the necessary considerations.[7]

European Databases

There are some databases in Europe similar to those of the TirePrint program and the Tread Assistant. One database in Belgium is a computerized database similar to that used by the MSP and RCMP and includes both car measurements such as track width but also other features of the vehicles, including the model year, number of doors, tire size, and so forth.[8]

Another resource in Europe is Tire Global Information. This company was founded in Austria in 1995 by Dr. Friedrich Lux and was originally named Tire Guides International. In 2003 the name was changed to Tire Global Information. This company produces tire guides for the tire market in Europe and Asia. More information can be found at their Web site: www.tgi.co.at.

SICAR TreadMate[9]

SICAR's TreadMate is an extensive international tire reference database currently comprising approximately 5,000 records from the United States, Europe, and Asia dating back to 2002. Each record is provided with brand and model information and notes on the tire's availability, including country of origin, dates of introduction, and withdrawal from the market. TreadMate groups together records from different manufacturers using the same tread pattern. This allows the user to take into consideration the range of possible tires that could have made the print and provides some indication of how common the pattern is. TreadMate can be used as either a stand-alone system or in conjunction with the footwear database, SICAR 6. As a stand-alone system records may be retrieved using manufacturer and model references or by using pattern coding, providing a means of identifying tread marks found at a crime scene. TreadMate is updated annually on DVD. Figure 12.12A shows the screen shot used during the coding of a tread design as used when entering or searching for a tire design. Figure 12.12B depicts a tire hit list produced when using TreadMate for a search of a tire design.[10]

[7] Dave Bicigo (Michigan State Police), personal communication, December 14, 2006.

[8] Gerrit Volckeryck, Federale Politie, Directie Technische en Wetenschappelijke Politie Centrale Eenheid, Notelaarstraat 211, 1000 Brussels, Belgium.

[9] SICAR TreadMate is produced by Foster & Freeman USA, Inc., 46030 Manekin Plaza, Suite 170, Sterling, VA 20166; www.fosterfreeman.com.

[10] Information and photographs provided by Amy Temenak, Foster & Freeman USA, Inc.

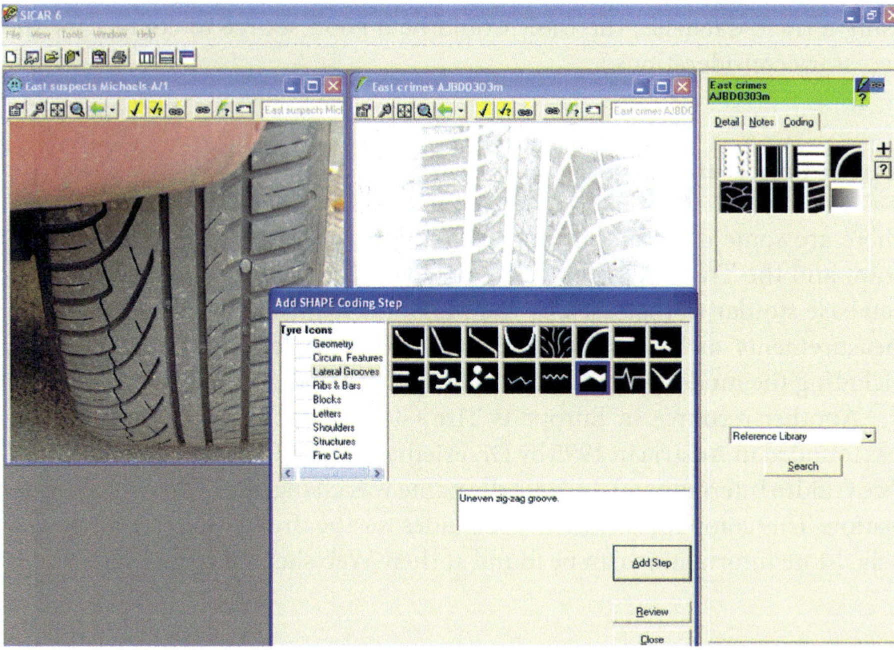

A

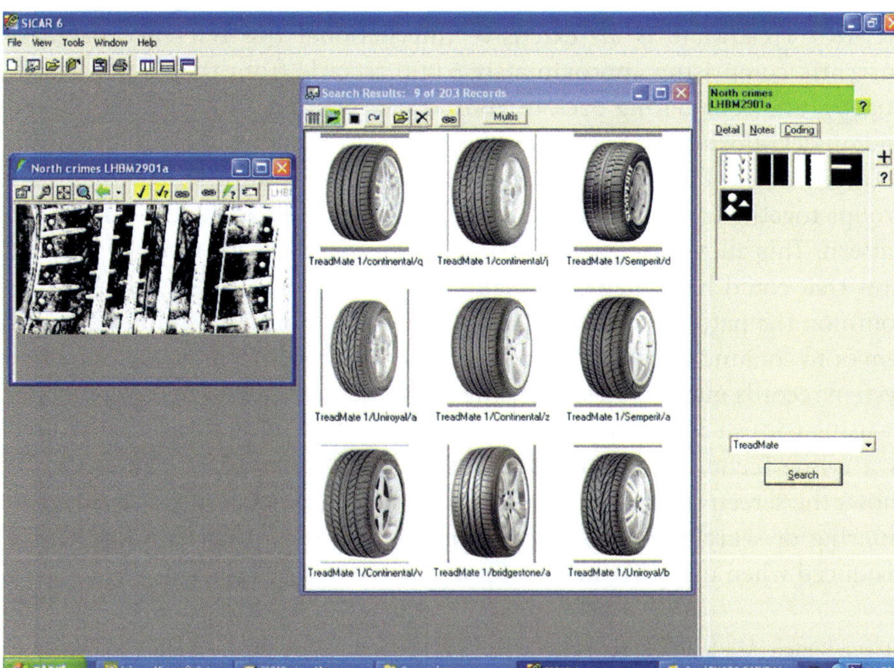

B

Figure 12.12A,B. SICAR program screen shot examples. (Courtesy of Foster & Freeman, USA.)

Books

See Bibliography for complete citations.

Tire Imprint Evidence *by Peter McDonald* In 1989, Peter McDonald, a tire engineer from the Firestone Tire and Rubber Company, wrote this book dedicated entirely to the forensic examination of tire impression evidence. Although this book is now dated in some regards, it provides good basic information about tires as well as some case examples. It is on the recommended reading list for forensic tire examiners.

Forensic Tire Impression Identification *by Lawrence A. Nause*[11] This book was written during the early 1990s as a training manual for RCMP examiners and scene of crime officers (SOCO) but was not published until 2001. The book contains much valuable information and should be read by all forensic tire examiners.

Tire Tracks and Tread Marks *by B. W. Given, R. B. Nehrich, and J. C. Shields* This 88-page book was written in 1977 and is a mixture of accident scene, tire impression tracking, and other information that could be recovered or observed at scenes. This book is currently out of print, but it is worthwhile reading if you can find it.

Tire Technology *by F. J. Kovac* The fifth edition of this 164-page book was published by the Goodyear Tire and Rubber Company in 1978. It contains basic information about the pneumatic tire.

The Pneumatic Tire *edited by A. N. Gent and J. D. Walter* *The Pneumatic Tire* was published by the National Highway Traffic Safety Administration in 2003 and is an 18-chapter, 700-page publication. It provides highly technical information about tires and tire performance. It is available from the University of Akron, Akron, Ohio (330-972-7814), or on the Internet at http://www.tiresociety.org/mainpages/nhtsa.html.

IAI **Recommended Course of Study for Footwear and Tire Track Examiners** The International Association for Identification published the *Recommended Course of Study* many years ago, covering the areas of footwear and tire examination. It was updated in 2006 by Lesley Hammer[12] and other members of the IAI Footwear and Tire Track Subcommittee. This course covers the topics of collection, documentation, photography, manufacturing, examination, conclusions, and providing testimony in the areas of footwear

[11] Nause, L. A., *Forensic Tire Impression Identification,* Canadian Police Research Centre, 2001, available through NRC Publication sales, Montreal, Ottawa, Canada (613)993-2054.

[12] Criminalist IV for the State of Alaska Crime Laboratory, Anchorage, Alaska.

and tire track evidence. The course sets objectives, and provides written and practical exercises, readings, and sample test questions for a trained examiner to use in the training of a future examiner. It is available through the IAI Web site www.theiai.org.

SWGTREAD (Scientific Working Group on Impression Evidence)

In September 2004 the Scientific Working Group on Impression Evidence (SWGTREAD) was formed and met for the first time. One of the roles of SWGTREAD is to write basic guides on various aspects of evidence recovery, training, and examination for the field of footwear and tire impression examination. These guides are published through the IAI Web site (www.theiai.org) for comment by practitioners in the field. All comments are considered and appropriate changes are made after which the guides are published in their final form. SWGTREAD also performs other functions related to the field of examination of footwear and tire impression evidence.

13 Case Studies

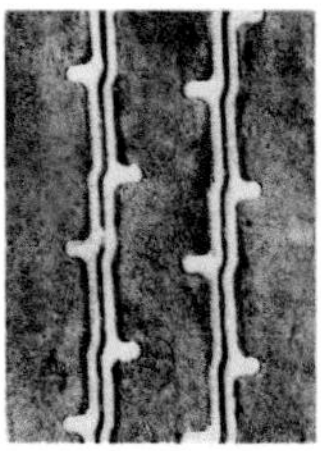

Kunz Family Homicides

On July 4, 1987, four members of the Kunz family were shot to death at their rural farmhouse in Athens, Wisconsin. Their bodies were discovered in the early morning hours the following day. All were shot at close range with a .22 caliber rifle. Missing was Helen Kunz, a fifth homicide victim whose body was not found until nine months later in a neighboring county approximately 18 miles away. The Marathon County Sheriff's department, after a lengthily and involved investigation, charged Christopher Jacobs III of Medford, Wisconsin with these homicides. Crucial evidence in the case involved a series of tire impressions on the dirt road leading to the front of the Kunz farmhouse, and .22 caliber casings found inside of the homicide scene. Although the .22 caliber rifle was never found, a rifle of that type that used the same type of .22 caliber ammunition was linked to Jacobs. More significantly, numerous spent .22 caliber casings were found at the Jacobs residence that were identified as being fired from the same weapon as the spent .22 caliber casings found at the crime scene. The possible motive for the crime was robbery. The Kunz family reportedly had large amounts of cash stashed in the home. After the slayings, this was confirmed when police found over $20,000 in coins and currency that still remained hidden within the house. There was no way to know if or how much other cash had been stolen. Jacobs was familiar with the Kunz family and had traveled to their farmhouse in the past to buy used cars or junk auto parts from them. Other circumstantial evidence linking Jacobs with this crime also existed.

The Kunz farmhouse was well off the main state road and was reached by first driving down a dirt road onto their farm and then turning down a second more narrow dirt road that led up to the farmhouse. When the police responded to this crime they recognized the presence of numerous tire impressions and were quick to preserve the entire area. Four family members-Clarence—Kunz, 76, Marie Kunz, 72, Randolph Kunz, 30, and Irene Kunz, 81—were found dead in the farm house. Helen Kunz, 70, the fifth family

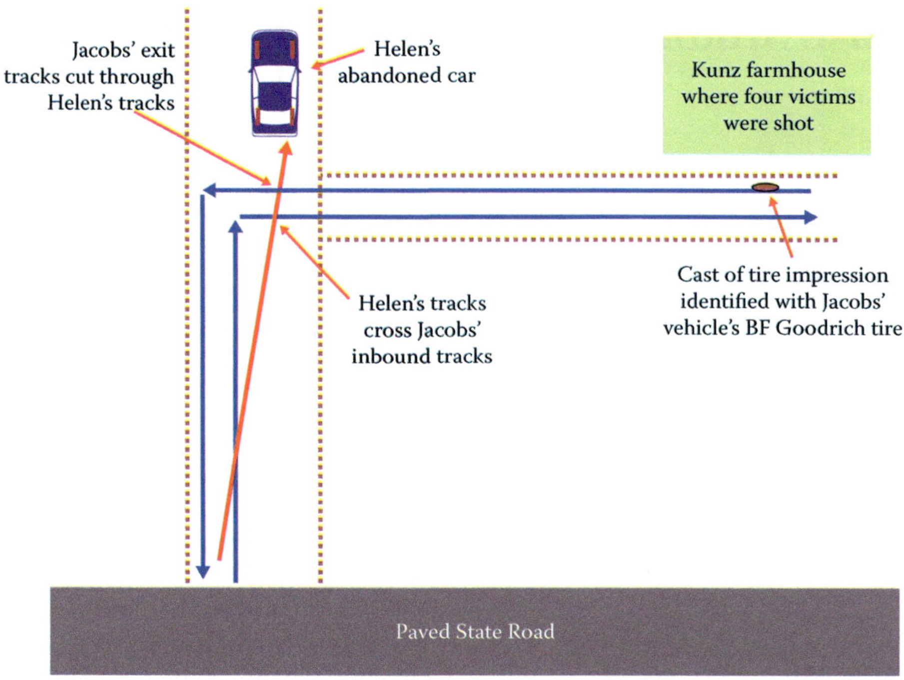

Figure 13.1. A diagram of the scene at the Kunz farmhouse.

Figure 13.2. A photograph of Helen Kunz's car found abandoned on the dirt road of the Kunz farm and just past the dirt road to the farmhouse.

member, was not found at the scene, but her car was abandoned and parked midway between the farmhouse and the state road. A diagram of this scene is depicted in Figure 13.1 and a scene photograph of part of this area including Helen's car is shown in Figure 13.2.

It was observed and documented that Helen's car had tracked over a set of tire tracks leading to the farmhouse while other exiting tracks of that same design had tracked over her inbound car tracks (Figure 13.1). This established that her vehicle arrived at the scene while the perpetrator's vehicle was still there. Over 100 photographs of the tire impressions were taken and seven long dental stone casts of tire impressions were poured.

About six months after the crime, police detained Jacobs for questioning and seized the four tires and spare tire from his old car. Those tires included two Duralon DS Premium tires, size G78-14, DOT VCL9 MB 6063, taken from the rear of the vehicle; a BF Goodrich Belted T/A tire, size P235 60/B14, DOT BFR1 600195, taken from the right front of the vehicle; a BF Goodrich Belted T/A tire, P245/60 B14, DOT BFR2 600195, taken from the left front of the vehicle; and the spare tire, a Duralon DS Premium tire, H78-14, DOT HYMB MB 6098.

The tire evidence was examined by the Wisconsin State crime laboratory whose examiner determined that the two Duralon DS Premium tires, size G78-14, corresponded in design and dimension with the crime scene impressions but could not be positively identified. Other impressions recovered from the same set of tracks at the scene did not match that found on Jacobs' vehicle. Months had passed before Jacobs' vehicle was seized and the possibility existed that tires on his vehicle might have been changed. It was also noted that the tire sizes on the front of the vehicle were not matched and the wheels of the front tires did not match the wheels of the rear tires. A former tire engineer from the tire industry was consulted and assisted in identifying the brand and line of tire that produced those impressions. A search warrant was issued and resulted in the seizure of two additional tires from the property of Jacobs. Those tires were both BF Goodrich Belted T/A P235/70 B14 tires. The Wisconsin laboratory examiner, in addition to determining that the two Duralon DS Premium tires on the vehicle when it was originally seized corresponded in design and dimension was now also able to determine the two BF Goodrich Belted T/A tires obtained via the search warrant, corresponded in tread design and dimension and were capable of having made the other crime scene impressions. He did not locate any individual characteristics that would support a positive identification of any of the tires. A small problem arose when the former tire engineer positively identified the Duralon tire taken from the left rear position of Jacobs' vehicle with one of the photographs from the scene. The Wisconsin examiner reviewed this conclusion but did not concur there was sufficient and confirmable individual characteristics to agree with the identification.

In an attempt to resolve these differences of opinion, on June 1, 1989, the FBI Laboratory was requested to examine all the tire evidence in this case. I prepared inked impressions of all seven tires, photographed all seven casts, and had certain negatives enlarged to natural size. As a result of my examination, I was able to positively identify one of the cast impressions as having been made by the BF Goodrich Belted T/A, P235/70 B14 tire, one of the tires obtained in the search warrant. A portion of that cast is depicted in Figure 13.3 and a portion of the known impression of that tire superimposed over the cast is depicted in Figure 13.4. Enlarged areas of the tire and cast are depicted in Figure 13.5 and Figure 13.6. Although the soil at the scene was mostly a dry powdery mix, portions of the cast held sufficient detail, including the general wear characteristics of the tire and an area of the tire where three clear individual characteristics were present. Both the Wisconsin examiner and the tire engineer concurred with my identification of this cast impression. In addition, I determined that tread design and dimension of some of the crime scene impressions corresponded with the two Duralon DS Premium tires, size G78-14; however, I was unable to confirm or agree with the identification made of one of these tires by the tire engineer and I specifically did not concur with the markings on a chart he prepared which pointed to several individual characteristics he claimed were present. None of those areas clearly depicted anything in my opinion nor in the opinion of the Wis-

Figure 13.3. A portion of one of seven casts made of tire impressions at the scene.

Figure 13.4. An inked impression of the BF Goodrich Belted T/A P235/70 B14 tire superimposed over the cast.

consin state examiner. I eliminated the spare tire (Duralon H78-14) and both BF Goodrich Belted T/A tires taken originally from the two front positions of the vehicle.

Jacobs was tried before a jury in October 1989 and, despite the identification of Jacobs's tire at the farmhouse; despite the fact that Helen's tire tracks crossed his and his tracks crossed Helen's, proving they were there at the same time; and despite the fact that the .22 caliber casings were identified with other casings found at Jacobs' residence, as well as other evidence, Jacobs was acquitted on all five counts of homicide.

Approximately four years after the trial, the State came into posses-

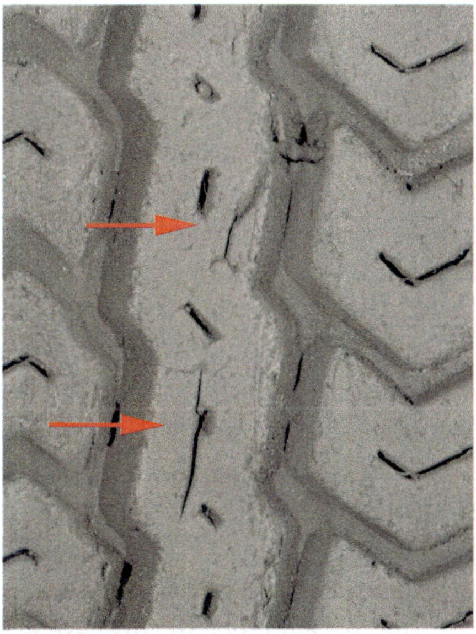

Figure 13.5. An enlarged area of the tire which contained individual characteristics also found in the cast.

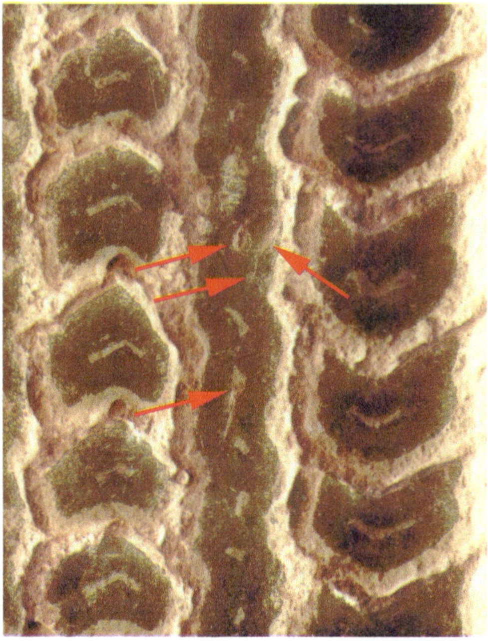

Figure 13.6. An enlarged view of the section of the cast containing the individual features with the inked impression superimposed.

sion of new evidence and charged Jacobs, this time with the false imprisonment and kidnapping of Helen Kunz. Although in Jacobs' first trial, he was charged with the murder of Helen, he had never been charged with kidnapping her and taking her to the final area where she was killed and her body later found. After attempts by the defense to dismiss these charges based on claims they violated the double jeopardy clause, in January 1996 the U.S. Seventh Circuit Court of Appeals upheld the lower court rulings and denied the motion to dismiss these charges. The new trial would be removed to St. Croix, Wisconsin. On June 8, 1998, the kidnapping and false imprisonment trial of Chris Jacobs III began. After hearing testimony from 58 witnesses, including my identification of Jacobs's tire at the farmhouse scene, the jury found Jacobs guilty on both counts on June 19, 1998.

Thanks to the hard work of the investigators, those who diligently recovered the evidence from the crime scene, the laboratory examinations, and the persistent efforts of the prosecutors in this case, the horrendous crime that took place on July 4, 1987, was finally solved, nearly 11 years later.

The tire evidence in this case was crucial and was interesting for several reasons. From the standpoint of the recovery, the initial securing of the area to prevent other vehicles from destroying the impressions likely saved the destruction of some, if not most, of the tire evidence. The extensive recovery of the tire evidence through many photographs and seven long dental stone casts, as well as recognizing and documenting the critical intersections of Helen's and Jacobs' tracks, were crucial to the proof of facts in the case. Next, the recognition by the Wisconsin State Laboratory examiner that some of the tire impressions did not match two of the tires eventually led to the search warrant that produced the two additional tires, one of which we both identified with one of the cast impressions. Finally, testimony in court by those recovering the evidence and the Wisconsin examiner and myself, provided demonstrable physical evidence to the jury that Jacobs' car was at the farmhouse and was present when Helen returned to the farm.

Mary Lou Arruda Homicide

Late in the afternoon of September 8, 1978, Mary Lou Arruda, a petite 15-year-old high school sophomore cheerleader, rode the school bus home to her house in the rural community of Raynham, Massachusetts. Upon exiting the bus, she headed to her friend's house to pick up her bicycle. She never returned home, and that night police and neighbors began searching for her. Her bicycle was found abandoned between her house and her friend's house, along the side of a dirt road. Witnesses in the small rural neighborhood had reported that day seeing a light green car on that street driven by a person unknown to them. Both witnesses provided sufficient details to result in facial composites of the driver of that vehicle.

For over two months Mary Lou remained missing. A task force composed of local, state, and federal personnel continued the investigation and the search for her. On November 11, 1978, two young boys out riding their bikes came upon a body tied to a tree in the Freetown State Park. Later, through dental records, the body would be identified as that of Mary Lou Arruda.

In late November, James Michael Kater, a 32-year-old manager of a donut shop, was arrested and charged with the kidnapping and homicide of Mary Lou. He had been a suspect since near the beginning of the case based on the facial composites that neighbors had provided. Kater, a prior known sex offender, had served little over six years of a 15- to 20-year sentence for the rape of a 15-year-old girl. He had been freed in January 1976 by parole officials. He owned a 1976 Opel Kadette, light green in color.

In the summer of 1979, Kater was brought to trial in New Bedford, Massachusetts. Investigation and physical evidence revealed that Kater, while driving his small light green Opel, knocked Mary Lou from her bicycle. The right side of the car and the handle grip of the bicycle came into contact with each other, resulting in a long, thin black mark along the right front fender of the car. On the soft shoulder of the road, Mary Lou's discarded bicycle laid on its side with its seat twisted. Tire impressions were found in the soft soil at this location and were photographed and later compared with the tires on Kater's green Opel. The witnesses identified Kater as the person they saw driving the light green car in the neighborhood during that afternoon.

Kater's 1976 Opel Kadette was equipped with original equipment BF Goodrich Radial ST tires, size 155 SR-13. These tires were manufactured by the Yokahama Rubber Company in Mishima, Japan, and were imported with the car into the United States. These tires were not sold as replacement tires in the United States, so unless someone specifically ordered a tire of this tread design and dimension, this tire would only find it way into the United States on a small number of new imported vehicles.

At the crime scene, a series of photographs had been taken of the long tire impression where it traveled off the main portion of the dirt road adjacent to Mary Lou's discarded bicycle. This road was an unpaved but a routinely packed and graded dirt road. The shoulder area where the long tire impression was found was a softer mix of soil and small rocks. No casts were taken of this impression. Natural-sized enlargements were made from several photographs that were of this impression. Full-circumference inked tire impressions were made of the BF Goodrich tires. One of the tires is depicted in Figure 13.7. It has a mixed sequence of three pitch lengths: small (S), medium (M), and large (L). My examination determined that the tread design and tread dimension, including the mixed pitch sequence that was evident in the crime scene photographs, depicted in Figure 13.8 and Figure 13.9, corresponded with and could have been made by the right front tire from Kater's Opel. One particular area of the mixed pitch sequence included an area where three consecutive small (S) pitch lengths occurred with certain adjacent pitch lengths of other sizes around it. No other tire size of this BF Goodrich tire design line had this same pitch sequence.

The examination also revealed considerable specific wear along the outside shoulder of the right front tire and the spare tire. On the shoulder of the tire, four small continuous sipes travel between each of the lateral grooves. On one side, all of these sipes are intact. On the other side, the outer most sipes were almost worn completely away except for the center area. The two red arrows in Figure 13.7 point to these sipes on each side of the tire, where the outer sipes on one side are completely present but on the other side are almost worn away except for a small area in its center. The spare tire was not mounted on a wheel but exhibited similar wear. When inked impressions were made of these tires on a flat hard surface, the area containing the specific worn sipe did not make contact with the ground and did not record. To record this portion of the tire, known impressions had to be made in sand. As the tire sank into the soil, the worn sipe on the outer area of the shoulder would record in the impression. Figure 13.10 is a photograph of a portion of the known impression. The arrows point to the same outer sipes as seen in Figure 13.7. The worn sipe characteristic was evident in the

Figure 13.7. A portion of one of the BF Goodrich tires on Kater's car.

photographs of the crime scene impression as well. This area of the tire would not normally contact the asphalt or concrete road surface and wear that far around the shoulder. Investigation revealed that Kater had gone to a service station to have repairs to the wheel bearings of the front wheel and for a car alignment. The service attendant stated the car was in such disrepair it was making considerable noise as it drove into the service station. Experts from the BF Goodrich tire company examined the tire and attributed the causes of wear to those typically caused by faulty alignment and worn wheel bearings. Other tires of this design and type on a properly maintained car would not wear in the area of that outermost sipe.

The case first went to trial in 1979, and on June 21 of that year the jury returned a verdict of guilty of murder in the first degree. The conviction was later overturned by the State Supreme Court over the use of hypnotically induced statements of some witnesses. A second trial ended in January 1986 with another conviction; however, again, the appellate court overturned the case. In December 1992 the third trial ended in a mistrial. Finally, in December 1996, Kater was convicted after a fourth trial. In the fourth trial, testimony was allowed that revealed Kater was convicted of an almost iden-

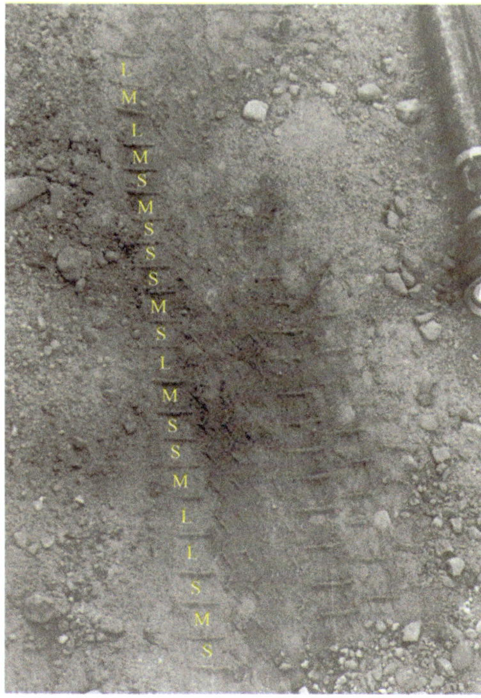

Figure 13.8. A photograph of the crime scene impression which revealed the easily distinguishable pitch sequence.

Figure 13.9. An overhead view of the same impression in Figure 13.8.

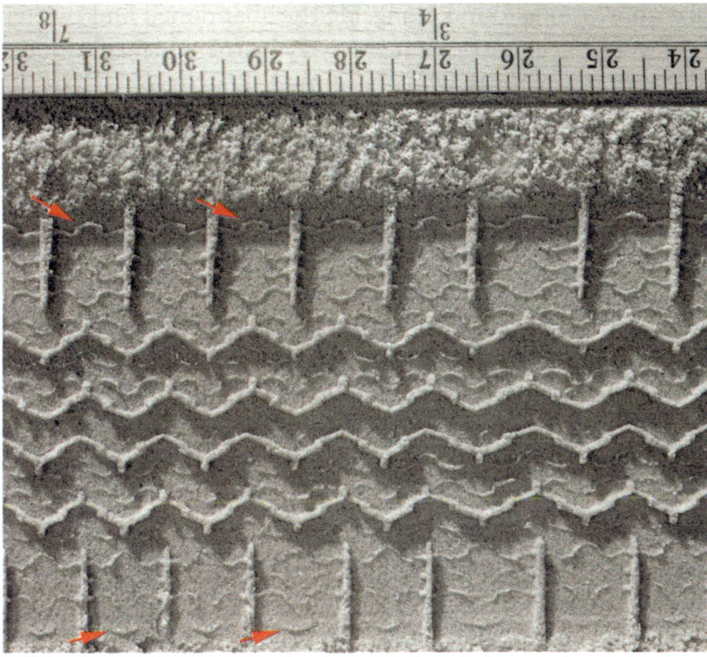

Figure 13.10. A portion of the known impression of the tire showing the worn outer sipe on one side. The arrows point to two sipes on each side to show the difference in wear on one side versus the other.

tical crime that occurred in 1968 when he abducted a 13-year-old girl as she walked her bicycle. He took her into the woods, tied her to a tree and assaulted her, and left her there to die. Fortunately in her case, she was able to free herself and survived. Unfortunately, Mary Lou was unable to escape. Kater was sentenced to life without parole and the case was upheld by the Massachusetts Supreme Judicial Court in 2000.

This case is a good example of tire evidence that is crucial, even when a positive identification was not made. The quality of the crime scene impression and the photographs taken of that impression had some limitations. Although natural-sized enlargements were made of those photographs, the detail was limited to the class characteristics of tread design, tread dimension, and wear. The fact that these tires were original equipment on an imported car and were not normally sold as replacement tires in the United States, and were not commonly found in the United States or Massachusetts, that the small, medium, and large pitch sizes of their pitch sequence were easily distinguishable and unique to that tire size; and that the specific and unusual wear could be attributed to the mechanical condition of Kater's Opel all contributed to the importance of the tire evidence. Kater had used his car to strike the victim as she rode her bike and then fled the scene with her held captive in his car. But the neighbors in this small rural subdivision saw both him and his green car. The tire impressions found alongside the abandoned and twisted bicycle of Mary Lou would help corraborate their eyewitness identification, and and convince the jury it was Kater who committed this crime.

Hit-and-Run Civil Case

Not all tire examinations involve criminal charges. Vehicles are often involved in traffic mishaps resulting in considerable injury or death. Accident reconstruction experts will normally interpret the skid marks and other tire-generated evidence related to speed, braking distances, and the like. In some cases, however, the tread impression evidence is also present and requires a forensic tire examiner to interpret or make comparisons of that evidence.

Although there can be a criminal component to these incidents, there also can be a civil component as well. On many occasions I have been retained in civil cases to assist counsel and to examine tire evidence and/or help interpret statements of witnesses or findings by other examiners. This is an actual example of such a case.

The incident occurred when an elderly female victim was crossing a four-lane street in the crosswalk along with the proper "walk" crossing signal. This was an intersection with two driving lanes on each side of two intersecting roads. The intersection had a traffic light and four crossing signs and crosswalks. As the victim crossed the street within the crosswalk, she entered the final lane and was almost to the other side of the street. At that moment, a large recycle truck that had stopped at the light began to move. The driver of this truck was driving from the right-hand side, permissible as he was making stops along the way to pick up recyclable items. But because he was in this position and despite several adjustable mirrors, his ability to see pedestrians, particularly those coming from the left side, was diminished. In this case the driver failed to see the victim. After he made a full stop, he began to make a right-hand turn on the red light. The truck struck and dragged the victim as it continued its wide right-hand turn. Eventually the left front tire of the truck, an 11-inch-wide Michelin Pilot XZY-1, ran over the victim's head, killing her instantly. Despite witnesses's attempts to flag down the truck, it continued away from the scene and failed to stop. Based on a description of the truck, the police rounded up numerous recycle trucks of the only company that serviced that area. Approximately four hours later, investigators were able to narrow the possible truck down to just one based on the recycle routes and other factors. The driver of the truck was insistent that he did not run over anyone, although he admitted driving through that area. Examination of the truck and examination of the victim initially failed to locate any transferred evidence. No evidence from the truck such as grease or impressions was found on the victim or her clothing and no blood, hair, or torn bits of clothing from the victim were found on the undercarriage of the truck or on its front left tire. It is noted that the left front tire was worn excessively. Reportedly, only a few areas of the tire's nearly 11-foot circumference were swabbed for blood with negative results. Several hours had elapsed since the hit-and-run occurred and the truck had traveled some distance during that time, possibly wearing away any blood that might have been on its surface.

I was first contacted in regard to photographs that had been taken of tire marks present on the white crosswalk lines. Even based on my limited knowledge of the case at this time, I could see no relevance to linking the truck's Michelin tire to any of these marks. This was because this truck normally passed over this crosswalk in its weekly route to pick up recycled items. White crosswalk lines at almost any intersection acquire an accumulation of black tire marks of various designs and qualities, and there is no way to accurately determine the age of any of these marks. To provide a complete and thorough evaluation of any potential tire evidence that might have been remained, I requested photographs of the victim and her clothing and any autopsy photographs as well. As is unfortunately typical after such requests, I was initially provided low-quality photographs printed from a computer, often called laser prints. Not surprisingly, I was unable to visually detect any tire impressions on the victim from these prints. I also received the normal 4 × 6-inch prints like those made at the local one-hour photo service. Although these were better quality in some regards, photographs of this type do not often reveal fine details because of the way they are printed. At this point, I was unable to detect any tire marks or contusions on either the victim or the victim's clothing. Finally I received a set of high-quality enlargements that were prepared directly from the original negatives of those photographs taken at the victim's autopsy.

Examination of these immediately revealed a set of contusions on the cheek of the victim. The contusions consisted of two sets of narrow parallel lines, as depicted in Figure 13.11. Figure 13.12 is the same picture with these parallel lines slightly enhanced. In addition to the parallel lines, each also revealed a fingerlike projection at a 90-degree angle to those parallel lines.

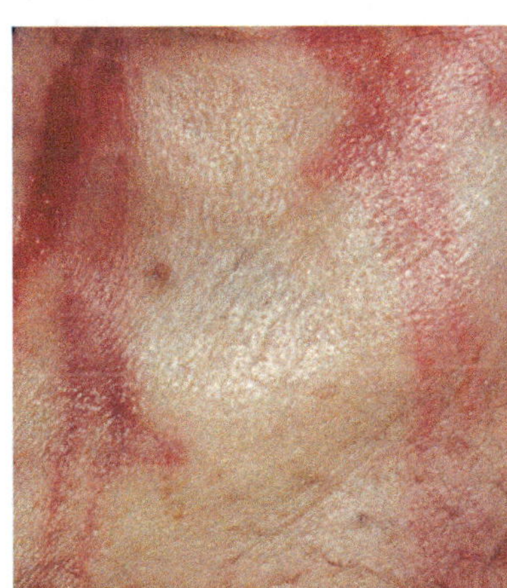

Figure 13.11. The blunt force injury contusions apparent on the cheek of the victim.

The front tires of the recycle truck were Michelin Pilot XZY-1 tires. This tire design was only manufactured in one size, 3.15/80 R22.5. The left

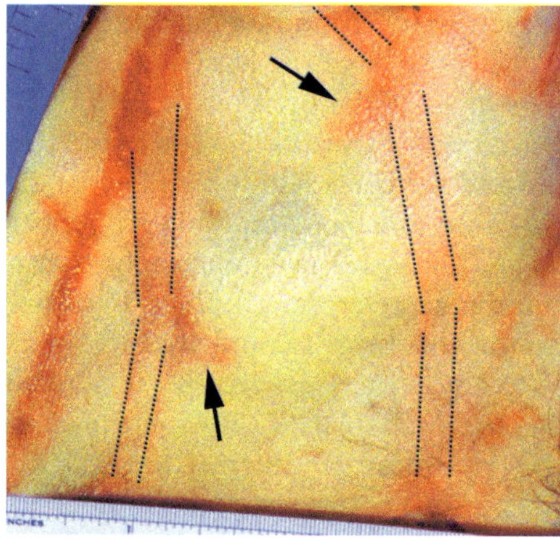

Figure 13.12. A slightly enhanced picture with dotted lines to illustrate the paths of the small parallel contusions. The arrows point to the fingerlike projections.

tire was the main tire in question because it would have been the one that was nearest the victim during the sharp right turn. The path the right tire took during the right turn would have placed it at considerable distance from where the victim was run over. The left front tire was excessively worn. Parts of the shoulder were worn beyond the tread wear indicator depth and some areas of the shoulder were even bald. In the center of the tire, the two central grooves still had some depth, and at the bottom middle of each groove was a raised strip of rubber the manufacturer included in the design to help prevent the retentions of stones and subsequent stone drilling. The tread surface was worn down to where these strips of rubber were now even with the tread. Figure 13.13 shows a Michelin XZY-1 tire when new next to the worn left

Figure 13.13. On the right is the new Michelin XZY-1 tire. On the left is the worn front tire from the recycle truck.

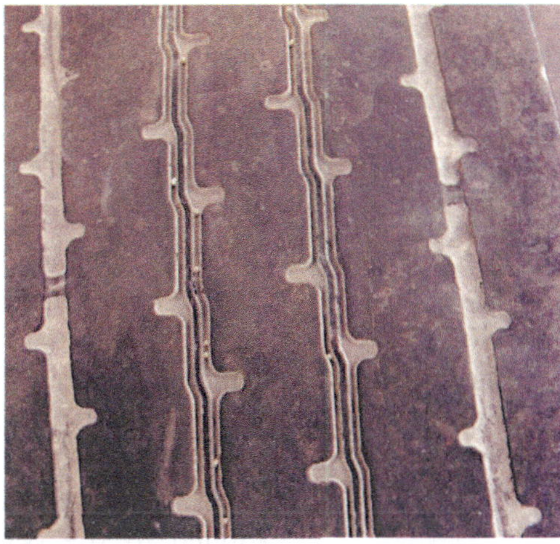

Figure 13.14. The front left tire in its advanced stages of wear. Two tread wear indicators are worn to the same level as the surrounding tread. In addition, the small rubber strips in the two center grooves are now even with the tread surface.

Figure 13.15. An enlargement comparing one of the center grooves of the worn front tire with the appearance and dimensions of the same groove on the new tire. The tapering of the groove has become narrower after wear. The small rubber strip deep in the bottom of the new tire has now become part of the tire design. The once square fingerlike projections on the new tire have been worn down to the smaller rounded projections on the worn tire.

front tire of the truck. Figure 13.14 depicts the central groove areas of the left front tire worn down below the tread wear indicators and also to the strips of rubber in the middle of the two center grooves. As depicted in Figure 13.15, the central grooves, when new, are significantly wider and have much greater depth than the well-worn tire. The width of the main grooves is reduced substantially in the worn tire due to the designed taper of these grooves. The rubber strip at the bottom of each new groove, because of the depth, would not be part of the impression process, whereas in the excessively worn front tire this strip now makes contact with road surface and has become part of the design. The fingerlike projections have a larger and rectangular profile on the new tread surface, and a small transverse groove is connected to them. As the tire wears down, the rectangular profile transitions to a smaller and more rounded projection. The small and shallow transverse grooves have been worn completely away.

In this case, the tire ran over the victim and the blunt force trauma produced a contusion on her cheek that retained details of the central area of the tire design and its excessive condition of wear. A contusion is produced when sufficient blunt force is rapidly applied to the skin's surface. That force causes subcutaneous hemorrhaging just below the skin's surface as the capillaries burst. Hemorrhaging creates the discoloration known as a contusion or more commonly called a bruise. In the case where the blunt force is applied by a patterned object, whether it is a shoe, tire, or other object, a blunt force pattern injury may occur. Figure 13.16 depicts a simple patterned object applying force to skin and the resulting blunt force pattern injury. When this patterned object strikes the skin with sufficient force, it forces the blood in the underlying skin to be moved away from that portion of the patterned object exerting the force, i.e., to the edges of that pattern. If sufficient force is applied rapidly enough and the proper conditions exist, the blood vessels will rupture in those areas, resulting in a replication of that pattern. Figure 13.17 depicts how this would occur with the center portion of the worn front tire. On the left is the tire design, including the small rubber strips that divide the two center grooves. On the right

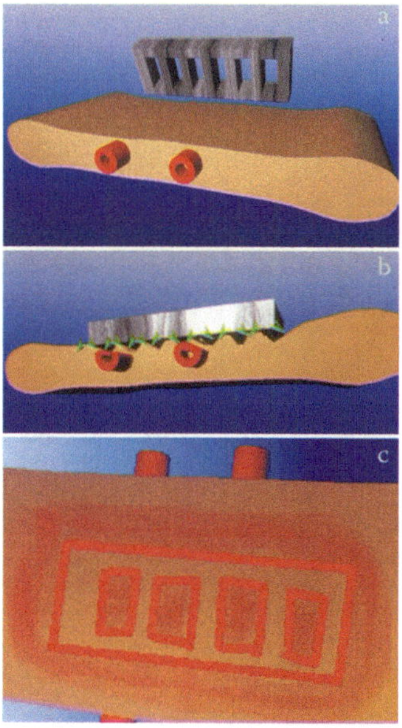

Figure 13.16. A simple patterned object applying force to skin and the resulting blunt force injury pattern. If the patterned object strikes the skin with sufficient force, it causes the blood in the underlying skin to be moved away from the pressure the patterned object exerts. This forces the blood to the edges or grooves of that pattern. If the force is applied rapidly enough and the proper conditions exist, the blood vessels can rupture in those areas, resulting in a replication of that pattern.

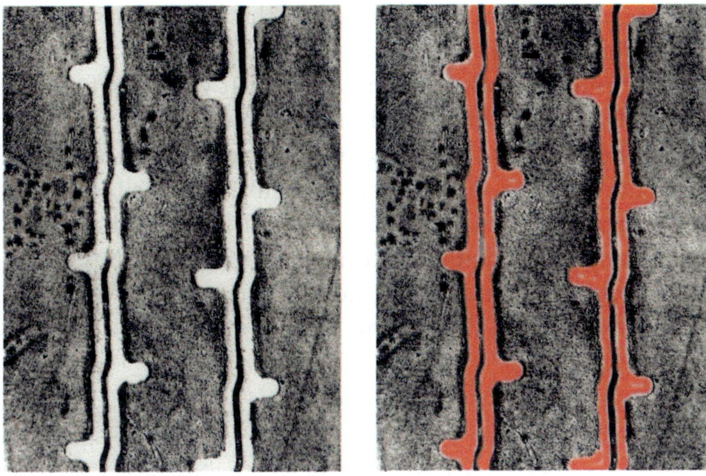
A B

Figure 13.17. The left side, marked *A,* is an impression of a small portion of the center two grooves of the front left tire. On the right, marked *B,* the areas in red are where the blood from ruptured blood vessels beneath the skin would replicate this pattern.

of Figure 13.17, the areas in red are the areas the blood would be forced to and would represent the resulting pattern injury.

In the hit-and-run case, the parallel lines and fingerlike projections evident on the victim's face are contusions that resulted from this type of action. As the tire exerted its pressure against the skin and blood was forced into those areas, the small blood vessels hemorrhaged, resulting in a blunt force patterned injury. Compare the two parallel lines and fingerlike projections in red in Figure 13.17 with the pattern injury on the cheek of the victim (Figures 13.11 and 13.12). The force of the Michelin tire in its worn condition caused the blood beneath the skin on the cheek of the victim to move to the areas of those two tiny grooves between the rubber strip and edges of the main groove as well as into the area of the fingerlike projections.

Contusions vary considerably in their detail due to the many variables involved in their production by a blunt patterned object. In some cases, a tire can roll over a victim and leave little or no pattern injury. In other cases, a more extensive and detailed pattern injury is possible. In this case, the initial assessment of the vehicle and victim were incomplete because one of the basic procedures of examination, i.e., that of looking at all of the most detailed evidence available, was not followed. Only until custom-printed enlargements made from the original autopsy negatives were made was the blunt force pattern injury on the victim's cheek visible. Even then, without an understanding of blunt injury formation, the patterned injury could have still gone unnoticed. The examination of the tire for blood was also incompletely carried out. At the scene, the investigating officer documented that blood was transferred from the victim to another location, one rolling tire circumference away from her body. It was therefore established that the tire did acquire some blood on it. Although it is entirely possible that in the few hours after the incident any blood on the excessively worn tire was worn off the tire's surface, it is also entirely possible that removing the tire and examining it with luminol would have produced some trace of blood that could have then been compared with the DNA of the victim. Unlike the initial investigation concluded, there was, in fact, a transfer of evidence from the truck to the victim.

The Tire Evidence in the Oklahoma City Bombing Case

14

On Wednesday, April 19, 1995, at 9:02 AM local time, at 5th and Harvey Streets in downtown Oklahoma City, Oklahoma, a catastrophic explosion disintegrated half of the Alfred P. Murrah Federal Building. One hundred and sixty-eight people died, either instantly or later from their sustained wounds. Over 500 others were injured, many losing eyes or limbs, and being so severely scarred, their lives would never again be the same. The property damage was assessed in the hundreds of millions of dollars.

The Murrah Federal Building was nine stories high. It had been named after Alfred P. Murrah, the youngest federal judge to be appointed in American history. Within this building worked a mixture of people, including Federal agents, military recruiters, citizens seeking social security payments or housing assistance, as well as many children in its day care center.

The explosion that morning was so powerful that people living in towns 30 to 40 miles away heard it. One survivor who was in the building stated she was working on her computer when literally the entire building blew up. She was thrown against the floor, and when able to stand up, all of the girls in the office she had worked with had totally disappeared along with the six floors now on top of them. She never saw them again.

The initial minutes and hours were filled with panic. The blast caused many fires within the office building and to nearby vehicles impacted by the explosion. The damage also extended through the interior portions of the building and in other directions and caused significant damage to adjacent buildings and their occupants.

Firemen, police, and helpful citizens responded to the scene to help extinguish the flames and tend to the victims's needs. The rescue operation for survivors continued for several days. Initially, it was a scene filled with dazed and injured victims, bodies and body parts, fires and smoke, and friends and relatives trying to reach their loved ones. It eventually turned into attempts to locate trapped and buried victims and the remains of those who were not so lucky.

The blast from the bomb was forceful enough to remove a major portion of the external structure of the building (Figure 14.1). The Ryder rental truck that contained the bomb had been parked almost midway at curbside in front of the office building. The explosion created a 30-ft-wide, 8½-ft-deep crater.

The blast had completely destroyed the Ryder truck and had sent debris from it in all directions. The axle of the truck wound up almost 600 feet away from ground zero, where it had smashed into a small red car (Figure 14.2). The early discovery of this axle had great significance. The axle contained an identification number, also shown enlarged in Figure 14.2. This number allowed investigators to trace the axle to the Ford Motor Company and to identify it as a 1993 20-foot Ford F700 Truck. That truck had been manufactured by Ford as part of an order of 400 trucks specifically made for the Ryder Rental Corporation. In short time investigators were able to determine the axle belonged to a specific truck that had been rented to an individual

Figure 14.1. An aerial view showing the damage to the Alfred P. Murrah Federal Building. The Ryder truck bomb had been parked in front of the building. A crater was now at this location and is covered by blue tarp, as indicated by the arrow.

Figure 14.2. The axle from the Ryder truck, now resting on the ground and indicated by the arrow, was blown almost 600 feet into this small car, smashing its hood and windshield. A VIN on the axle allowed investigators to identify the Ryder Ford truck that was used as the bomb.

who listed his name on the rental agreement as Robert Kling. The rental of this truck had been made at Elliott's Body Shop in Junction City, Kansas. Interviews by FBI agents at Elliott's Body Shop resulted in an artist's composite of the individual who had rented the truck using the name of Robert Kling (Figure 14.3). That composite led to the identification of Timothy McVeigh later that same day by the owner of the Dreamland Motel in Junction City where McVeigh had stayed during the preceding days.

A search of McVeigh's name through the National Criminal Information Center (NCIC) showed that a Timothy James McVeigh had been arrested on April 19 by the Oklahoma Highway Patrol (OSP) and was still lodged in the Noble County jail in Perry, Oklahoma. McVeigh, after leaving the Ryder truck bomb parked in front of the Murrah building, had driven away in his recently acquired Mercury Marquis, depicted in Figure 14.4. He previously had parked the Mercury nearby as a means of escape. Shortly after the bomb detonated as he was leaving Oklahoma City, he was pulled over by the OSP for failure to have a license plate on the car and was arrested for both that as well as

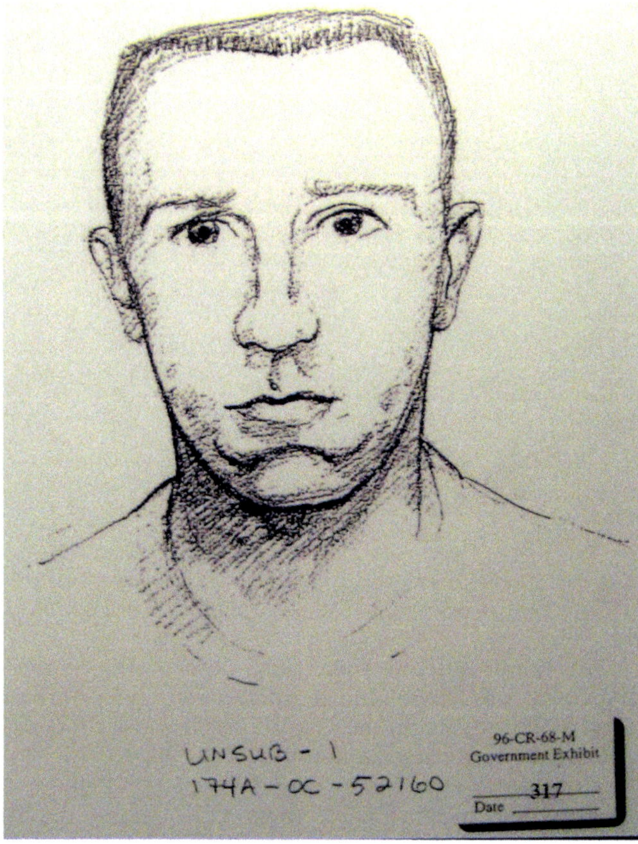

Figure 14.3. The artist's composite created from witnesses at Elliott's Body Shop, later identified as Timothy McVeigh.

Figure 14.4. The Mercury Marquis McVeigh was driving on the way out of Oklahoma City when he was arrested for driving without any license plates.

SATURDAY
OKLAHOMAN & TIMES

OKLAHOMA CITY, OK — SATURDAY, APRIL 22, 1995 — 94 PAGES — 50¢

BOMB SUSPECT CHARGED

Man Upset By '93 Raid Near Waco

This story was written from reports by staff writers Nolan Clay, Diana Baldwin, John Parker, Robby Trammell, Randy Ellis and Michael McNutt.

Figure 14.5. The headlines of the *Oklahoman & Times* newspaper on April 22, 1995, showing the FBI taking custody of Timothy McVeigh.

carrying a concealed weapon. He was turned over to FBI custody and on Friday, April 21st, was charged with the bombing, as shown in Figure 14.5.[1]

After identifying McVeigh, investigation led the FBI to Terry Nichols, a former army buddy of McVeigh and a resident of Herington, Kansas. In Herington, Nichols and McVeigh had rented a storage shed under the alias name of Shawn Rivers. Agents believed it was here that the 55-gallon drums and other materials used to build the bomb had been stored. Investigation was focused on this locker where it was noticed there was a set of very deep dual assembly tire tracks directly in front of it. The truck would have been here just prior to the Wednesday morning bombing. There had been considerable rain and the sand and gravel mixture that was in front of the rented storage contained a set of two deep dual-axled tracks. Terry Nichols had allegedly returned to this locker after the bombing, possibly to clean out any evidence that might remain. A set of tire tracks leading from the main dirt road and

[1] Oklahoman & Times, April 22, 1995, front page.

curving around through a grassy area to the front of the storage locker were believed to be from Nichols pickup truck.

At 9 AM on Saturday, April 22, I received a call from the Assistant Director of the FBI Laboratory to proceed to Herington, Kansas to recover and examine these tracks. I arranged to have someone at the FBI Academy in Quantico, Virginia transport 200 pounds of dental stone to the Manassas, Virginia airport. I was flown to Kansas on the Bureau's small jet and then continued the travel to Herington by car. Arriving approximately one-half hour prior to dark, I quickly took several general scene photographs. Figure 14.6 is one of those photographs overlooking the incoming dirt road. On the left is the building housing storage locker #2 that Nichols and McVeigh rented, and on the right, cutting through the grassy area, were tire tracks believed to be made by Nichols' pickup truck. One of the FBI's Emergency Response Teams was present in Herington to process Nichols' residence, and part of that team was present at the storage facility to assist me in the recovery of the tire evidence.

The areas of interest had already been marked with red cones and the entire area had been closed off with crime scene tape. The dual tire tracks that were suspected of being from the Ryder truck were directly centered in front of shed #2 and are pictured in Figure 14.7 and Figure 14.8. The sand and gravel mixture was not a substrate that would retain great detail. Further, it had rained since the day of the bombing, and the rain had washed away any tread design that might have originally been retained. Even though the rain had eroded any tread design from the tracks, the ridges created between each set of dual assembly tires were still present. The industry track width for a

Figure 14.6. A long-range view of the storage locker area showing storage locker #2, second door from left, and the grassy area on the far right, believed to contain impressions from Nichols's GMC truck.

Figure 14.7. The dual assembly tracks were perfectly centered on storage locker #2.

Figure 14.8. The track width measurements and the distance from the building to each point where the tracks ended were taken.

dual assembly vehicle is measured from the center point in-between the tires on one side to the same point between the tires on the other side, indicated by the arrow running between the tracks in Figure 14.8. Even with the heavy rainfall, the center point of these ridges would remain the same and the distance between them was measured at several locations. Each measurement yielded track width of 73.5 inches. Although the impressions themselves were weathered, some measurements from the outside and inside borders were also taken. In addition, measurements were made from the point where each dual tire track ended in order to determine the distance that remained between the end of the tracks and the shed. This would allow a determination as to whether that particular Ryder truck could have backed up this close to the storage locker and, if so, how much clearance would remain.

Because the truck used in the bombing was totally destroyed, an identical Ryder 20-foot truck was used to obtain these known measurements. The truck used was located in Alexandria, Virginia, only a 30-minute drive from the FBI lab, and was one of 400 Ford F700 trucks from that Ryder order. Each of the 400 trucks had sequential vehicle identification numbers (VIN) as well as identical components, including the axles, wheels, and Bridgestone tires. The truck I examined in Alexandria was therefore identical in all respects to the truck rented by McVeigh. The center-to-center track width measured on that truck was 73.5 inches, the same that had been measured at numerous locations in the tracks in front of storage locker #2. The outside-to-outside and inside-to-inside measurements taken at the scene were not as accurate because the outer and inner edges of the tires were notched and because of the considerable amount of erosion that had occurred due to the rain. Those measurements, as expected, were 3/8 inch and 5/8 inch off, an insignificant amount under the circumstances. The distance between the tire tracks and the shed door had been measured at the scene and compared against the Ryder truck in Virginia. The clearance that would have remained between the rearmost part of the truck and the storage shed was 17.5 inches on one side and 20.5 inches on the other side. The truck had been backed up to within less than 2 feet of the shed. Figure 14.9A depicts the side view of the truck. Figure 14.9B depicts the rear view with the ramp pulled out. The ramp was a slide-out ramp built into the rear of the truck. It would only slide straight out, but its width would allow it to fit through the doorway of the storage locker. The fact that the tracks were centered perfectly on the locker door and the truck had backed up so close indicates the ramp was probably pulled directly into the storage locker, not only providing a ramp for loading but also providing privacy. Of all the tracks and track widths that could have been found in front of this locker, rented by McVeigh and Nichols under a fictitious name, these dual assembly tracks were identical to those of the Ford F700 Ryder rental truck that had been used as the truck bomb and had been rented by McVeigh. A summary of the track measurements is included in Figure 14.10A and 14.10B.

The other tracks I recovered and examined were those that agents believed were made by the 1984 GMC pickup truck of Terry Nichols, depicted in Figure 14.11. These tracks were located both throughout the gravel mix area running up to the front of storage locker #2, as well as through the grassy area where the clay soil there retained more detailed impressions. Further, these tracks had been made more recently and since the rain had ended. Eight tire tracks could be seen leaving the main gravel road where they crossed over the softer clay soil and through the grass. The arrows in Figure 14.12 indicate the location of these eight tracks near cones 6 through 10. The tracks represented

A

B

Figure 14.9A,B. Side and rear views of the Ryder truck examined in Alexandria, Virginia identical to the Ryder truck used in the bombing. The ramp pulls straight out of the rear of the truck bed.

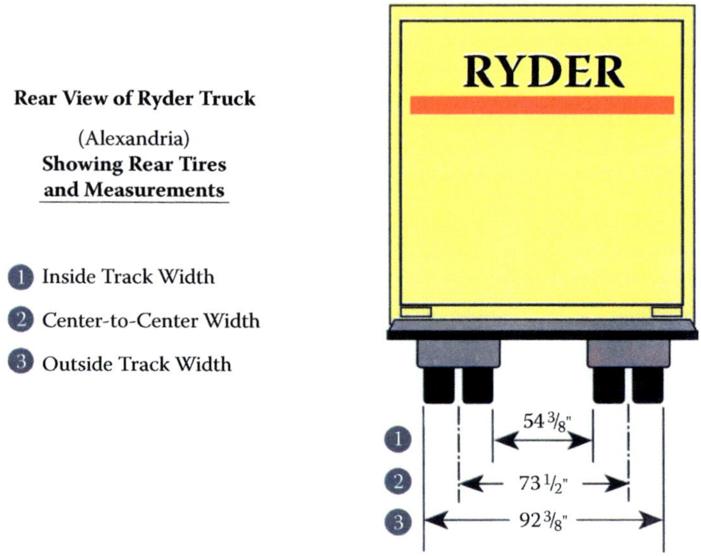

Figure 14.10A. The track width measurements obtained from the Ryder truck in Alexandria, Virginia.

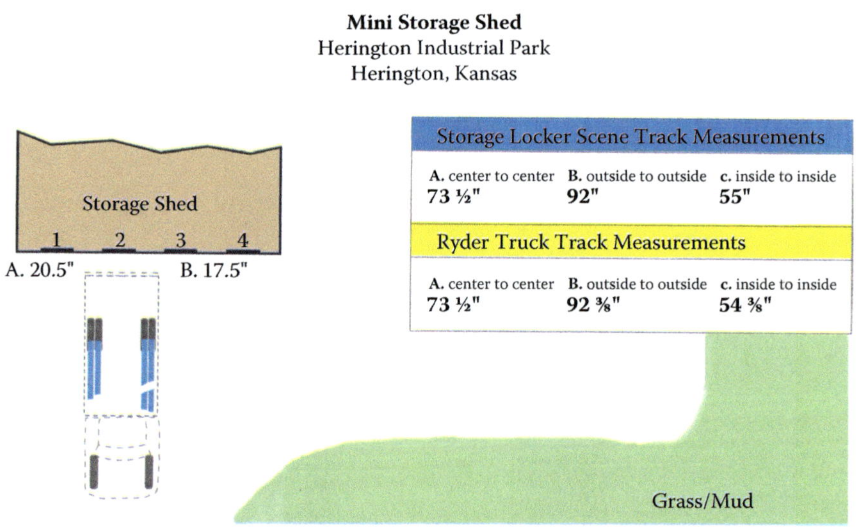

Figure 14.10B. On the right is a comparison of the track width measurements made at the storage shed scene in Herington, Kansas, and the measurement taken from the Ryder truck in Alexandria, Virginia. On the left is depicted the amount of clearance that would remain if that truck had backed up to the storage shed and stopped at the point where the tracks had ended.

Figure 14.11. The GMC truck belonging to Terry Nichols.

Figure 14.12. Another general scene photograph, taken before dark and depicting the eight tracks that left the gravel road and crossed over the grassy area. The tracks continued to curve around and could be followed to the front of storage locker #2.

two different designs, represented in blue and red in Figure 14.13. The GMC truck of Nichols had been seized and was stored in a garage at the Herington Police Department, only minutes away. I traveled to the police department and made the preliminary observation that the two tire designs represented in those eight tracks corresponded with the tire designs on Nichols' truck. The left front and left rear tires as well as the front right tire on the truck were of one design, a Firestone Triumph M/S Radial 2000 tire. The right rear tire was a different design, a Cooper Multi-Mile Radial XL tire.

Numerous sequential photographs were taken of each of the eight tire tracks. A long tape measure was laid down alongside of each track and remained in that position during the entire sequence of examination quality photography along a length of each impression (Figure 14.14). The

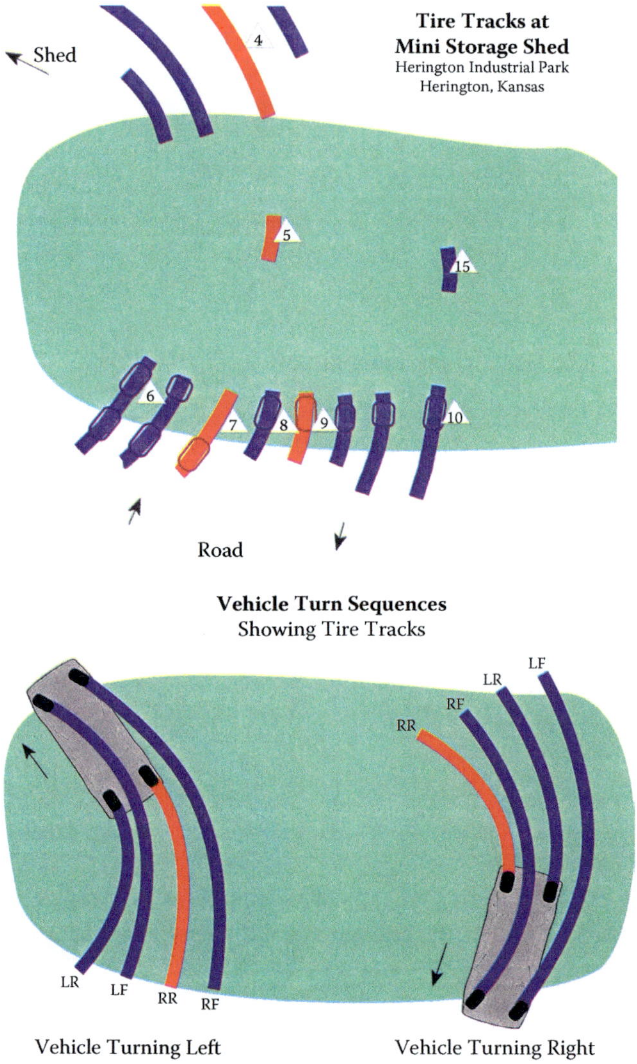

Figure 14.13. The top is a drawing depicting the eight tracks in Figure 14.12 and additional continuations of those tracks that were also recovered. The red tracks were those made by the Cooper Multi-Mile tire mounted serial side out on the right rear position of Nichols's truck. The blue color represents those tracks of the Triumph 2000 tires. The bottom of this drawing depicts the right rear tire (red) tracks in relation to the other tires when turning left in toward storage locker #2 and when turning right exiting from storage locker #2.

Figure 14.14. A long tape measure was laid out along the length of each separate track to help keep track of the individual examination-quality photographs taken.

examination quality photographs were taken using an additional metric ruler in each of these exposures as the scale. Figure 14.15 depicts an examination-quality photograph of a segment of one of the impressions in the grassy area.

After photography, 200 pounds of dental stone was used to pour 13 large dental stone casts to recover portions of the tire tracks that appeared to contain the best detail. At least once cast was made of each of the eight tracks.

Figure 14.15. A 300-mm ruler was used as the scale for the examination quality photographs taken of each impression.

Inked impressions were made of all four tires. The Cooper Multi-Mile tire on the right rear position had been mounte d serial side out. Because this tire had directional noise treatment, it was determined that the tracks left by the right rear tire on both the inbound and outbound scene impressions were made by a tire that was mounted serial side out as well. Figure 14.13 distinguishes the positions of tracks of the Multi-Mile tire in red. A photograph taken of the casts made in this area was previously depicted in Figure 3.25 in Chapter 3.

The examination concluded the photographed and cast impressions corresponded in tread design, tread dimension, and general wear with the respective Triumph 2000 and Multi-Mile tires on Nichols' truck. Both of these tires were replacement tires. The combination of both designs in the same respective positions on both the vehicles and as evidenced in the scene tracks corresponded. In addition, the right rear tire was mounted serial side out, a situation that would not be frequently found on another vehicle having a tire of that particular design and size. No individual characteristics were present, in part because much of the tracks traveled through either a gravel mix or grassy area, but also in part because the tires contained very few individual characteristics.

Beyond the grassy area, the continuing tracks from Nichols' truck turned toward and continued to the front of storage shed #2. Night photographs of these tracks, taken with halogen lighting, are depicted in Figure 14.16 and Figure 14.17 and were used to document the path of the tracks. Figure 14.18 and Figure 14.19 depict two of the trial charts prepared to demonstrate the examination of the tires on Nichols' truck, one showing the Firestone Triumph 2000 design and the other the Cooper Multi-Mile design.

On May 13, 1997, I testified in the McVeigh trial in U.S. District Court in Denver, Colorado, regarding the dual assembly tracks and my conclusion regarding the track width and other measurements obtained from in front of the storage locker. The tire tracks played a very small role in the trial, but nevertheless, were part of the proof of facts that proved the case against both

Figure 14.16. One of the photographs taken at night with the halogen lights providing oblique lighting. These tracks come from the grassy area and curve toward the storage locker.

Figure 14.17. Another night photograph showing a continuation of the tracks in Figure 14.16 leading up to the front of storage locker #2.

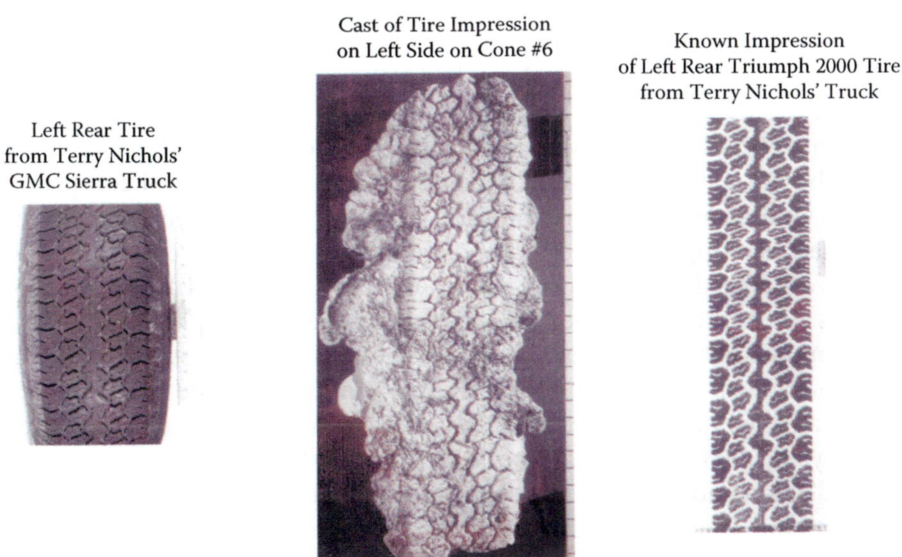

Figure 14.18. A trial chart showing the Firestone Triumph 2000 tread design (left), one of the casts from the left side of cone #6, and the corresponding wet media film inked impression of that segment of the tire.

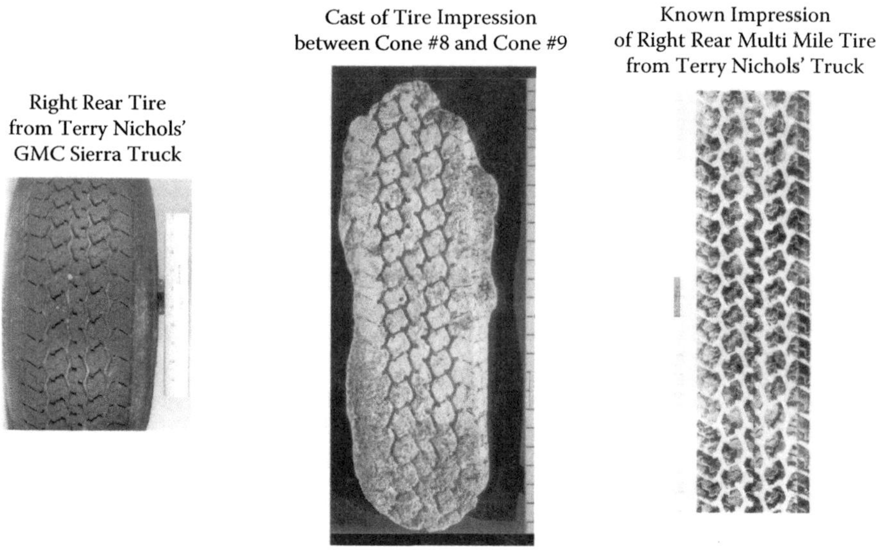

Figure 14.19. A trial chart showing the Cooper Multi-Mile tread design (left), one of the casts from between cones #8 and #9, and the corresponding wet media film inked impression of that segment of the tire.

McVeigh and Nichols. The jury reached a verdict of guilty for McVeigh on three counts of conspiracy and eight counts of murder. On June 11, 2001, at 7:14am, Timoth McVeigh, age 33, was executed by lethal injection as a result of his attack in Oklahoma City that killed 168 people and wounded hundreds more. It was the first federal execution since 1963.

Terry Nichols, age 43 was tried in U.S. District court separately. On December 23, 1997, jurors found Nichols guilty on one count of conspiracy to use a weapon of mass destruction and on eight counts of involuntary manslaughter resulting in the deaths of eight federal law enforcement officers. He was sentenced to life imprisonment on June 4, 1998. The federal trial of Nichols and McVeigh only pertained to the eight federal employees that were killed in the explosion. When Nichols was not given a death sentence in that trial, the state of Oklahoma tried him for the murders of the other 160 victims. I testified to the tire tracks at that trial, held in McAlester, Oklahoma. On May 26, 2004, Nichols was found guilty of first-degree murder, conspiracy and arson and again, he was sentenced to life imprisonment.

Not long after the investigation was over, the remains of the Alfred P. Murrah Federal Building were professionally demolished and removed. A fence was placed around what had become sacred ground. After the bombing, Oklahomans and their neighbors, visitors, and complete strangers had visited the fence to pay their respects or mourn their loved ones, leaving behind a variety of stuffed animals, pictures, flowers, shirts, and other symbols. On April 19, 2000, exactly five years after the bombing, a museum and a permanent memorial to the bombing, featuring 168 stone and glass chairs, each one inscribed with the names of one of the dead, was

Figure 14.20. The glass chairs and reflecting pool outside the Oklahoma City National Memorial & Museum located on the former site of the Alfred P. Murrah Federal Building.

Figure 14.21. A portion of the fence has been preserved at the memorial and museum site.

dedicated (Figure 14.20). A portion of the original fence has been preserved (Figure 14.21).

Glossary

Aggressive design A tire design that has a more complex tread design, normally with many grooves and sipes.

Air pressure The force exerted by air within the tire, normally expressed in pounds per square inch (psi). The air pressure is held within the tire by the liner.

Aspect ratio The ratio that expresses a tire's section height to section width proportion. If a tire's sidewall height were 55% of its section width, its aspect ratio would be 55. In the tire size expressed as 205/55-15, the number 55 is the aspect ratio.

Asymmetric tread pattern A tread where the design on one side is not identical to the other side. Larger tread elements may be used on the outer portion of the tire to increase performance. Also called an uneven tread design.

Balance The even distribution of weight on a mounted wheel and tire The state in which a tire and wheel assembly spins with all its weight distributed equally.

Bald tire A tire that has worn away all of its tread design or that has been manufactured without any tread design.

Beads Two rubber insulated multistranded hoops made of very strong steel wires that hold the tire on the rim.

Belts Two wide strips of rubber-coated steel wires placed circumferentially over the plies and just beneath the tread. They reinforce the tread area, provide puncture resistance, and help the tire make better contact with the road

Bias tire A tire that has two plies that cross diagonally over one another at an angle (on a bias). Also known as diagonal construction as designated on a tire with the letter "D."

Bias-belted tire A tire that has two plies that cross diagonally over one another at an angle (on a bias) plus two reinforced belts that lie beneath the tread. Bias-belt construction is designated on a tire with the letter "B."

Camber The inward or outward tilt of the tire as viewed from the front of the vehicle. Negative camber tilts inward and positive camber tilts outward.

Carcass The portion of the tire that includes the liner, plies, and bead and that forms the foundation for the tread, belts, bead, and sidewall.

Caster The angle of the steering axis that supports the wheel and tire assembly. Caster relates to steering feel and stability. It is referred to as positive and negative caster.

Center rib A rib that runs circumferentially and is centered between identical tread design on each side.

Chunking The breaking away of pieces of the tire tread.

Contact patch The contact area a tire tread makes against a flat surface when under load. Also known as a tire footprint.

Cord Fabric placed under tension and covered with rubber used to form the plies of the tire. Cords are usually be made of rayon, nylon, or polyester.

Deflection The reduction in the distance between the wheel axis or center and the supporting surface when the tire is placed under load. Free radius minus the loaded radius.

Dimples Very small indentations or small round or elliptical sipes.

Directional tread Directional tread designs are those having a "one-way" tread pattern that is optimized to work best when rotating in one direction only. Arrows or other symbols are on the sidewalls and indicate the direction of rotation, which determines the side of the vehicle they are mounted on.

DOT number A series of molded letters and numbers in the sidewalls of all tires, prefixed by the letters "DOT" and mandated by the U.S. Department of Transportation.

Elliptic design A variation of the radial tire that has very thick sidewalls that runs on higher inflation pressures. Elliptic construction is designated on a tire with the letter "E."

Footprint The contact area a tire tread makes against a flat surface when under load. Also known as a contact patch.

Green tire The completely built tire before it goes through vulcanization in the mold cure process.

Grooves The space or channels between the tread ribs and elements. Circumferential grooves run around the circumference of the tire. Transverse or lateral grooves, also known as slots, run across the tire. Grooves allow for water to be channeled from beneath the tire's surface.

Inner liner A thin layer of a butyl rubber compound that holds the pressurized air inside the tire.

Load rating A numerical code that indicates the maximum load a tire can support at a given service condition.

Low profile A term describing a tire that has a low aspect ratio, thus a short sidewall.

Lug nut The nuts securing the wheel to the axle.

Mold The cavity that contains the tread and sidewall designs that are transferred to the green tire under heat and pressure in a process known as vulcanization.

Mold parting line The dividing line between two halves of a shell mold, or between the segments of a segmented mold.

Mold rotation A misalignment of the two halves of a shell mold, occurring when the devices that align the halves are worn or broken. If there is sufficient mold rotation, the misalignment will be noticeable in the finished tire along the parting line in the center of the tire.

Negative offset A wheel whose mounting surface is closer to the inside of the wheel, resulting in the mounted tire being moved outward from the neutral position.

Noise treatment The tire industry's efforts to reduce noise generated by tires, particularly using a mixed arrangement of tread block sizes.

Notches Small void areas that extend off of grooves or slots.

Offset The positive or negative distance from the wheel's centerline to the wheel's mounting surface.

Overall diameter The diameter of an inflated tire without any load.

Pitch length Circumferential length allotted for a tread block.

Pitch sequence The arrangement of tread bocks of varied sizes to reduce tire noise.

Plus sizing A current trend that involves using a larger diameter wheel with a lower profile tire, thus maintaining the overall diameter of the tire and keeping speedometer changes minimal. Plus sizing is done primarily for aesthetics.

Ply Rubber-coated parallel cord fabric that is placed over the liner and forms the tire carcass when locked around the beads. Bias plies run across the tire at angles, whereas radial plies run at 90 degrees to the bead straight across the tire.

Pneumatic tire A tire filled with air under pressure.

Positive offset A wheel whose mounting surface is closer to the outside of the wheel resulting in the mounted tire being moved inward from the neutral position.

Radial ply tire A tire whose plies run from bead to bead at right angles to the centerline of the tread. Radial construction is designated on the tire with the letter "R."

Retread A used tire to which a new tread has been added.

Rib A row of continuous rubber or disconnected tread blocks tread blocks that run circumferentially around a tire to form the tread pattern. Further distinguished as center ribs and shoulder ribs. Some tires have tread blocks in a mixed arrangement instead of a more defined rib and groove arrangement.

Rim A metal support for a tire assembly upon which the beads are seated.

Rim diameter The diameter of the rim seat that supports the tire bead. It is expressed in inches, such as 13″, 16″, 16.5″, etc.

Rim width The distance between the rim flanges of the wheel.

Rolling circumference The linear distance traveled by a tire in one revolution. This will vary with load and inflation.

Rotation The practice of moving tires from side to side or front to rear on a vehicle in a prescribed way to achieve uniform wear on all tires.

Run-flat tires Tires made in a number of ways, such as a tire within a tire or a tire with a thicker sidewall, that allow for use, even after puncture or excessive air loss. See *Self-supporting tire.*

Section height The distance from the rim seat to the tread surface of an unloaded tire.

Section width The linear distance between the exterior sidewalls of an inflated tire, exclusive of any lettering or designs.

Self-supporting tire Self-supporting tires appear like conventional radial tires yet have very thick sidewalls. This allows them to be driven to the nearest service center, even when flat.

Shoulder The portion of the tire where the sidewall and tread meet and provides continuous contact with the road, especially during sharp maneuvers.

Sidewall The sides of the tire that connect the tread and the bead.

Sipes Small, slit-like grooves molded in tread blocks and/or ribs. They add flexibility by allowing more movement and provide additional traction edges, thus increase traction.

Slots Lateral grooves.

Spare tire A tire that is kept in the car or truck for use in the event one of the primary tires fail. Traditionally spare tires were full-size tires mounted on identical wheels, and many vehicles still have these traditional spare tires. Smaller spare tires are also used to save space and are often referred to as *Temporary spares* or *Space-saver spares*.

Speed symbol Symbols molded on the sidewall that indicate a tire's maximum speed rating.

Symmetrical tread pattern Both halves of the tread pattern are the same.

Temporary spare A temporary spare tire is a special tire meant for use in emergencies only. It is more compact than the original equipment tire. It is intended to be used only as a means of getting the vehicle to a local service center where the original equipment can be repaired or replaced. Temporary spare tires are designated on the sidewall with the letter "T." A space saver spare is another form of temporary spare and is often stored unflated to save additional room.

Tie bar Rubber connecting one tread block to another to reduce the effects of side forces and squirm to improve tread wear.

Tire life The number of miles a tire lasts before it wears down to the tread wear indicators and must be replaced.

Toe A measure of whether the fronts of the tires, as viewed from above, are closer in (toe in) or father apart (toe out) than the rear portion of the tires.

Track width The distance from the center of one wheel or tire to the center of the opposing wheel or tire.

Tread The designed part of the tire that comes into contact with the road.

Tread blocks Those shapes of tread that together make up the design of the tread.

Tread depth Tread depth is a vertical measurement between the top of the tread and the bottom of the tire's deepest groove, measured in 32nd of an inch. Tread depth is best measured with a tire tread depth gauge.

Tread depth gauge A device used to measure the depth of the tread.

Tread wear indicator Bands of raised rubber, sometimes called "wear bars," that are 2/32 inches above the bottom of the main grooves.

Tread width Tread width is the distance between the outer edge and the inner edge of the tread of a tire. Treads having a square profile are more easily measured. There is no industry standard pertaining to "how much" of a rounded shoulder tire's tread should be included in the tread width measurement. At the crime scene, tread width refers to the width of the tread as left in a particular impression, as well as any width characteristics within that impression.

Turning diameter The diameter of the smallest circle in which a vehicle can complete a U-turn. This depends on the wheelbase of the vehicle (longer vehicles usually need more space to turn around) and maximum steering ability.

UTQG Uniform Tire Quality Grading. The DOT–mandated tire rating system with regard to tread wear durability, traction, and temperature resistance.

Valve A device that is mounted in the wheel as a way of letting air in and out of the tire.

Vent holes Small holes drilled in the tread and sidewall surfaces of a mold to allow for air to escape during mold cure.

Ventless mold Tread portions of newer molds are made in a jigsaw puzzle manner that allows air to flow between the tiny interfaces of these pieces but does not allow rubber to pass through. This process prevents the need to drill vent holes.

Void ratio The amount of open space in the tread design. Low void ratios mean more rubber and more contact with the surface. Higher void ratios mean less rubber and more grooves and sipes, thus increasing the ability to drain water and/or eject mud.

Wheel base The distance between the centers of the front and rear wheels.

Zero offset A wheel whose mounting surface is at the centerline of the wheel.

Bibliography

Adair, T., Lemay, J., McDonald, A., Shaw, R., and Tewes, R. "The Mount Bierstadt Study. An Experiment in Unique Damage Formation in Footwear." *Journal of Forensic Identification* 57(6) (2007): 199-205.

Adair, T., Tewes, R., Bellinger, T., and Nicholls, T., "Characteristics of Snow and Their Influence on Casting Methods for Impression Evidence." *Journal of Forensic Identification* 57(6), (2007): 807–822.

Adair T., Shaw, R., "The Dry-Casting Method: A reintroduction to a simple method for casting snow impressions." *Journal of Forensic Identification* 57(6) (2007): 823–831.

Bessman, C., and Schmeiser, A. "Survey of Tire Tread Design and Tire Size as Mounted on Vehicles in Central Iowa." *Journal of Forensic Identification* 51 (2001): 587-596.

Blitzer, H., Hammer, R., Jacobia, J., "Effect of Photographic Technology on Quality of Examination of Footwear Impressions." *Journal of Forensic Identification* 57(5) (2007): 641–657.

Bodziak, W. J. *Footwear Impression Evidence: Detection, Recovery and Examination.* 2nd ed. Boca Raton, FL: CRC Press; 2000.

Bodziak, W. J. *Encyclopedia of Forensic Sciences.* Kent, UK: Academic Press, Harcourt Publishers Ltd., 2000. Authored units on Pattern Evidence: Footwear Marks, and Pattern Evidence: Vehicle Tire Marks and Tire Track Measurements.

Bodziak, W. J. *Forensic Evidence.* Sacramento, CA: California District Attorney's Association, 1999: Chapter 9 "Footwear and Tire Tread Evidence."

Bodziak, W. J. *Forensic Science: An Introduction to Scientific and Investigative Techniques.* Boca Raton, FL: CRC Press; 2002. Authored chapters on Footwear Impression Evidence (Chapter 16) and Tire Impression Evidence (Chapter 17)

Bodziak, W. J. "Shoe and Tire Impression Evidence." *FBI Law Enforcement Bulletin* July (1984): 2-12.

Bodziak, W. J. "Some Methods for Taking Two-dimensional Comparison Standards of Tires." *Journal of Forensic Identification* 46 (1996): 689-701.

Bodziak, W. J. "Tire Impression Variables: Variations in Tire Deflection on Soft versus Hard Road Surfaces." Presented at the IAI Meeting, Ottawa Canada, July 7-11, 2003.

Bodziak, W. J., and Hammer, L. "An Evaluation of Dental Stone, Traxtone and Crime Cast." *Journal of Forensic Identification* 56 (2006): 769-787.

Bolhouse, R. J. "Tires and Computers." *RCMP Gazette* 52 (1)(1990): 1–11.

Bolhouse, R. J. "The Identification of Vehicles from Wheelbase and Tire Stance Measurements." *Identification News* June (1984): 5-6.

Carlsson, K. "A New Method for Securing Impressions in Snow." *Crime Laboratory Digest* December (1982): 1-4.

Chavigny, M. "Tracks of Vehicles." *American Journal of Police Science* 1 (1930): 156-178.

Cook, C. W. "Footprints and Tire Tracks." *Identification News* 31 (1981): 7-10.

Cycling Trade Review. Part 3: Tires. Versailles, MO: Clark Cycle Tire Company, March 1897.

Eckerman, E., *World History of the Automobile* (Vom Dampfwagen zum Auto, 1989), translated by Peter L. Albrecht, republished by Society of Automotive Engineers, Inc. Warrendale, PA. 2001.

Federal Motor Carrier Safety Administration. Part 571: Federal Motor Vehicle Safety Standards. Revised June 1, 2007.

Geller, J. "Casting on Road Surfaces." *Journal of Forensic Identification* 40 (1990): 279-282.

Gent, A. N., and Walter, J. D. *The Pneumatic Tire.* Washington, DC: National Highway Traffic Safety Administration, U.S. Department of Transportation, August 2005.

Given, B. W., Nehrich, R. B., and Shields, J. C. *Tire Tracks and Tread Marks.* Houston, TX: Gulf Publishing Company, Book Division; 1977.

Grogan, R. J., and Watson, T. R. "Tyres and Crime." *Journal of the Forensic Science Society* 11 (1971): 3-14.

Hamm, E. D. "Locating an Area on a Suspect Tire for Comparative Examination to a Questioned Track." *Journal of Forensic Identification* 38 (1988): 143-151.

Hamm, E. D. "Historical Overview of Footwear and Tire Tread Evidence." Presented at the International Symposium on the Forensic Aspects of Footwear and Tire Impression Evidence, FBI Academy, 1994.

Hamm, E. D. "The Value of Shadow in Footwear and Tire Track Evidence Recovered by Photographic Techniques." *Journal of Forensic Identification* 38 (1988): 91-97.

Hamm, E. D. "Tire Tracks and Footwear Identification." *Identification News* 25 (1975): 3-6.

Hammer, L., and Wolfe, J. "Shoe and Tire Impressions in Snow: Photography and Casting." *Journal of Forensic Identification* 53 (2003): 647-655.

Hersley, J., Tongate, L., and Burke, B. *Simple Truths: The Real Story of the Oklahoma City Bombing Investigations.* Oklahoma City, OK: Oklahoma Heritage Association; 2004.

Hueske, E. E. "A Superior Method for Obtaining Test Prints from Footwear and Tires." *Journal of Forensic Identification* 41 (1991): 165-167.

Hueske, E. E. "Photographing and Casting Footwear/Tire Track Impressions in Snow." *Journal of Forensic Identification* 41 (1991): 92-95.

Kovac, F. J. *Tire Technology.* 5th ed. Akron, OH: Goodyear Tire & Rubber Company; 1978.

Lief, A. *The Firestone Story: A History of the Firestone Tire and Rubber Company,* New York: McGraw-Hill; 1951.

Lloyd, J. B. F. "Luminescence of Tyre Marks and Other Rubber Contact Traces." *Journal of the Forensic Science Society* 16 (1976): 5-19.

Ludas, J. M., and Leonard, J. L. "Why 'No-scale' Photographs Are Not Always a Dead-end: A Homicide Case Study." Presented at the International Symposium on the Forensic Aspects of Footwear and Tire Impression Evidence, FBI Academy, 1994.

McDonald, P. *Tire Imprint Evidence.* Boca Raton, FL: CRC Press; 1989.

Miller, T. A. "Tire Tread Design Combinations as Mounted on a Vehicle." Poster session at the International Symposium on the Forensic Aspects of Footwear and Tire Impression Evidence, FBI Academy, 1994.

Motor Vehicle Manufacturers Association. *Specifications Form for Passenger Cars.* Detroit, MI: Motor Vehicle Manufacturers Association of the United States, Inc.; nd.

National Highway Traffic Safety Administration, U.S. Department of Transportation. CFR Title 49, Chapter V, Part 571, § 571.119, Standard 119; New pneumatic tires for vehicles other than passenger cars. Washington, DC: NHTSA.

National Highway Traffic Safety Administration, U.S. Department of Transportation. CFR Title 49, Chapter V, Part 571, § 571.139, Standard 139; New pneumatic radial tires for light vehicles. Washington, DC: NHTSA.

National Highway Traffic Safety Administration, U.S. Department of Transportation. CFR Title 49, Chapter V, Part 575, § 575.104, Standard 104; Uniform tire quality grading standards. Washington, DC: NHTSA.

Nause, L. A. *Forensic Tire Impression Identification.* Ottawa, Ontario, Canada: National Research Council of Canada, 2001.

Nause, L. A. "Forensic Tire and Vehicle Track Identification." *RCMP Gazette* 52: 5-15.

Nause, L. A. "The Science of Tire Impression Identification." *RCMP Gazette* 49 (1987): 1-25.

Nause, L. A. "Tire Impressions as Evidence." *RCMP Gazette* 44 (1982): 10-27.

O'Reilly, *The Goodyear Story.* 1983, The Goodyear Tire & Rubber Company.

Osterburg, J. W. *The Crime Laboratory: Case Studies of Scientific Criminal Investigation.* New York: Clark Boardman Company, Ltd., 1982.

Paessler, R. T. "The Cessaro Case." *Journal of Criminology, Criminal Law and Police Science* 1: 193-206.

Piette, H. "The Identification of a Tyre Track." *International Criminal Police Review* 152 (1961).

Radial Tire Conditions Analysis Guide. Alexandria, VA: American Trucking Association, Technology and Maintenance Council, 2004. (3rd Ed.)

Sarkissian, G., The Analysis of Tire Rubber Traces Collected after Braking Indicents using Pyrolysis-Gas Chromatoraphy/Mass Spectrometry." JFS September, 2007 vol. 52, No. 5, pp. 1050–1056.

Sharma, B. R. *Foot Prints Tracks and Trails in Criminal Investigation and Trials.* Allahabad, India: Central Law Agency, 1980: 123-139.

Standards Testing Laboratories, Inc. Tire technology seminar, Massillon, Ohio, October 14-16, 1997.

Stone, R. "Footwear Examinations: Mathematical Probabilities of Theoretical Individual Characteristics." *Journal of Forensic Identification* 56 (2006): 577-599.

Thomas, M. "Tire Design and Manufacture." Presented at the 78th Annual IAI Educational Conference, July 28, 1993.

Tuthill, H., and George, G. *Individualization: Principle and Procedures in Criminalistics.* Jacksonville, FL: Lightning Powder Company, 1994.

Vandiver, J. V. "Tire Marks." *Law and Order Magazine* 25 (1977): 16.

Volckeryck, G. "Database of Tire Tread Stance, Wheelbase, Tire Size and Driving Shaft of Passenger Vehicles." Presented at the International Symposium on the Forensic Aspects of Footwear and Tire Impression Evidence, FBI Academy, 1994.

Volckeryck, G. "Identification of Vehicles through Tire Tread Stance and Wheelbase Measurements: A Computer Database." Gent, Belgium: Laboratorium voor Technische en Weterschappelijke Politie, 2002.

Zeldes, I. "Footwear and Tire Track Examination in the Soviet Union." *Journal of Forensic Identification* 39 (1989): 367-374.

Index

Page references given in *italics* refer to figures.
Page references given in **boldface** type refer to tables

T

Z

9780849372476